MAY 0 1 2017

The New Kansas Cookbook

The New
KANSAS COOKBOOK

RURAL ROOTS, MODERN TABLE

FRANK AND JAYNI CAREY

WITH ILLUSTRATIONS BY LOUIS COPT

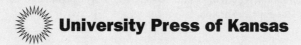
University Press of Kansas

© 2016 by Frank Carey and Jayni Carey
All rights reserved
Cover and interior illustrations © 2016 by Louis Copt

Published by the University Press of Kansas (Lawrence, Kansas 66045), which was organized by the
Kansas Board of Regents and is operated and funded by Emporia State University, Fort Hays State
University, Kansas State University, Pittsburg State University, the University of Kansas, and Wichita State
University

Library of Congress Cataloging-in-Publication Data

Names: Carey, Frank, 1949– author. | Carey, Jayni, author.
Title: The new Kansas cookbook : rural roots, modern table / Frank and Jayni
Carey ; with illustrations by Louis Copt.
Description: Lawrence, Kansas : University Press of Kansas, [2016] | Includes index.
Identifiers: LCCN 2016023586 | ISBN 9780700623198 (cloth : alk. paper)
Subjects: LCSH: Cooking, American—Midwestern style. | Cooking—Kansas. | LCGFT: Cookbooks.
Classification: LCC TX715.2.M53 C366 2016 | DDC 641.59781—dc23
LC record available at https://lccn.loc.gov/2016023586.

British Library Cataloguing-in-Publication Data is available.

Printed in the United States of America

10 9 8 7 6 5 4 3 2 1

The paper used in this publication is recycled and contains 30 percent postconsumer waste. It is acid free
and meets the minimum requirements of the American National Standard for Permanence of Paper for
Printed Library Materials Z39.48-1992.

Contents

Preface

So, what's cooking in Kansas?

In *The Kansas Cookbook: Recipes from the Heartland*, published in 1989, we looked back at the early foodways of Kansas. The book focused on recipes based on farm traditions, early settlers' ethnic heritage, and favorite family recipes. Let's fast-forward twenty-seven years. Kansans continue to be proud of their rural roots but there is a new twist on the way we cook. The current trend is to eat fresh and local but it is no mere fad. It's a lifestyle—a lifestyle based on rural traditions with modern appeal.

The "farm-to-table" trend is growing in Kansas, as well as nationally, and there is no place where it is more evident than your local farmers' market. Kansas is also a source for many of the wholesome foods that we need and desire. If Kansans can't grow it themselves, they want to purchase it locally, seasonally, and freshly harvested. In more populated areas, farmers' markets have become colorful family events intertwined with the identity of the community. It's the place to be on Saturday morning. People are digging deeper to uncover more ways to purchase and share whole foods. Community Supported Agriculture (CSA) programs and "you-pick" farms offer opportunities to get fresh fruits and vegetables at their peak of ripeness. Some farms invite folks to visit and buy organic meats, eggs, cheeses, and other farm-made products right at their source. Some schools are growing their own produce to augment the school lunch program and even sell the surplus to the public. Parents want their kids to know where their food comes from so they are planting vegetable gardens, herb beds, salsa gardens, an asparagus patch, or just a couple of berry bushes in the backyard. The desire to drop seeds into the earth is fueled by the joy of watching the plants spring forth, as if completing the circle to eat what we have sown for ourselves.

When interviewing people around the state, we learned what Kansans cook with the abundance of fresh, seasonal, and local ingredients available to them. What could be more local to Kansas than a simple wheat berry pilaf with black walnuts and sunflower seeds? It reminds the contributor of the wheat crop and the walnut trees on the family farm. A deer hunter sends us her venison chili recipe and another cook, who loves growing strawberries, describes how to make her favorite pie.

To honor Kansans' love of beef, we grilled steaks and concocted a sauce of mushrooms and locally made bourbon, pressure-cooked a brisket for sloppy joes, and embellished a salad of fresh and cooked vegetables with thin slices of steak. Chefs, some from small-town cafes and others from award-winning urban restaurants, generously offered their most popular recipes, never failing to mention their passion for sourcing foods from local purveyors or even their own gardens. One small-town establishment shares a zucchini and corn casserole and a "perfected" sweet cornbread recipe, while another eatery provides a deliciously inventive method for slow-roasting pork shoulder for its popular pork shoulder sandwich. And, for something with a little panache, several award-winning restaurants share recipes such as smoked duck empanadas, rainbow trout with a spicy crust, and roast pork tenderloin with Port wine and prunes. A farmer raising poultry tells how to make the best chicken and noodles and a rancher shares her recipe for ground grass-fed beef stuffed and baked in yellow squash. Thanks to the many options that keep cooks in seasonal produce, a bounty of recipes for vegetables such as stuffed acorn squash, Brussels sprouts roasted with bacon and apples, sweet corn with shallot and tarragon, and many recipes using fresh tomatoes found their way into the book. And after all, since Kansas is the "Wheat State," family and consumer science educators share their expertise on making breads, rolls, and desserts.

Features are peppered throughout the book to showcase the people, places, and perhaps the future of our diverse agricultural state. We think that readers will be pleasantly surprised, as we were, to learn that chestnuts are grown in Kansas and that a nationally renowned poultry farmer is on a mission to save his heritage turkeys and chickens. For more than fifty years, a western Kansas town has been hosting a farm-to-table dinner for fifteen hundred diners with all the ingredients grown by local farmers and prepared by community volunteers. A six-generation wheat-farming family tells us how the modern wheat harvest has changed the traditional harvest meals, and two former Kansas governors share their enthusiasm for turkey hunting. To amuse us, a cheesemaker tells us why she prefers goats to cows, while a brewery, a winery, and a distillery all express their dedication and passion to their crafts.

The New Kansas Cookbook: Rural Roots, Modern Table is filled with 220 well-tested recipes from contributors, as well as ourselves, that reflect how Kansans cook today. Thirty-one features are inserted among the recipes to paint a backdrop of our state's current foodways and its unique individuals. Though Kansas is a state that is large in area and diverse in character, we have discovered again that when it comes to sharing a meal, it still has a neighborly feel.

Acknowledgments

Writing *The New Kansas Cookbook: Rural Roots, Modern Table* has given us the opportunity to collaborate with many Kansans who shared their recipes, comments, and stories with us. We offer our heartfelt thanks to the Kansas cooks, chefs, farmers, ranchers, and family and consumer science educators who submitted recipes or allowed us to interview them for their unique stories. We wish to express our deep appreciation to Marci Penner, who was instrumental in helping us get the word out as we were searching for contributors, and a warm thank-you to our dear friends, Karen Waite, for assisting with recipe testing, and Susan Schott, Mike Briggs, and Ann Hagedorn, who gave us sage advice and encouragement while we were working on the book.

Our sincere thanks to Charles T. Myers, director of the University Press of Kansas, for his enthusiasm and support of this project; to Kim Hogeland, acquisitions editor, for her guidance; and to Kansas artist Louis Copt for the beautiful book cover and illustrations. We extend our gratitude to the staff of the University Press of Kansas for their creativity and advice, and for seeing the book through to publication.

Chapter 1
Starters and Small Plates

Try not to wince when you hear these words, "Could you please bring an hors d'oeuvre or snack to the party?" It's not unusual these days for a party invitation to include a small request to help out the host. Think of it as a compliment and, besides, Kansas cooks like to contribute. That's where this chapter comes in.

Whether it's a game day, a potluck, or a holiday dinner party, this chapter provides some great recipes to fit any occasion. To heighten team spirit during the playoff game, you'll find a variety of tasty snacks for your friends to munch on like "Chipotle Meatballs," "Chile-Apricot-Glazed Chicken Wings," or "Gella's Grebble with Sunflower Seed Pesto."

Dips and spreads are perennial favorites at casual parties. Start with "Toasted Baguette Slices" and select from an array of dips and spreads including these two easy toppings—"Sun-Dried Tomato Spread" and "Eggplant Dip."

For a special dinner party that calls for offering your guests a small plate serving to begin the meal, try "Smoked Duck Empanadas" or "Goat Cheese-Stuffed Prosciutto Rolls with Salad Greens." Or combine several small plates for an entire menu with choices like "Warm Shrimp and Bacon with Sherry Brussels Sprouts and Champagne Crema" and "Lamb Chops with Cheese Grits."

Gella's Grebble with Sunflower Seed Pesto

In 2003, Ellis County was recognized as the "German Capital of Kansas." Hays and other cities around the county celebrate their German heritage with festivals, feasts, traditional German music, and a variety of entertainment throughout the year. Gella's Diner and Lb. Brewing Co. exemplifies some of these traditions by serving award-winning beers and dishes, such as grebble, on their restaurant menu. "Grebble is a local Volga German dish and tended to be baked on Sunday, the traditional baking day. Grebble was created from the excess dough and revered as a special treat," Chef Manuel Hernandez tells us.

The Sunflower Seed Pesto, made with fresh herbs, spinach, and sunflower seeds, is also a staple on the menu. "I love the versatility of our pesto, and we use it in a number of dishes. Serve it with Gella's Grebble, toss it with pasta, or serve atop grilled chicken."
—Chef Manuel Hernandez, Gella's Diner and Lb. Brewing Co., Hays

12 TO 16 SINGLE SERVINGS

Grebble:
¾ cup butter
1½ cups all-purpose flour
¾ teaspoon baking powder
3 tablespoons sugar
⅛ teaspoon salt
2 large eggs

Sunflower Seed Pesto:
1 cup fresh basil leaves, packed
¼ cup fresh parsley leaves, lightly packed
¼ cup fresh spinach leaves, lightly packed
½ cup roasted, salted sunflower seeds
2 cups grated Parmesan cheese
2 garlic cloves

½ teaspoon salt, or to taste
¼ teaspoon white pepper
2 cups olive oil

Canola or vegetable oil, for deep-fat frying

CONTINUED ➡

Grebble: Melt the butter in a small saucepan over low heat and allow to cool. In a mixing bowl, sift the flour and baking powder together. Stir in the sugar and salt. Add the eggs and melted butter. Mix with a silicone spatula or a spoon until all ingredients are incorporated. Scrape the dough from the bowl, wrap in plastic wrap, and refrigerate overnight.

Prepare the pesto before frying the grebble. It can be served immediately or kept in the refrigerator for up to six days.

Sunflower Seed Pesto: Place the basil, parsley, spinach, sunflower seeds, grated cheese, garlic, salt, and white pepper in a food processor and blend until ingredients are finely chopped. With the processor running, slowly add the olive oil through the feed tube and blend until smooth. Makes 3½ cups.

To fry the grebble, heat the oil over high heat to 345 degrees in a large, heavy-bottomed saucepan or Dutch oven. Dust the work space with flour. Shape the dough into a loaf and cut into ½-inch slices. Flatten the slices into an oval shape ¼ inch thick and make two slits in the middle of each, cutting all the way through. Fry the grebble in small batches for 2 minutes on each side, or until golden brown. Drain on paper towels.

Serve the grebble with Gella's sunflower seed pesto.

Variation: The grebble can be served with warm maple syrup in place of the sunflower seed pesto.

Chipotle Meatballs

These bite-size meatballs make a spicy snack for a tailgate or potluck party. Serve them with a cold beer, preferably from one of the many fine Kansas breweries.—Frank and Jayni

40 TO 45 SINGLE SERVINGS

3 tablespoons olive or vegetable oil, divided
1 cup onion, finely chopped

1½ pounds lean ground beef
1 (7-ounce) can chipotle peppers in adobo sauce
1 teaspoon cumin seed, coarsely ground
1 teaspoon salt
½ teaspoon black pepper

1½ cups smooth tomato salsa (not chunky-style), divided

Heat 1 tablespoon of the olive or vegetable oil in a small skillet over medium-low heat. Add the onion and cook, stirring occasionally, until lightly browned and tender. Cool to room temperature.

Place the ground beef in a large bowl. Add the cooked onion. Remove 2 or 3 chipotle peppers from the can of chipotle peppers in adobo sauce. Wear plastic gloves to protect your hands. Cut the peppers open and scrape out the seeds. Finely chop enough of the peppers to equal 2 tablespoons. Add the chopped peppers to the beef along with 1 to 2 tablespoons of the adobo sauce. Add the cumin, salt, and pepper. Combine the ingredients using a fork to avoid compressing the meat too much. Form the meat into 1-inch balls. The recipe makes 40 to 45 meatballs. Preheat the oven to 375 degrees.

Heat the remaining 2 tablespoons of the oil in a large nonstick skillet over medium-high heat. Brown the meatballs on all sides in batches. Transfer the browned meatballs to a baking dish. Add more oil to the skillet if necessary and reduce the heat as needed to prevent burning.

Top the browned meatballs with just enough of the salsa to lightly coat them. Place them in the oven and roast for 5 to 10 minutes, until cooked through.

Transfer the meatballs to a decorative platter and serve with the remaining salsa.

Chile-Apricot-Glazed Chicken Wings

On game day, serve this winning platter of sweet and spicy chicken wings. Score one for you!
—Frank and Jayni

16 TO 20 SINGLE SERVINGS

2 to 2¼ pounds chicken wings, split
    at the joints, tips removed
Salt and black pepper, to taste

Chile-Apricot Glaze:
½ cup apricot preserves
1 tablespoon lime juice
2 teaspoons hot red chile powder
1 teaspoon cumin seed, coarsely
    ground
⅛ teaspoon garlic granules
⅛ teaspoon onion granules
⅛ teaspoon cayenne pepper
    (optional)

Cut the chicken wings at the joints and discard the tips, or purchase them precut. Pat the wings dry with paper towels. Season them with salt and black pepper and place them on an oiled rimmed baking sheet. Place the wings in a 425-degree oven and roast for 15 minutes, turn them over, and roast for 10 minutes more. While the wings are cooking, make the glaze.

Chile-Apricot Glaze: Place the apricot preserves and lime juice in a small bowl and whisk in the chile powder, cumin, garlic granules, onion granules, and cayenne pepper, if using.

After the chicken wings have cooked for 25 minutes, heat the chile-apricot glaze in the microwave for a few seconds to warm it. Brush the chicken wings generously with the glaze on both sides using a basting brush. Return the wings to the oven and bake for 5 to 10 minutes more, until they are cooked through and tender.

Transfer the chicken wings from the baking sheet to a warm platter and serve immediately.

Chicken and Sweet Corn Quesadillas

Quesadillas, typically found on the menu in most Mexican restaurants across Kansas, are flour or corn tortillas filled with a savory mix of cheese, chiles, meat, or vegetables. If you prep all ingredients ahead, you can assemble and brown them quickly on a hot griddle. Quesadillas taste best freshly made, when they are hot and crunchy.—Frank and Jayni

12 TO 18 SINGLE SERVINGS

2 skinless, boneless chicken
    breasts, about 6 ounces each

Marinade:
1 tablespoon fresh lime juice
1 large garlic clove, minced
⅛ teaspoon crushed red pepper
⅛ teaspoon salt
⅛ teaspoon black pepper
2 tablespoons olive oil

Filling:
2 ears sweet corn, shucked
2 tablespoons canola or vegetable
    oil
1 cup onion, chopped
1 jalapeño pepper, seeded and
    finely diced
2 garlic cloves, minced
1 teaspoon cumin seed, coarsely
    ground
¼ cup fresh cilantro leaves,
    chopped
Sea salt and black pepper, to taste

6 (8-inch) flour tortillas

Canola or vegetable oil
Red or green salsa of choice
2 cups pepper jack cheese, shredded

Garnishes:
2 ripe avocados, peeled and sliced
    (optional)
Sour cream (optional)

Place the chicken breasts on a cutting board. Place your hand on top of one chicken breast and carefully cut it in half, horizontally. Repeat with the remaining breast. Place them in a single layer in a baking dish.

Marinade: Combine the lime juice, garlic, crushed red pepper, salt, and pepper in a small bowl. Whisk in the olive oil. Pour the marinade evenly over the chicken and turn to coat. Cover and refrigerate up to 1 hour, or let stand at room temperature for 30 minutes before cooking.

Prepare a gas or charcoal grill for cooking over medium-high heat. Remove the chicken pieces from the marinade and place on the cooking grate. Cover the grill and cook for 2 to 4 minutes each side. Transfer the chicken to a cutting board, tent with aluminum foil, and let rest 5 to 10 minutes. Cut the chicken into bite-size pieces.

CONTINUED ➡

Filling: Cut the corn kernels off the cobs using a sharp knife. Heat 2 tablespoons of oil in a medium skillet over medium-high heat. Add the corn kernels and chopped onion and sauté until the mixture begins to turn golden. Add the jalapeño pepper, garlic, and cumin, and continue cooking until the pepper is soft, 2 to 3 minutes more. Off heat, stir in the cilantro, the grilled chicken, and season with salt and pepper. Warm the mixture briefly over low heat for a minute or two, if needed.

Heat a griddle or large nonstick skillet over medium heat. Brush one side of each flour tortilla generously with canola or vegetable oil. Place one tortilla at a time on the griddle, or in the skillet. Place about ⅓ cup of the chicken and corn filling onto one half of the tortilla. Top with salsa and sprinkle with cheese. Fold the tortilla over to form a half circle. Cook for 2 to 3 minutes, until lightly browned. Slide a spatula under the open side of the tortilla and carefully flip it over. Cook for 2 to 3 minutes more. Repeat with remaining tortillas and filling.

Open tortillas and add a few slices of avocado and sour cream, if desired. Cut each tortilla in half or thirds, to form triangles. Serve immediately.

Dips and Spreads

The very presence of something tasty offers a warm welcome to your guests. Parking some dips and spreads at the busy intersection where treats and conversation collide will intentionally cause some happy accidents.

Due to heavy traffic, your guests must slow down and use both hands to spread a creamy eggplant dip or load on a dollop of spicy chopped sun-dried tomatoes, olives, capers, and herbs. But to deliver the savory goodness to their mouths, these drivers will need a vehicle, and that's where the toasted baguette slices come in. Also known as a croute or crostini, baguette slices—golden, crunchy, rubbed with oil and sometimes garlic—make the perfect carrier for dips, spreads, or other toppings.

Following is a recipe to make a basket of toasted baguette slices that will put some savory crunch under any dip or spread. Choose one or more of the four delicious toppings that follow.

Toasted Baguette Slices

MAKES ABOUT 40 SINGLE SERVINGS

1 baguette
Olive oil
1 garlic clove, peeled (optional)
Sea salt

Slice the baguette into ⅜-inch slices. Brush both sides of each slice with olive oil and place them on a baking sheet. Bake in a 325-degree oven for 10 minutes, turn and bake for 8 to 10 minutes more, or until light gold. Rub a peeled garlic clove over one side of each baguette slice, if desired. Sprinkle them lightly with sea salt. Transfer the slices to a baking rack to cool. Store in an airtight container if not using within an hour or so.

Sun-Dried Tomato Spread

The intense sweet-tart flavor of sun-dried tomatoes, blended with rosemary, garlic, Parmesan cheese, walnuts, and olive oil, makes a spread that will pack a lot of punch at your next party.—Frank and Jayni

MAKES 1½ CUPS OF SPREAD

1 cup (lightly packed) sun-dried tomatoes in olive oil, drained
1 tablespoon fresh rosemary, chopped
2 small to medium garlic cloves, chopped
⅓ cup Parmigiano-Reggiano cheese, grated
¼ cup English walnuts
½ teaspoon crushed red pepper
⅓ cup sun-dried tomato oil or extra-virgin olive oil

Toasted baguette slices

Place the sun-dried tomatoes, rosemary, garlic, cheese, walnuts, and crushed red pepper in a food processor and pulse to a fine mince. Add the oil and blend for a few seconds to combine. Scrape the spread into a small decorative bowl. Cover and refrigerate for at least 2 hours before serving.

Bring the spread to room temperature about 30 minutes before serving. Drizzle with extra olive oil and serve with toasted baguette slices.

Olive and Sun-Dried Tomato Spread

A dab of this tasty concoction on a toasted baguette slice, with a glass of wine or spirits in hand, signals that the party has begun.
—Frank and Jayni

MAKES 1¼ CUPS OF SPREAD

⅓ cup Kalamata olives, pitted
¼ cup pimiento-stuffed Spanish olives
½ cup (lightly packed) sun-dried tomatoes in olive oil, drained
2 small to medium garlic cloves, chopped
¼ cup Parmigiano-Reggiano cheese, grated
1 tablespoon capers, rinsed and drained
1 teaspoon fresh thyme leaves
⅓ cup extra-virgin olive oil (or half olive oil, half sun-dried tomato oil)

Baguette slices

Place all ingredients for the spread in a food processor and pulse to a fine mince. Scrape the spread into a small decorative bowl. Cover and refrigerate for at least 2 hours before serving.

Bring the spread to room temperature about 30 minutes before serving. Serve with toasted baguette slices.

Eggplant Dip

The Pendletons grow eggplant and other vegetables to sell at the local farmers' market and at their country market, located on their farm in rural Douglas County.

"This is an eggplant dish that our family loves. I really like the fact that, in the summer months, most of the ingredients are available locally."—Karen Pendleton, Pendleton's Country Market, Lawrence

15 TO 20 SINGLE SERVINGS

2 medium eggplants
Juice of 1 lemon

½ cup olive oil
1 medium onion, diced
2 garlic cloves, minced
1 red bell pepper, seeded and diced
1 hot pepper, diced

1 cup pitted canned black olives, chopped
2 tablespoons tomato paste
1 cup water

8 ounces plain yogurt
Pinch of sugar, or to taste
Lemon juice, to taste
Salt, to taste
Freshly ground black pepper, to taste
½ cup fresh parsley, chopped

Toasted baguette slices

Peel the eggplants, cut them into small cubes, and place in a large bowl. Add the lemon juice and toss to coat.

Heat the olive oil over medium heat in a large skillet, sauté pan, or Dutch oven. Add the eggplant, onion, garlic, bell pepper, and hot pepper. Cover and cook the mixture over medium heat. Stir occasionally until the vegetables are cooked throughout.

Stir in the olives, tomato paste, and 1 cup of water. Bring the mixture to a boil and cook for 2 minutes, stirring frequently. Remove the skillet from the heat and cool completely.

Transfer the cooled eggplant mixture to a food processor or blender and purée until smooth. Pour the dip into a large bowl and stir in the yogurt. Add the sugar and lemon juice, and season with salt and pepper. Add the parsley. Cover and chill the dip for at least 1 hour before serving.

Pour the dip into a decorative bowl surrounded by toasted baguette slices.

Variation: Serve the eggplant dip with a tray of fresh sliced vegetables for dipping.

Goat Cheese Spread with Olives

This light and easy-to-make goat cheese spread travels well to a party. We offer it to our dinner guests with a glass of white wine or Champagne upon arrival. Make the spread a day ahead to save time.—Frank and Jayni

MAKES 1 CUP OF SPREAD

8 ounces fresh goat cheese
Zest of 1 lemon
2 tablespoons lemon juice
1 large garlic clove, pressed or
    minced
1 tablespoon fresh lemon thyme,
    rosemary, or dill, finely chopped
Sea salt, to taste

1 tablespoon extra-virgin olive oil
Fresh herb sprigs, or 1 tablespoon
    finely chopped herb of choice,
    for garnish
½ cup mixed gourmet olives
Toasted baguette slices

Place the goat cheese in a small bowl and break it up with a fork. Add the lemon zest and juice and blend until smooth. Mix in the garlic and chopped herb of choice. Season the spread with sea salt. Cover and refrigerate until 30 minutes before serving.

When ready to serve, mound the goat cheese spread on a decorative plate and drizzle with 1 tablespoon of olive oil. Garnish with a few herb sprigs, or sprinkle 1 tablespoon of chopped herb over the goat cheese spread. Surround the spread with olives and serve with toasted baguette slices.

Southeast Asian-Style Frog Legs

Mike Hayden, former Kansas governor and secretary of the Kansas Department of Wildlife, Parks, and Tourism, grew up in Atwood catching frogs in the nearby ponds and lakes.

"Back then, I served the legs battered and fried, but when I served in Vietnam during the war in 1969 through 1970 as an infantry officer, I saw for the first time the use of lemongrass and peanut oil for cooking frog legs. This recipe is as close as I have come to replicating the Vietnamese version."
—Mike Hayden, Lawrence

12 SINGLE SERVINGS

6 pairs frog legs

Soy-Lemongrass Marinade:
1 stalk lemongrass
½ cup low-sodium soy sauce
¼ cup seasoned rice vinegar
¼ teaspoon red pepper flakes
2 tablespoons peanut oil

¼ cup peanut oil, for frying
1 or 2 mangoes, peeled and diced
2 kiwifruit, peeled and sliced
4 lime wedges
¼ cup fresh cilantro leaves, snipped

Pat the frog legs dry with paper towels. Split the pairs of legs in half through the pelvic bone. Set aside.

Soy-Lemongrass Marinade: Cut off the tough green top and the root end of the lemongrass stalk and discard. Remove the tough outer leaves and finely chop the stalk. Place the chopped lemongrass in a small bowl. Add the soy sauce, seasoned rice vinegar, and red pepper flakes. Whisk in 2 tablespoons of peanut oil.

Place the frog legs in a plastic storage bag. Pour the marinade over them and seal the bag or place the frog legs in a baking dish and cover with the marinade. Refrigerate the legs for 2 to 3 hours and occasionally turn the bag over, or turn the legs in the baking dish.

To cook the frog legs, heat ¼ cup of peanut oil over medium-high heat in a nonstick skillet or sauté pan. Remove the legs from the marinade and drain them briefly on paper towels. When the oil is hot, add the legs in two batches and sear until golden and crisp, about 3 to 4 minutes each side. Reduce the heat as needed to prevent burning.

To serve, arrange frog legs on a platter and garnish with diced mango, sliced kiwi, and lime wedges. Sprinkle with cilantro. Serve warm.

Curried Egg Salad with Mango Chutney and Pita Chips

"We live in rural Douglas County where we keep a flock of seventeen laying hens and a small, productive garden. Every summer the hens go into overdrive, producing dozens of eggs. Among other things, the garden yields a fine crop of shallots. I'm always looking for ways to serve both, and this recipe fills the bill. I make this curried egg salad to take to potluck dinners, or when we have several guests at home. I serve it with mango chutney, or a plum sauce I make every summer when the Italian plums are in season."—Shirley Domer, Lawrence

30 SINGLE SERVINGS

1 dozen eggs

Curry Dressing:
1 cup mayonnaise, plus more to
    moisten if needed
1 teaspoon curry powder
1 teaspoon turmeric
1 tablespoon prepared mustard
1 teaspoon cider vinegar
½ to 1 teaspoon salt, to taste

¼ cup shallot, minced, or ½ cup
    green onion, thinly sliced
1 red bell pepper, seeded and diced

Mango chutney, homemade or
    purchased
Toasted pita chips, crackers, or
    tortilla chips

Put the eggs in a 2-quart saucepan, cover with water by at least 1 inch, and bring to a boil over high heat. As soon as the water comes to a boil, remove the pan from the heat, cover and let stand for 13 minutes. Pour off the hot water and cover the eggs with cold water. Allow the eggs to cool while preparing the dressing.

Curry Dressing: In a small bowl, combine the mayonnaise, curry powder, turmeric, prepared mustard, cider vinegar, and salt. Stir to combine.

When the eggs are cool, peel and coarsely chop them, and place them in a large bowl. Add the shallot or green onion, and red bell pepper. Mix gently to combine. Mix in the dressing. Add more mayonnaise to moisten, if needed.

Serve the egg salad immediately, or cover and chill until ready to serve. Serve with a small bowl of mango chutney and toasted pita chips, crackers, or tortilla chips.

Option: To serve as a salad, place lettuce leaves on six to eight salad plates and top with some of the egg salad. Garnish with mango chutney and toasted pita chips, crackers, or tortilla chips.

Winter Tomato Soup

A small serving of this tasty tomato soup is a warm way to welcome your guests. Serve in stemless cocktail glasses or small bowls as a first course for a dinner party. On winter nights, we like to meet our guests upon arrival with mini servings in espresso cups.—Frank and Jayni

MAKES 18 TO 24 SMALL SERVINGS

3 tablespoons butter
1½ cups onion, chopped
1 garlic clove, chopped
⅛ teaspoon crushed red pepper
¼ teaspoon salt
1 (6-ounce) can tomato paste
4 cups low-sodium chicken broth, divided
4 ounces red cherry tomatoes, cut in half

3 tablespoons crème fraîche, slightly thinned with milk to a pouring consistency
Freshly ground black pepper

Melt the butter in a saucepan over medium-low heat. Add the chopped onion and cook until softened, about 5 minutes. Add the garlic, crushed red pepper, and salt, and cook for 1 minute. Stir in the tomato paste and cook for 1 minute more. Stir in 1 cup of the chicken broth. Pour the mixture into a blender, add the cherry tomatoes, and blend until smooth. Return the soup to a clean saucepan and add the remaining 3 cups of broth. Simmer over medium-low heat for 5 minutes. Taste and add more salt, if needed.

To serve, ladle the soup into stemless cocktail glasses, small bowls, or espresso cups. Top each with a drizzle of crème fraîche and a bit of freshly ground black pepper.

Vanilla Bean Buffalo Sweat Maple Bread

Tallgrass Brewing Company in Manhattan encourages its fans to explore the many flavors and unique characteristics of the beers, not just by drinking them but also by incorporating them into recipes. This recipe for the Tallgrass Brewing Company's maple bread calls for its Vanilla Bean Buffalo Sweat Stout, a variation of its Buffalo Sweat Oatmeal Cream Stout.

While the maple bread bakes, the folks at Tallgrass suggest you pour yourself a beer, relax, and take a deep breath.—Tallgrass Brewing Company, Manhattan

12 SERVINGS

1¾ cups all-purpose flour
1 teaspoon baking soda
½ teaspoon baking powder
½ teaspoon salt

6 tablespoons butter, softened
¾ cup dark brown sugar
2 large eggs
½ teaspoon vanilla extract
½ cup sour cream
½ cup Tallgrass Vanilla Bean Buffalo
    Sweat Stout Beer, or other stout
    beer
¼ cup maple syrup
½ cup walnuts or pecans, chopped

3 tablespoons powdered sugar

Combine the flour, baking soda, baking powder, and salt in a bowl and set aside.

In a large mixing bowl, beat the butter and brown sugar with a hand mixer on high speed until well blended. Add the eggs, one at a time, and beat well. Blend in the vanilla extract and sour cream. Add the beer, maple syrup, and chopped nuts and mix well. Beating on low speed, gradually add the flour mixture, mixing just until combined.

Spray a 9 × 5 × 3-inch loaf pan with baking spray. Pour the batter evenly into the loaf pan. Bake in a 350-degree oven for 45 to 50 minutes, until an inserted toothpick comes out with moist crumbs. Cool the bread for 15 minutes before removing it from the pan. Place the bread on a cake rack to cool completely.

Just before serving, pour the powdered sugar into a sifter or fine wire-mesh strainer. Sift the powdered sugar over the top of the bread, until evenly covered. Slice into 12 servings.

Smoked Duck Empanadas

Chef Carl Thorne-Thomsen is the chef-owner of Story, an award-winning restaurant in Prairie Village. He is committed to sourcing the best ingredients and letting their flavors shine in his creative American cuisine at Story. He believes that quality of ingredients and sound basic cooking technique are most important for a cook to produce a successful dish. In 2014, Chef Thorne-Thomsen was named Food & Wine *magazine's "The People's Best New Chef." Story is a recipient of* Wine Spectator *magazine's "Best of Award of Excellence."*

Chef Thorne-Thomsen's "Smoked Duck Empanadas" make an exciting starter to a special dinner and are sure to impress your guests. To save time, prepare the smoked duck in advance.—Chef Carl Thorne-Thomsen, Story, Prairie Village

8 OR 9 SMALL PLATE SERVINGS

1 pound duck leg or duck breast meat

1 tablespoon olive oil
Salt and black pepper, to taste
½ small yellow onion, minced
½ carrot, peeled and shredded
1 garlic clove, minced
1½ teaspoons tomato paste
1 cup duck or chicken stock
1½ teaspoons lemon juice
½ teaspoon fresh thyme, chopped

3 to 4 tablespoons apple wood smoking chips

Empanada Dough:
8 ounces all-purpose flour
½ teaspoon salt
2½ ounces rendered duck fat or canola oil
2 ounces water

Canola oil, for deep frying

Guacamole or sauce of choice

Remove any bones and fat from the duck meat. Finely dice the meat with a sharp knife, or grind in a meat grinder.

Heat a large sauté pan or a rondeau over high heat. Add 1 tablespoon of olive oil and brown the duck meat, stirring occasionally. Season with salt and pepper. Add the onion, carrot, garlic, and tomato paste. Reduce the heat to medium and cook for 4 to 5 minutes, stirring occasionally. Add the duck or chicken stock, lemon juice, and fresh thyme, and season with additional salt and pepper, if desired. Cover the pan, reduce the heat to medium-low, and simmer for 30 minutes, stirring occasionally.

To smoke the duck meat, place a piece of aluminum foil in the bottom of a cast iron or stainless steel Dutch oven, or other large heavy-bottomed pot with a lid. Place 3 to 4 tablespoons of apple

CONTINUED ➡

wood smoking chips (small pieces work best) on the foil. Cover the pot and heat over high heat until the wood smolders, about 5 to 10 minutes.

Transfer the cooked duck meat to one of the following: a stainless steel vegetable steamer that will fit into the pot, a shallow tinfoil pan, or a piece of heavy-duty foil formed into a shallow container. Place it in the pot on top of the smoking wood chips. Cover the pot with foil to help seal in the smoke and replace the lid. Turn off the heat and smoke the meat for 15 to 20 minutes. Remove the smoked meat from the pot and cool completely before making the empanadas. Note: To avoid smoke in the kitchen, turn on a kitchen exhaust fan while smoking, or smoke the meat outdoors on the side burner of a gas grill.

Empanada Dough: Place the flour and salt in a bowl. Stir in the rendered duck fat or canola oil until the mixture appears sandy or pebbly. Add the water, a little at a time, stirring until the dough forms a ball and can be handled. Shape

the dough into a thick disk, wrap in plastic wrap, and chill for 1 hour. When ready to make the empanadas, allow the dough to come to room temperature before rolling it out, about 30 minutes.

Divide the dough into three or four pieces. Roll each piece into a thin sheet on a lightly floured surface. Using a 3-inch ring cutter, cut circles out of the dough. Place 1 teaspoon of the smoked duck meat on each circle and fold into a half-moon. Seal with the tines of a fork. If the dough does not stick together, dip your index finger in water and lightly moisten the edges of the dough. The recipe makes 24 to 28 empanadas.

Pour the canola oil to a depth of 2 inches in a Dutch oven or heavy-bottomed pot. Heat the oil over high heat to 350 degrees. Fry the empanadas, a few at a time, until they are light brown in color. Remove the empanadas from the pot with a slotted spoon and drain them on paper towels.

To serve the empanadas as a small plate course for a dinner party, arrange three empanadas on each plate with a spoonful of guacamole or a sauce of your choice.

Option: For a larger crowd, serve the empanadas as a party appetizer on a decorative serving plate accompanied by a bowl of guacamole or sauce of choice.

Goat Cheese–Stuffed Prosciutto Rolls with Salad Greens

Rolling thin slices of prosciutto around a goat cheese filling and nestling them among salad greens makes an elegant small plate starter. As an alternative, the prosciutto rolls and salad greens can be arranged as a divider between meats and cheeses on an appetizer tray.—Frank and Jayni

6 SMALL PLATE SERVINGS

4 ounces fresh goat cheese, chilled
¼ cup crème fraîche, chilled
2 teaspoons lemon zest
1 to 2 teaspoons fresh rosemary, minced

4 ounces prosciutto, sliced paper thin

Extra-virgin olive oil
Freshly ground black pepper

Salad Greens:
5 ounces mixed salad greens
12 cherry tomatoes, halved
12 oil-cured black olives, pitted
Red wine vinegar
Olive oil
Salt and black pepper, to taste

Combine the goat cheese with the crème fraîche in a small bowl, blending with a fork until smooth. Stir in the lemon zest and minced rosemary. Spoon the cheese mixture into a small plastic storage bag and chill in the refrigerator for at least 1 hour.

Cut the prosciutto into strips about 3 inches wide and 3 to 4 inches long. Snip the tip off one bottom corner of the storage bag containing the goat cheese mixture. Squeeze some of the mixture across one end of each strip of prosciutto and roll up firmly.

Pour 2 or 3 tablespoons of olive oil onto a small, shallow serving tray that is just large enough to hold the rolls. Grind some black pepper over the oil. Arrange the prosciutto rolls, seam side down, on the tray. Drizzle the tops of the rolls generously with more olive oil and grind more black pepper over the tops. Cover and refrigerate the prosciutto rolls for at least 3 hours before serving. Remove them from the refrigerator about 15 minutes before serving.

Salad: Place the salad greens in a salad bowl. Add the tomatoes and olives. Drizzle the salad greens with olive oil, sprinkle with the red wine vinegar, and toss gently to coat. Sprinkle with salt and pepper and toss again. Taste and adjust seasonings, if needed.

Arrange small piles of the salad on six small plates. Place two prosciutto rolls on each plate.

The Wonders of Goat Cheese

More than three decades ago, when goat cheese began showing up on restaurant menus and in specialty food stores, Americans fell in love. We have the cheese makers in France to thank for developing the many varieties, styles, and textures of tart and creamy goat's milk cheese. And, now that a few Kansas farmers are raising goats and making cheese, it is becoming easier to find and taste some local varieties.

Kathy Landers, owner of Landeria Farm in Olathe, raises goats and makes artisanal goat cheeses. Her family had cows and made cow's milk cheeses when she was growing up. She bought her first goat and started making cheese in 1972. "Goats are easier to manage than cows because of their small size. Unlike cows, it doesn't hurt when they step on your toes, they can't slap you across the face with their tails, and they poop cute little pellets instead of pies," Kathy says jokingly. The eighty goats at Landeria Farm were all born on the farm and have names like Lilac, Honey, Molasses, and Mandy. They are very tame, make good pets, and even come when they are called.

Kathy makes three types of handmade cheeses. They include hard cheese such as Swiss, jack-cheddar, and Gouda, twelve varieties of fresh chèvre, and three bloomy rind cheeses. Kathy enjoys educating people about cheese and teaching cheese making classes. She sells her cheeses at several farmers' markets and some large supermarkets near Olathe.

Goat cheese is popular with almost everyone.

It is relatively inexpensive and its versatility is amazing. If you are searching for an easy starter or small plate for your next party, the key is goat cheese!

With very little effort, goat cheese can be used to make a variety of impressive appetizers in minutes. Blend fresh, creamy goat cheese with lemon juice and herbs and it becomes a spread for toasted baguette slices or crackers. Enrich it with crème fraîche and it turns into a filling for prosciutto rolls. Or serve a combo platter of aged hard, soft, and bloomy rind goat cheeses "au natural" and simply savor its flavors and textures.

Bourbon & Baker Brussels Sprouts

"These Brussels sprouts have been a favorite small plate, and one of the top sellers at Bourbon & Baker since opening in the fall of 2013, often garnering responses like, 'I never liked Brussels sprouts until now.'"—Executive Chef Cadell Bynum, Bourbon & Baker, Manhattan

4 TO 6 SMALL PLATE SERVINGS

12 ounces Brussels sprouts
Kosher salt

4 to 6 slices pecan-smoked bacon

1 tablespoon extra-virgin olive oil
6 tablespoons dry white wine
3 tablespoons fresh-squeezed
    lemon juice
1½ tablespoons apple cider vinegar
1 tablespoon light brown sugar
1 teaspoon Himalayan sea salt
1 ounce (⅓ cup) Parmesan cheese,
    grated

Remove any damaged outer leaves from the Brussels sprouts and rinse well. Shave or thinly slice each sprout crosswise. Break apart the layers of the sliced sprouts. Bring a pot of well-salted water (kosher salt) to a boil. Add the Brussels sprouts and blanch for 2 minutes. Pour them in to a colander and rinse with cold water. Drain well.

Cook the bacon in a small skillet over medium heat until crispy. Drain and dice into small pieces and set aside.

Heat a medium sauté pan or skillet over medium-high heat. Add the olive oil and bacon and sauté for 30 seconds. Add the blanched Brussels sprouts, increase the heat to high, and sauté for 1 minute. Add the white wine and cook, stirring often, until most of the liquid is absorbed. Stir in the lemon juice, apple cider vinegar, brown sugar, and sea salt. Stir occasionally, until about ¾ of the liquid has been absorbed. Stir in the Parmesan cheese and toss to combine.

To serve, divide the Brussels sprouts among four to six small plates.

Option: The Brussels sprouts also make a great side to pork chops or grilled bratwurst.

Mussels Steamed in White Wine

Many people order mussels in a restaurant but never think of preparing them at home. Mussels are easy, elegant, and an affordable seafood option for small plate servings. Serve the mussels with baguette slices for sopping up the delicious broth.—Frank and Jayni

4 TO 6 SMALL PLATE SERVINGS

2 pounds fresh mussels

1½ tablespoons unsalted butter
⅓ cup shallot, minced
1 large garlic clove, peeled and smashed
1¼ cups dry white wine
3 fresh parsley sprigs

Black pepper, freshly ground (optional)

Baguette slices

Just before cooking the mussels, scrub and rinse them in several changes of cold water. Remove the beards and discard any mussels with cracked shells. Tap or press any open mussels to see if they are alive. If they do not close, discard them.

In a large sauté or braising pan with a lid, melt the butter over medium-low heat. Add the minced shallot and cook for about 3 minutes, until soft, stirring often. Add the smashed garlic clove, wine, and parsley sprigs. Cover the pan and simmer the liquid for 3 minutes over medium-low heat.

Raise the heat to medium-high and bring the liquid to a boil. Remove the lid and quickly add the mussels to the pan. Sprinkle them with pepper, if desired, and cover the pan. Cook until the mussels open, about 5 minutes. Do not overcook.

Using a slotted spoon, transfer the cooked mussels to four to six small soup bowls or pasta bowls. Discard any unopened mussels, the garlic, and parsley sprigs. Strain out the shallots, if desired, and pour some of the broth over each bowl of mussels. Serve immediately with baguette slices.

Warm Shrimp and Bacon with Sherry Brussels Sprouts and Champagne Crema

Chefs Colby Garrelts and Megan Garrelts were celebrated for their first restaurant, Bluestem, in Kansas City, Missouri, in 2004. Eight years later they opened Rye in Leawood, which celebrates the Midwestern foods they grew up eating.

Colby and Megan are proud Midwesterners, and Rye gives them the opportunity to showcase dishes that they have enjoyed with several generations of their families. Their cuisine offers traditional Midwestern dishes from a chef's point of view while preserving the important heritage of the dishes.—Chef Colby Garrelts, Bluestem and Rye, Leawood

4 SMALL PLATE SERVINGS

2 tablespoons butter
8 ounces slab bacon, cubed into
    16 pieces
2 large shallots, minced
4 garlic cloves, minced
16 medium shrimp, peeled and
    deveined

16 Brussels sprouts, cut in half,
    cored, and leaves peeled
¼ cup sherry vinegar
Salt and black pepper, to taste

Champagne Crema:
1 tablespoon cooking oil
1 large shallot, minced
4 garlic cloves, minced
1½ cups dry Champagne
1 cup cream
1 tablespoon honey
1 large tarragon sprig
2 tablespoons crème fraîche or
    sour cream
Salt and black pepper, to taste

Melt the butter in a large sauté pan over medium heat. When it begins to foam, add the cubed bacon and cook until browned, about 5 minutes. Add the minced shallot and garlic and cook until translucent, about 3 minutes, lowering the heat if necessary to prevent burning. Add the shrimp and cook through, about 5 minutes.

Transfer the bacon and shrimp mixture to a warm dish, reserving about 2 tablespoons of the bacon fat in the sauté pan. Raise the heat to high and add the Brussels sprout leaves. Sauté quickly until the leaves begin to crisp, about 3 minutes. Add the sherry vinegar to deglaze the pan. Return the bacon and shrimp mixture to the pan, toss to combine, and season with salt and pepper.

To serve, divide the shrimp mixture among four small plates or shallow bowls and drizzle each with the Champagne Crema.

Champagne Crema: Heat the cooking oil in a small saucepan over medium heat. Add the minced shallot and garlic and sauté until soft, about 3 minutes. Add the Champagne and continue to cook until reduced by half, about 5 minutes. Add the cream,

CONTINUED ➡

honey, and tarragon, and continue cooking for another 5 minutes. Remove the pan from the heat and discard the tarragon. Allow the crema to cool to room temperature. Pour the crema into a blender, add the crème fraîche, and purée until smooth. Return to a clean saucepan, season with salt and pepper, and keep warm until ready to serve.

Fried Shrimp with Smoky Cocktail Sauce

Who doesn't love fried shrimp? Served as a small plate prior to the main course, this recipe is a sure winner. Smoked sea salt and smoked Spanish paprika deliver a touch of smokiness to the cocktail sauce.—Frank and Jayni

6 SMALL PLATE SERVINGS

Cocktail Sauce:
½ cup ketchup
1 tablespoon prepared horseradish
⅛ teaspoon smoked sea salt
1 teaspoon smoked Spanish paprika
1 teaspoon lemon juice
Dash Worcestershire sauce

18 medium to large shrimp
Sea salt

2 egg whites
¼ cup all-purpose flour
1 cup Panko* breadcrumbs

Canola or vegetable oil, for deep-frying

6 lemon wedges
Fresh parsley sprigs

Cocktail Sauce: In a small bowl, combine all the ingredients for the sauce. Let stand for 30 minutes to allow the flavors to blend.

Shell and devein the shrimp, leaving the tails intact. Wipe the shrimp or pat dry with paper towels. Sprinkle the shrimp lightly with sea salt.

Whisk the egg whites and flour together in a small bowl. Place the breadcrumbs on a plate.

Pour the canola or vegetable oil to a depth of 1½ inches in a large saucepan or pot. Do not fill the pan more than halfway up to avoid hot oil bubbling over when frying the shrimp. Heat the oil over high heat to 360 to 375 degrees, or until hot enough to sizzle a test drop of the egg white mixture. Dip three or four shrimp at a time into the egg white mixture to coat, shake off the excess, then coat them generously with the breadcrumbs. Place the shrimp in the hot oil and cook for about 1½ minutes, or until golden and cooked through. Remove the fried shrimp with a slotted spoon and drain on paper towels. Repeat with the remaining shrimp.

To serve, divide the shrimp among six small plates. Place a tiny container of the cocktail sauce, or a spoonful, on each plate and garnish with lemon wedges and parsley sprigs. Serve immediately.

* Panko breadcrumbs are Japanese-style dried breadcrumbs. They are available in most supermarkets and Asian markets.

Option: To serve the shrimp for a small party, arrange the fried shrimp on a large platter surrounding a bowl of the cocktail sauce. Garnish with lemon wedges and parsley sprigs.

Lamb Chops with Cheese Grits

Not long ago, most lamb chops were only available packaged from New Zealand. These days, there is a growing opportunity to purchase local, organically raised lamb in Kansas.

A generous roasted lamb chop served on a mound of creamy cheese grits makes an elegant small plate serving for dinner guests.—Frank and Jayni

4 SMALL PLATE SERVINGS

1 rack of lamb (about 1 pound, 8 ribs), frenched

2 to 3 garlic cloves
¼ teaspoon salt
¼ teaspoon black pepper
1 teaspoon dried herbes de Provence
2 teaspoons olive oil

2 tablespoons vegetable or peanut oil

Cheese Grits:
¾ cup whole milk
½ cup water
¼ teaspoon salt
½ cup corn grits
1 tablespoon butter, softened
⅓ cup (room temperature) sharp cheddar cheese, shredded
¼ teaspoon white pepper

Fresh rosemary or thyme sprigs

CONTINUED ➡

Remove the layer of fat from the meaty side of the rack of lamb and set the rack aside.

Using a mortar and pestle, crush the garlic with the salt and pepper. Add the herbes de Provence and crush until the mixture resembles a paste. Stir in the olive oil.

Spread the garlic and herb mixture onto the meaty side of the rack and place it on a plate or in a baking dish. Let stand at room temperature for 30 minutes, or cover and refrigerate if cooking later. If refrigerated, let stand at room temperature for 30 minutes before cooking.

Heat a stainless steel (oven-safe) skillet over medium-high heat. Add 2 tablespoons of vegetable or peanut oil to the skillet and place the rack in the skillet, meaty-side down. Cook for 2 to 3 minutes, until browned. Turn the rack over and brown for about 30 seconds. Place the skillet with the lamb rack in a 500-degree oven and roast for about 7 to 10 minutes, until the meat registers 130 to 135 degrees for medium-rare. Transfer the rack of lamb to a cutting board, tent with aluminum foil, and let rest for about 10 minutes. While the lamb is resting, prepare the cheese grits.

Cheese Grits: Pour the milk and water into a heavy-bottomed saucepan. Add the salt and

bring to a boil over medium-high heat. When the liquid boils, slowly stir in the grits. Reduce the heat to low and cook for 4 to 5 minutes, stirring frequently, until the liquid is absorbed and the grits thicken. Remove the pan from the heat and immediately stir in the butter, cheese, and white pepper. Cover and let the grits stand for 5 minutes before serving.

To serve, cut the rack of lamb into four double chops, two ribs each. Place a large dollop of cheese grits in the center of each small plate. Arrange a double chop on top. Garnish with fresh rosemary or thyme sprigs.

Chapter 2
Soups, Stews, and Chili

From the early days of Kansas settlement to today, mention soup or stew, and the very words evoke memories of aromas wafting from the kitchen, patient simmering, and complex flavors. Home cooks add a secret ingredient—perhaps it's something mystical—when they stir together a meal in a single pot.

The reasons for cooking soups, stews, and chili vary beyond the convenience of a meal-in-one, but melding harmonious flavors together over time is what this chapter's recipes have in common. Whether you begin with the aromatics—onion, carrot, celery—or build a flavorful base from browned meats, once you pour in the stock, the tempo slows to the rhythm of a gentle murmur. You monitor a simmering pot at the pace of the day, knowing that warmth, comfort, and nourishment will be served at your convenience.

Soups tend to be lighter than stews and cook in less time. They can be served as the first course, such as "Gella's Beer Cheddar Soup," or be the entire meal, like "Vegetable Beef Soup." Soups can be composed of fresh, uncooked ingredients, as is "Gazpacho," or made of cooked vegetables that are then puréed in the blender and served chilled, as in "Cold Buttermilk-Golden Beet Soup."

Stews usually include meat and vegetables covered in water or stock and simmered slowly until the meat is fork tender. The ingredients seem to conspire, producing a rich potion intended to sooth stressful times, such as the recipe for "Chicken and Green Chile Stew." For the cook with less time to prepare dinner, we offer "Pork Country Ribs and White Bean Stew" made in a pressure cooker. A stew can also take a creative twist, such as "Campfire Stew in Spaghetti Squash Bowls."

Chili is another matter. A bowl of hearty chili can fire up the fans on game days, be the center of attention when hosting a potluck, or recharge the weary after shoveling the sidewalk on a snowy day. Bold, spicy, and never shy, chili spells party time! Its ingredients vary widely, but the common characteristic is the promise of fun, such as in "Venison Chocolate Chili," "Spicy Turkey Chili," and "Dan's Lucky Chili."

Perfect Potato Soup

Bobbi Luttjohann likes to make this recipe on cold, snowy days in Kansas. "My girls love this recipe, and I know it's a hit every time I make it," says Bobbi. "I've used this recipe countless times for office parties, 4-H fundraisers, and potluck dinners. I believe I even served it on Easter once." Bobbi buys her veggies from the local farmers' market when she can, or purchases organic products when available.

"The milk or cream I use is raw and from a lovely family who milks three cows in the next county over," she says. The bacon she prefers is from a neighbor who butchers his own hogs. If that's not available, she buys brands marked "From the Land of Kansas." Bobbi says, "All these fresh local ingredients create a wonderful healthy soup my entire family loves."—Bobbi Luttjohann, Topeka

6 SERVINGS

6 cups potatoes, peeled and cubed
¼ cup onion, chopped
2 medium carrots, chopped
2 celery ribs, chopped
¼ teaspoon black pepper
6 cups homemade chicken broth

1 cup homemade cream cheese
    made from raw local whole
    milk, or 1 cup raw local cream*

½ to 1 cup shredded cheddar
    cheese, to taste
6 bacon strips, fried and crumbled
Salt and black pepper, to taste

In a large pot or Dutch oven, combine the cubed potatoes, onion, carrots, celery, and pepper. Pour in the chicken broth, bring the mixture to a boil over medium heat, and cook until the potatoes are tender, about 10 minutes.

Using a potato masher, mash a few of the cooked potatoes to release their starch for thickening (this step is very important). Reduce the heat to low and add the cream cheese a little at a time. Stir frequently until the cream cheese melts. This step takes awhile, so be patient. Whisk the soup gently to blend, if needed. Cream may be added in place of the cream cheese. Heat the soup just until simmering.

CONTINUED ➡

Remove the pot from the heat and immediately stir in the shredded cheddar cheese and crumbled bacon. Taste and season with salt and pepper, if desired.

* Raw milk for making homemade cream cheese, or raw cream as a substitution for the cream cheese, is not always available to cooks. A high-quality or organic cream cheese or heavy whipping cream from a natural foods store or supermarket may be substituted.

Harry's Deli Cream of Wild Mushroom Soup with Toasted Pecans and Goat Cheese

Harry's Deli, owned and operated by Harry's, a fine dining restaurant in downtown Manhattan, offers casual, cafeteria-style service with soups, sandwiches, and hot daily specials.

"We added this soup to our offerings at Harry's Deli around 2011. It is a great soup to make during the fall or winter months. Feel free to try different mushrooms that will change the flavor, depending on the choice. We usually use a blend of shiitake, cremini, and portabella mushrooms."
—Executive Chef Cadell Bynum, Harry's Deli, Manhattan

4 TO 6 SERVINGS

5 cups (about 12 ounces) fresh wild mushrooms of choice, or a combination of shiitake, cremini, and portabella mushrooms
2 tablespoons butter or olive oil

2 tablespoons butter
½ cup yellow onion, finely chopped
¼ cup carrot, finely chopped
¼ cup celery, finely chopped

1 teaspoon kosher salt
1 teaspoon black pepper, coarsely ground
1 pinch dried thyme
1 pinch dried tarragon
2 tablespoons all-purpose flour

4 cups chicken broth
2¼ cups heavy cream

1 cup fresh goat cheese
½ cup pecans, toasted*

Extra toasted pecans for garnish (optional)

Clean and trim the mushrooms and stem shiitakes, if using. Thinly slice the mushrooms. In a medium saucepan heat 2 tablespoons of butter or olive oil over medium heat and sauté the mushrooms until tender. Set aside.

In a large saucepan, heat 2 tablespoons of butter over medium heat and sauté the chopped onion, carrot, and celery until lightly caramelized. Add the kosher salt, pepper, thyme, and tarragon. Sprinkle the flour over the vegetables and herbs and stir until the mixture is lightly browned.

Add the chicken broth to the vegetables and herbs and simmer over medium-low heat, stirring occasionally, until lightly thickened. Add the cream and bring to a simmer.

In a blender, combine the goat cheese and toasted pecans with about 1 cup of the soup base and slowly purée until very smooth. Add the puréed mixture to the remaining soup base and simmer over low heat until thickened, 5 to 10 minutes. Add the reserved mushrooms and cook for 2 minutes more.

Ladle the soup into bowls and garnish with extra toasted pecans, if desired.

*Toasted Pecans: Place pecan halves on a microwave-safe plate and microwave on high for 2 to 4 minutes, or until lightly browned. Or place the pecans on a baking sheet and toast in a 350-degree oven for 5 to 8 minutes, turning once.

Gella's Beer Cheddar Soup

In 2014, the Huffington Post *honored Gella's Diner & Lb. Brewing Co., as "the ONE thing you must do" in Kansas. And the Weather Channel's storm chasers regularly tell viewers, "If in Hays, go to Gella's."*

Gella's Diner & Lb. Brewing Co. is located "just off the beaten path" in downtown Hays. The restaurant and microbrewery draws its unique name from the community's rich Volga-German heritage. Lb. Brewing Co. pays homage to the bygone days of the settlers when beer and bread sometimes played interchangeable roles. When in the field, workers couldn't always stop to eat lunch. So, they drank it. Hence, the "Lb." in the company name stands for "liquid bread."

"Whenever possible I like to incorporate Lb. Brewing Co.'s award-winning beers into our recipes, and our 'Beer Cheddar Soup' became a favorite."—Chef Manuel Hernandez, Gella's Diner & Lb. Brewing Co., Hays

8 TO 10 SERVINGS

¼ cup butter
1 medium onion, finely chopped
1 carrot, peeled and finely chopped
1 celery rib, finely chopped
¼ cup garlic, finely chopped
1 tablespoon fresh thyme, chopped
3 tablespoons all-purpose flour

2 cups chicken broth
2 cups heavy cream
2 cups Lb. Brewing Co. IPA, oatmeal
    stout, or beer of choice
1 bay leaf
1 pound cheddar cheese,
    shredded
Salt and white pepper, to taste

Heat the butter over medium heat in a Dutch oven or large saucepan. Add the chopped vegetables, garlic, and thyme and cook until the vegetables are tender, stirring frequently. Stir in the flour and cook for 1 to 2 minutes more.

In a separate large saucepan, heat the chicken broth and heavy cream over high heat until it comes to a boil. Slowly pour the liquid into the vegetable mixture, stirring constantly. Add the beer and bay leaf and return to a boil. Reduce the heat to low and stir in the cheese. Blend the soup with an immersion blender or a wire whisk. Pour the soup through a wire-mesh strainer and discard the vegetables and bay leaf. Season the soup with salt and white pepper. Serve immediately.

What's Brewing in Kansas?

Nothing was really hoppin' in Kansas until 1987. Forgive the pun, but brewing beer was outlawed in the Kansas Constitution back in 1881. As the law was enforced, Kansas towns, many with large German populations, witnessed the closing of their local breweries and, along with them, their revered beer gardens. The beer gardens were truly social centers with educational events, food saloons, and amusements for the entire family. With the purchase of a schooner of beer, you could join in the conviviality, dine, walk among the flowerbeds, bowl, and waltz to a brass band. Though the national prohibition years came and went, Kansas's strict laws continued to discourage alcohol production and consumption.

All that changed when an enterprising University of Kansas student took a break from his studies. Chuck Magerl developed an interest in home-brewing beer in the 1970s. After a decade of research and self-training, he believed he was ready to open a brewpub and sell his brew. But to do that he first had to set aside his brewer's apron for a necktie. His timing was good; the attitudes about liquor laws in Kansas were changing. Single-handedly, Chuck lobbied lawmakers to include microbreweries in the legislation. The law passed, and in 1989 Free State Brewing Company became the first legal brewery in Kansas in more than one hundred years.

The Free State brewpub opened its doors in Lawrence to an enthusiastic crowd. Patrons soon learned that beer tastes better fresh. Chuck's vision of restoring Kansans' historic love of beer had become a reality bolstered by the growing interest in craft brews nationally and by those who had travelled to Europe. Conviviality, an essential component, appeared to be brewed in.

"For me, making beer is not about reaching the pinnacle of culinary achievement, or producing a rarefied product for the elite," Chuck says. "I want to contribute to the enjoyment of life, make a product with flavor, and provide an atmosphere that could be shared with family and friends. It's about enhancing the flavor of life."

The enthusiasm for craft beers over the last twenty-six years has resulted in more than twenty breweries across Kansas. Tallgrass Brewing Company has been brewing beer since 2007 in Manhattan, and now sells beer across the country. In 2015, The Tallgrass Tap House opened to an eager audience in downtown Manhattan. Gella's Diner & Lb. Brewing Co. in Hays was touted in the *Huffington Post*'s 2014 article as "the ONE thing you must do" in Kansas. Hays, located in Ellis County, is recognized as the "German Capital of Kansas." The Lb. Brewing Co., with its award-winning beers, exemplifies the county's German heritage.

Some brewpubs continue to honor the traditions of the long-ago beer gardens of Kansas by hosting a variety of social events. Although you may hear more bluegrass and jazz than oompah these days, the bands play, the food is delicious, and the conversation is lively. For those aficionados who can't resist foaming at the mouth, the Kansas Craft Brewers Expo, an annual event held every March in Lawrence, gives beer lovers the opportunity to try beers from the professional craft breweries around Kansas. If that's still not enough to encourage you to take a seat at the bar, consider the motto at Free State Brewery: "Because without beer, things do not seem to go as well."

Bolita Bean Soup

A pot of bean soup is just as satisfying to Kansans today as it was to past generations. These days, take advantage of our pressure cooker. The beans don't need to soak and they cook much faster.

There is an endless variety of heirloom beans to choose from. One of my favorites for this soup is bolita beans because they have a bold, rich flavor and creamy texture. For an additional flavor boost, I sometimes add a smoked ham hock while cooking the beans, or toss in small cubes of ham at the end while thickening the soup. If you can't find bolita beans, try other heirloom varieties when making this recipe.—Jayni

6 SERVINGS

1 pound dried bolita beans, or
    other heirloom beans, inspected
    and rinsed

2 tablespoons olive or vegetable oil
1 medium onion, chopped
2 medium carrots, peeled and
    chopped
1 rib celery, chopped
1 garlic clove, minced

8 quarts water
3 tablespoons tomato paste
1 bay leaf

1 tablespoon cold butter
1 tablespoon all-purpose flour
Salt and black pepper, to taste

Rinse and sort through the beans to eliminate small pebbles or debris. Drain well and set aside. (The beans do not need to be soaked if using a pressure cooker.)

Set an electric pressure cooker* on "sauté" and add 2 tablespoons of oil to the cooking pot. When hot, add the onion, carrots, and celery and sauté until tender, about 5 minutes. Add the garlic during the last minute of cooking.

Add the beans to the pressure cooker pot and pour in 8 quarts of water. Stir in the tomato paste and add the bay leaf. Cover and lock the cooker lid into place. Cook on high pressure for 40 minutes. Let the steam release naturally. Taste, and if the beans haven't reached the desired tenderness, reset the pressure cooker and cook for 10 to 15 minutes more, or simmer the soup in the pressure cooker pot until done.

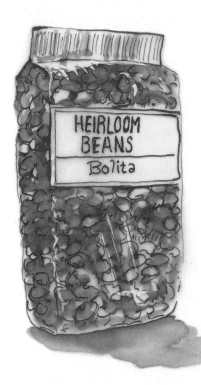

To thicken the soup, set the pressure cooker on "brown" and bring it to a boil. Mash the cold butter and flour together using a fork and form it into a ball. Pinch off bits of the butter and flour ball and stir them into the soup until the desired thickness is reached. Change the setting to "simmer" and let the soup simmer gently for 2 to 3 minutes. Season with salt and pepper. Ladle the soup into wide soup bowls to serve.

*If using a stovetop pressure cooker, follow the manufacturer's instructions when preparing this recipe.

Option: The soup may be made in a Dutch oven or soup pot on the stovetop. Rinse and sort the beans. Soak them in water overnight, then drain and rinse them. Prepare the soup as directed. Simmer the soup uncovered over low heat for 1½ to 2 hours, or until the beans are tender. Add more water to the beans while cooking, if needed. Thicken the soup as directed.

Quinoa Vegetable Soup with Feta Cheese

Quinoa, known as a super-grain, is delicious, versatile, and really good for you. It is the basis for this vegetable soup. Although quinoa is actually the seed of a leafy plant distantly related to spinach, it is classified and treated as a grain. Quinoa is considered to be high in protein and unsaturated fats and low in carbohydrates. It also provides a rich and balanced source of vital nutrients. Quinoa is available in several colors, but we prefer the red quinoa for this soup because of its chewiness and slightly earthy flavor.—Frank and Jayni

6 TO 8 SERVINGS

1 cup red quinoa, rinsed well

3 tablespoons olive oil
1 garlic clove, finely chopped
⅛ teaspoon crushed red pepper
1 teaspoon cumin seed, coarsely
    crushed
10 to 12 ounces red potatoes,
    peeled and cut into ½-inch dice
4 ounces carrots, peeled and cut
    into ¼-inch dice
½ cup onion, finely chopped
⅓ cup celery, finely chopped
½ teaspoon salt
⅛ teaspoon black pepper

4 cups chicken or vegetable broth
2 cups ripe tomatoes, peeled and
    chopped, or 1 14.5-ounce can
    diced tomatoes
1 small bunch (about 6 ounces)
    fresh spinach, stemmed, rinsed,
    and chopped

4 to 6 ounces feta cheese, crumbled

Bring 6 cups of water to a boil over high heat in a large saucepan. Add the quinoa and return the water to a boil. Stir, reduce the heat to medium-low, and simmer for 10 minutes. Pour the quinoa through a wire-mesh strainer to drain, reserving 2 cups of the cooking water. Set aside.

Heat the olive oil in a Dutch oven or large soup pot over medium-low heat. Add the garlic, crushed red pepper, and cumin. Cook for about 1 minute, stirring. Add the potatoes, carrots, onion, celery, salt, and pepper and cook for 5 to 8 minutes, stirring frequently, until the vegetables begin to soften.

Add the chicken or vegetable broth, tomatoes, and the 2 cups of reserved cooking water to the pot. Raise the heat to high. When the soup begins to boil, reduce the heat to medium-low and maintain a gentle simmer. Cook until the vegetables are tender, 15 to 20 minutes. Stir in the cooked quinoa and spinach and simmer for 2 to 3 minutes more.

Remove the pot from the heat and add the feta cheese. Season the soup with additional salt and pepper, if needed.

Creamy Chicken Soup with Leeks, Spinach, and Wild Rice

"This soup calls to me the moment I feel the first whisper of cold weather. It's so nourishing, and it satisfies the entire family on a wintry Kansas night."—Karen Waite, Lawrence

4 TO 6 SERVINGS

6 cups chicken broth
2 skinless, boneless chicken breasts

3 cups water
¾ cup uncooked wild rice blend
1 teaspoon salt

2 tablespoons butter
5 ounces bacon (5 strips), diced

2 medium leeks, cleaned and
   chopped*
2 celery ribs, chopped
5 cups baby spinach leaves
2 carrots, peeled and chopped
5 garlic cloves, finely chopped
4 sprigs fresh thyme, tied with
   kitchen twine

1 cup heavy cream
Salt and black pepper, to taste

Lemon juice
Parmesan cheese shavings
French baguette, warmed

Pour the chicken broth into a pot or large saucepan. Add the chicken breasts and simmer over low heat, partially covered, until tender, 20 to 25 minutes. Remove the chicken from the broth and cool briefly. Dice the chicken into bite-size pieces and reserve the broth.

Bring 3 cups of water to a boil in a large saucepan. Add the wild rice blend and salt. Cover, reduce the heat to low, and simmer until tender, about 30 minutes. Drain the water from the rice.

In a stockpot or Dutch oven, melt the butter over medium heat. Add the diced bacon and cook until crispy. Lower the heat to prevent the bacon from burning, if needed. Using a slotted spoon, remove the bacon and drain on paper towels. Leave the dripping in the pot and reserve the bacon to garnish the soup.

Add the chopped leeks, celery, spinach, and carrots to the drippings in the stockpot. Cook over medium-low heat to soften, about 3 minutes. Add the garlic and cook for 2 minutes more. Raise the heat to high and add the reserved chicken broth, diced chicken, cooked rice, and thyme sprigs. Bring the soup to a boil, reduce the heat to low, cover and simmer for about 10 minutes, until the leeks and carrots are tender.

CONTINUED ➡

Remove the thyme sprigs. Stir in the heavy cream and return the soup to a gentle simmer over low heat. Season with salt and pepper.

To serve, ladle the soup into bowls. Sprinkle each with a few drops of lemon juice and top with Parmesan cheese shavings and the reserved diced bacon. Serve with a warm baguette.

* To clean and chop the leeks: Cut off the dark green tops of the leeks, leaving about 2 inches of the lighter green area. Remove the roots. Slice the leeks in half, lengthwise, and rinse under cold running water, separating the layers to remove any sand or dirt. Drain well. Chop the leeks into ½-inch pieces.

Vegetable Beef Soup

One winter day, we entered the butcher shop and, influenced by the cold weather, spied a large, meaty beef shank. These days, vegetable beef soup is often made with precut beef stew meat to simplify the process, but instead, we went old school, anticipating the comforting aroma of a slow-simmering beef shank permeating throughout the house. We decided to modernize the soup by adding dried porcini mushrooms to amplify the broth with a smoky, rich flavor and, along with the usual vegetables, tossed in kale, for added nutrition, color, and texture.—Frank and Jayni

6 TO 8 SERVINGS

2 cups water
½ -ounce dried porcini mushrooms

2 pounds (1 or 2) meaty crosscut
    beef shanks, 1 to 2 inches thick
Salt and black pepper
2 tablespoons olive oil

¼ cup onion, finely chopped
¼ cup carrot, finely chopped
¼ cup celery, finely chopped
2 garlic cloves, minced
1 (14.5-ounce) can beef broth
6 cups water
1 small bay leaf

½ cup frozen pearl onions
2 cups fresh tomatoes, peeled and
    chopped, or 1 14.5-ounce can
    diced tomatoes

2 or 3 medium carrots, peeled and
    sliced into ¼-inch thick coins
2 medium celery ribs, thinly sliced
8 to 12 ounces red potatoes, peeled
    and cut into ½-inch dice
2 cups kale, chopped and lightly
    packed
4 ounces green beans, cut into
    1-inch pieces
¾ cup fresh or frozen sweet corn
    kernels
½ teaspoon salt, or to taste
¼ teaspoon black pepper, or to taste

Bring 2 cups of water to a boil. Place the porcini mushrooms in a small bowl and pour the boiling water over them. Let stand for 10 minutes.

Pat the beef shanks dry with paper towels and season generously with salt and pepper. Heat the olive oil over medium-high heat in a Dutch oven or soup pot. Add the shanks and brown on all sides. Transfer them to a small bowl or plate, reserving the dripping in the pot.

Add the finely chopped onion, carrot, and celery to the pot. Reduce the heat to medium-low and cook until softened, about 5 minutes. Add the garlic and cook for 1 minute more. Stir in the beef broth and raise the heat to medium-high. Bring to a simmer and stir up the browned bits. Return the beef shanks to the pot and add 6 cups of water. Add the bay leaf. Strain the broth from the porcini mushrooms and add it to the pot. Chop the porcini mushrooms into small pieces and reserve them to add later. Bring the soup to a boil and reduce the heat to low. Partially cover the pot and maintain a gentle simmer for 2 hours, or until the beef is very tender and falling off the bone.

Transfer the shanks to a cutting board and let cool. When cool enough to handle, remove the meat from the bones. Remove and discard any excess fat and cut the meat into 1-inch pieces. Set aside. Pour the broth through a wire-mesh strainer; remove and discard the vegetables and bay leaf. Pour the broth into a fat separator and separate the fat, or let it stand in a large bowl for about 30 minutes to allow time for the fat to rise to the top. Skim off the fat and discard.

Return the beef and defatted broth to a clean Dutch oven or large pot. Place the frozen pearl onions in a microwave-safe bowl and microwave on high for 30 to 60 seconds to defrost and warm them. Add the pearl onions, tomatoes, carrots, celery, potatoes, kale, and reserved porcini mushrooms to the pot. Bring the soup to a simmer over medium-low heat for about 10 minutes, or until the vegetables are almost tender. Add the green beans and corn and continue simmering for 20 minutes more, or until all the vegetables are very tender. Season the soup with ½ teaspoon of salt and ¼ teaspoon of pepper. Taste and adjust seasonings, if needed.

Cold Buttermilk-Golden Beet Soup

Beets are planted in early spring, so you'll find them freshly harvested in the markets in early summer. Though red beets are more common, choose golden beets for this chilled summer soup. It's a great starter for a summer dinner party, or pair it with a green salad for lunch. It makes a cheery bowl of sunshine!—Frank and Jayni

4 SERVINGS

1 pound medium-sized golden
    beets
Olive oil

½ teaspoon salt
1½ cups buttermilk, or more if
    needed

Fresh dill, chopped

Trim the beet stems to within ½ inch of the beets and leave the roots intact to prevent bleeding while roasting. Rinse the beets well and pat dry with paper towels. Place them on a piece of heavy-duty aluminum foil and coat with a small amount of olive oil. Roast them in a 400-degree oven for 1 to 1½ hours, until very tender, depending on the size of the beets. When the beets are just cool enough to handle, remove the tops and roots, and peel them. Cut the beets into quarters.

Place the beets and salt in a blender. With the blender running, pour in the buttermilk through the feed tube. Purée until smooth. Pour the beet soup into a large bowl or container. If the soup is too thick, add extra buttermilk, up to ½ cup. Taste and add more salt, if needed.

Cover and chill for at least 3 hours. Serve the soup in small bowls topped with fresh chopped dill.

Variation: Chioggia (striped) beets can be substituted for golden beets to make a pretty pink soup.

Gazpacho

In Kansas, we can't wait for the tomato season. Be careful what you wish for because once the tomatoes begin to ripen, most gardeners can't use up their crop fast enough. We make gazpacho, a Spanish-style cold soup, as a delicious, no-cook way to use a few pounds of tomatoes—not to mention the overflow of bell peppers, cucumbers, and onions. Purée the vegetables in the blender or food processor and in minutes you'll have a refreshing bowl of summer's bounty. Serve it as a starter or a main course.—Frank and Jayni

6 TO 8 SERVINGS

3 pounds ripe, juicy tomatoes
1 medium red or green bell pepper
12 ounces cucumbers, peeled
1 cup yellow onion (sweet variety), peeled
1 large garlic clove, chopped
3 tablespoons sherry vinegar
1 teaspoon sea salt
¼ cup extra-virgin olive oil

Croutons

Rinse the vegetables, core, seed, and roughly chop them into 1-inch pieces. Place the tomatoes in a blender or food processor. Blend for a few seconds to break them down. Add the remaining vegetables, garlic, sherry vinegar, sea salt, and olive oil. Blend until smooth.

Pour the gazpacho into a large bowl or container, cover and chill in the refrigerator for several hours, or overnight, to allow time for the flavors to meld. Taste and add more vinegar or salt if needed.

To serve, ladle the gazpacho into small bowls and top each with a few croutons.

Chicken and Green Chile Stew

Many Kansans love Southwestern flavors, especially in the western and southwestern parts of the state. In late summer, green chile peppers begin to appear in the markets, or perhaps in your own garden. The aroma of roasting green chiles in the oven, or on the grill, is all the inspiration you'll need to prepare this spicy chicken stew. For additional background flavor, we add our homegrown tomatillos and use masa harina, the Mexican corn flour, to add body to the stew.—Frank and Jayni

6 SERVINGS

12 to 16 ounces Hatch or Anaheim green chile peppers

3½- to 4-pound whole chicken, cut up
8 cups water
1 medium carrot, peeled and cut into 3 pieces
1 celery rib, cut into 3 pieces
½ medium onion, cut in half
1 teaspoon salt
¼ teaspoon whole black peppercorns

1 pound fresh tomatillos
3 tablespoons of olive oil, divided

1½ cups onion, cut into ½-inch dice
2 garlic cloves, minced
1 teaspoon cumin seed, coarsely ground
½ teaspoon dried oregano

1 tablespoon masa harina
1 (15.5-ounce) can golden hominy, drained

Salt and black pepper, to taste
⅓ cup fresh cilantro leaves, snipped

Sour cream
Corn or flour tortillas, warmed

To roast the green chile peppers, put them on a foil-lined baking sheet and place them about 6 inches under the oven-broiler, or roast them on a hot grill grate, until charred and blistered on all sides. Immediately enclose the charred chiles in a plastic or paper bag and let them "sweat" for about 20 minutes for easier peeling. Peel the chiles and remove the stems and seeds. Chop into ½-inch dice and set aside.

Place the chicken pieces in a Dutch oven or large pot. Cover with 8 cups of water. Add the carrot, celery, onion, salt, and peppercorns.

Bring to a boil over high heat. Once boiling, immediately reduce the heat to low and maintain a steady but slow simmer, uncovered, for 45 to 50 minutes. Transfer the cooked chicken pieces to a cutting board to cool. Remove the skin and bones and shred the meat. Pour the broth through a wire-mesh strainer into a large bowl to remove the vegetables and peppercorns. Let the broth stand in the bowl or pour it into a fat separator for about

15 minutes, then skim or pour off the fat. Measure 5 cups of broth and reserve the remaining broth.

Remove the papery husks from the tomatillos. Rinse off the sticky substance and dry them with paper towels. Cut the tomatillos into halves or quarters, depending on their size. Add 2 tablespoons of the olive oil to a skillet over medium-high heat. When hot, add the tomatillos. Turn the tomatillos or shake the skillet occasionally, until they are lightly browned and begin to break down. Cool the tomatillos to warm, then place them in a blender and purée until smooth.

In a large Dutch oven, heat the remaining tablespoon of olive oil over medium heat. Add the chopped onion and cook until soft and caramelized, stirring often. During the last minute or so of cooking, add the garlic, cumin, and oregano and stir constantly.

To the Dutch oven, add the roasted and chopped green chiles, 5 cups of chicken broth, and the puréed tomatillos. Bring the mixture to a gentle simmer over medium-low heat for 10 minutes. In a small bowl, whisk together ¼ cup of the reserved cooled chicken broth and the masa harina. Slowly stir the mixture into the stew and return it to simmering. This will very lightly thicken the stew to give it body. Add the shredded chicken and hominy and simmer for about 5 minutes more. Season the stew with additional salt and pepper, if needed. Off heat, stir in the snipped cilantro just before serving.

To serve, ladle the stew into bowls and garnish with a dollop of sour cream. Serve with warm corn or flour tortillas.

Option: If fresh tomatillos are not available, substitute one (11-ounce) can of tomatillos. Drain the tomatillos and purée them in a blender until smooth.

Pork Country Ribs and White Bean Stew

Nothing warms the home on a winter evening like a full-flavored stew of pork ribs and white beans. When it's cold outside and your hungry family is eager to sit down to dinner, let your pressure cooker shorten the simmering time to just thirty minutes. While the stew is cooking, bake a batch of corn muffins.—Frank and Jayni

6 SERVINGS

1 cup dried great northern beans, inspected and rinsed

2 pounds boneless pork country ribs
2 tablespoons olive oil
Salt and black pepper, to taste
1 cup onion, finely chopped
½ cup celery, finely chopped
2 garlic cloves, minced
1 cup tomato, peeled and chopped
1 pound thick carrots, peeled and cut into 1-inch coins
4 cups chicken broth
3 sprigs each of fresh parsley, rosemary, and thyme
3 fresh sage leaves

1 tablespoon cold butter
1 tablespoon all-purpose flour

Rinse and sort through the beans to eliminate small pebbles or debris. Drain well. (The beans do not need to be soaked if using a pressure cooker.)

Pat the pork ribs dry with paper towels. Set an electric pressure cooker* on "brown" and add 2 tablespoons of olive oil to the cooking pot. When hot, add the ribs in two batches and brown on all sides, about 5 to 6 minutes for each batch. Transfer the ribs to a plate or tray and season with salt and pepper. Set the pressure cooker on "sauté" and add the chopped onion, celery, and garlic to the pot. Cook, stirring frequently, until tender. Add the beans, then stir in the chopped tomato. Arrange the pork ribs on the beans and tomatoes and place the carrots on top. Pour in the chicken broth. Tie the parsley, rosemary, thyme, and sage leaves together with a string and tuck the bundle into the pot. Cover and lock the cooker lid into place. Cook on high pressure for 30 minutes. Let the steam release naturally.

Using a slotted spoon, transfer the pork ribs and carrots from the pot to a cutting board or large bowl. Separate the pork ribs into chunks, or leave whole, and remove excess fat. Discard the herb bundle. Pour the broth with the beans and bits of tomato through a wire-mesh strainer into a large fat separator or bowl. Reserve the beans and tomato. Let the broth stand for about 15 minutes to separate, or skim the fat if using a bowl. Transfer the pork, carrots, beans, and tomato to a Dutch oven or large saucepan. Add the defatted broth and heat over medium heat to simmering.

Mash the cold butter and flour together using a fork and form it into a ball. Pinch off bits of the ball and whisk or stir them into the simmering broth. Use as much as needed to slightly thicken the broth. Season with salt and pepper, if needed. Ladle the stew into wide soup bowls to serve.

*If using a stovetop pressure cooker, follow the manufacturer's instructions when preparing this recipe.

Option: The stew may be prepared in a Dutch oven or soup pot on the stovetop, but first soak the beans overnight. Prepare as directed, but add 2 extra cups of chicken broth and simmer, covered, over low heat for 1½ hours, or until the meat and beans are tender.

Beans on the Ceiling

The home pressure cooker appeared in America's kitchens after it was introduced at the world's fair in 1939. The new appliance was able to cook food 25 to 50 percent faster because the small amount of liquid in the pot was under pressure, and the steam produced inside reached a temperature approaching 250 degrees, which was a higher cooking temperature than simple boiling. Pressure-cooking was a boon for home cooks during the war years because the moist heat helped tenderize less expensive cuts of meat, concentrated flavors, and preserved vitamins—all this in a shorter amount of time. A major disadvantage was that the cook couldn't see into the pot to check the food for

doneness without removing the lid and stopping the cooking process.

The convenience of saving time came with a bit of danger, however. Those who have witnessed an old pressure cooker in action would recall its constant hissing as if it were a warning of impending disaster. Children were scolded to steer clear. Good advice, it seems. It was not uncommon for the lid to blow off and splatter beans all over the ceiling. Apparently, ingredients such as dried beans produce a foam when cooking. And, as the foam expanded, it would clog the pressure relief valve, resulting in an explosion. To avoid injury, more than one pressure cooker ended up on the back porch as the dog's water bowl.

Times have changed. The pressure cooker has been retooled, rediscovered, and is now enjoying a renaissance. The newly manufactured models have more than one safety mechanism, and the lid cannot be removed until all the pressure is safely gone. Electric versions are convenient, and many have nonstick coatings, making cleanup easy. Not everything can be cooked in a pressure cooker, but it's surprising how many kinds of foods do well. Inexpensive cuts of meat are popular ingredients, of course, but beans, grains, and rice are real winners. Today's cooks are experimenting with techniques such as "steam roasting" and even "pan-in-pot" baking. Concentrating flavors and quick cooking in the pressure cooker is still a benefit. Gone is the risk.

Beef Stew

In a cattle state, beef stew is a universally loved comfort food, and everyone seems to have his or her own recipe for preparing it. We make our version with organic Kansas beef. Whether you prefer beef that is grass or grain finished, certified organic, or traditionally raised, Kansas has many choices to offer.

Fresh herbs, along with red wine and beef broth, give this stew a heavenly aroma as it gently simmers on the range top. The addition of pearl onions, carrots, and tiny potatoes turns the stew into a complete meal.—Frank and Jayni

4 TO 6 SERVINGS

3 bacon strips, coarsely chopped
1 tablespoon olive oil, or more as needed
2½ to 3 pound beef chuck roast, cut into 1-inch pieces
Salt and black pepper, to taste

½ cup onion, finely chopped
1 carrot, peeled and finely chopped
1 celery rib, finely chopped
1 garlic clove, finely chopped
2 teaspoons tomato paste
2 cups beef broth, divided

2 cups dry red wine, Cabernet Sauvignon or Zinfandel preferred
2 to 3 sprigs fresh rosemary
2 to 3 sprigs fresh thyme
1 bay leaf

½ cup frozen pearl onions
3 medium carrots, peeled and cut into ½-inch thick coins

8 ounces small yellow or white potatoes (about ½-ounce each), peeled, or 8 ounces medium potatoes, peeled and cut into 1-inch cubes

2 tablespoons cold butter, diced
2 tablespoons all-purpose flour

Fry the chopped bacon in a large skillet over medium heat. Remove the bacon and reserve it. Add 1 tablespoon of olive oil to the bacon drippings and, when hot, brown the beef in batches. Add more oil to the skillet as needed. Transfer the beef to a Dutch oven or large pot. Season with salt and black pepper.

Add the chopped onion, carrot, celery, and garlic to the skillet drippings. Add another tablespoon of olive oil, if needed. Cook the vegetables over medium heat, stirring often, until softened, about 5 minutes. Stir in the tomato paste and add 1 cup of the beef broth. Bring the mixture to a simmer, scraping up the browned bits. Pour the mixture into the pot with the beef.

CONTINUED ➡

Pour the remaining beef broth and red wine into the pot. Tie the rosemary and thyme sprigs together with kitchen twine and add to the pot along with the bay leaf and the reserved bacon. Cover the pot and simmer over low heat for 1 hour.

After 1 hour, place the frozen pearl onions in a microwave-safe bowl and microwave on high for 30 to 60 seconds to defrost and warm them. Add the pearl onions to the stew along with the carrots. Cover and simmer the stew for 15 minutes. Add the potatoes and simmer for 15 to 30 minutes more, or until the vegetables and beef pieces are tender. Remove the herb bundle and bay leaf and discard.

To thicken the stew, mash the butter and flour together using a fork and form it into a ball. Pinch off bits of the ball and add to the stew, a little at a time, stirring until the liquid thickens slightly. Use only as much as needed. Simmer the stew for 2 to 3 minutes more.

Campfire Stew in Spaghetti Squash Bowls

Campfire stew, made with ground beef, is a favorite with children. In the past, this stew was commonly made with canned vegetable soup and frozen vegetables, but this version brightens up the flavor by using a variety of fresh vegetables. Serving the stew in roasted spaghetti squash "bowls" makes it a fun meal for the kids. —Jayni

6 SERVINGS

Campfire Stew:
1½ pounds ground beef
1 medium onion, chopped
1 celery rib, chopped
1 teaspoon salt
¼ teaspoon black pepper

1 large green pepper, seeded and
    chopped into 1-inch pieces
2 medium carrots, peeled and
    chopped into ½-inch pieces
4 ounces button mushrooms, thinly
    sliced

4 ounces green beans, cut into
    1-inch pieces
1 large garlic clove, minced
1 teaspoon dried oregano

3 cups fresh tomatoes, peeled and
chopped, or 2 (14.5-ounce) cans
diced tomatoes
1 cup sweet corn kernels, fresh or
frozen
1½ cups beef broth

3 spaghetti squash, about 2 pounds
each
Olive oil
Salt and black pepper

Campfire Stew: Heat a large pot or Dutch oven over medium heat. Add the ground beef, breaking it up. Add the onion, celery, salt, and pepper. Cook, stirring frequently, until the beef is browned. Spoon off excess fat, if desired.

Add the green pepper, carrots, mushrooms, green beans, garlic, and oregano to the pot. Cook for 3 minutes, then stir in the tomatoes, corn kernels, and beef broth. Bring the mixture to a simmer, reduce the heat to low, and partially cover the pot. Cook the stew for 50 minutes, or until the vegetables are tender. Season with additional salt and pepper, if needed. While the stew is simmering, roast the squash.

To roast the spaghetti squash, cover a large baking sheet with aluminum foil. Split the squash in half, lengthwise. Using a large spoon, scrape out the seeds and discard. Brush or rub the cut sides of the squash halves with olive oil and season generously with salt and pepper. Place the squash halves cut side down on the foil and roast in a 400-degree oven for 30 to 35 minutes, or until the flesh is tender.

To serve, place squash halves cut side up on dinner plates or in wide pasta bowls. Scraping with a fork, fluff the squash to resemble spaghetti. Ladle some of the warm stew into each squash cavity and serve immediately.

Beef Chili with Hominy

When the temperature drops, our desire for a bowl of chili rises. Midwesterners love chili, but unlike Southwest-style chili, chili made in the Midwest usually involves ground beef, tomatoes, and beans, and everyone has his or her own version. As a nod to the Southwest influence in Kansas, we like to use pure red chile powder, substitute hominy for beans, and add a spoonful of masa harina (corn flour) to thicken and enhance the flavor of the chili.—Frank and Jayni

6 SERVINGS

2 pounds ground beef
1 cup onion, chopped

3 to 4 garlic cloves, chopped
2 teaspoons cumin seed, coarsely crushed
2 tablespoons pure New Mexico red chile powder (mild or medium-hot)
1 teaspoon dried oregano
1 teaspoon salt
½ teaspoon black pepper

1 (14.5-ounce) can diced tomatoes
2 cups water
1 (7-ounce) can chipotle peppers in adobo sauce

1 tablespoon masa harina (corn flour)
1 (15.5-ounce) can hominy, drained
Salt and black pepper, to taste

Corn muffins, warm tortillas, or carrot sticks

Place the ground beef and chopped onion in a Dutch oven and brown over medium heat. Stir occasionally to break up the beef. If the juices are fatty, spoon off the fat, or drain the juices from the beef and pour into a fat separator. Let stand for about 10 minutes, then pour the defatted juices into a cup or small bowl. Reserve the juices to add to the ground beef later.

Once the beef is browned, add the garlic, crushed cumin seed, chile powder, oregano, salt, and pepper. Cook for 2 minutes to toast the spices, stirring frequently.

Add the tomatoes, 2 cups of water, and the reserved defatted juices, if using, to the ground beef. Wearing plastic gloves, remove three or four chipotle peppers from the can. Cut the peppers open, scrape out the seeds, and finely chop them. Stir the chopped peppers into the beef mixture along with 2 tablespoons of the adobo sauce from the can. Add more peppers and adobo sauce for hotter chili.

Bring the chili to a boil over medium heat. Partially cover the pot and reduce the heat to low. Simmer for about 45 minutes, stirring occasionally, until the beef is tender. Sprinkle the masa harina over the chili and stir to combine. Add the drained hominy and continue cooking, uncovered, for 15 minutes more. Season with additional salt and pepper, if needed.

Serve the chili with corn muffins, warm tortillas, or carrot sticks.

Dan's Lucky Chili

Dan Schriner describes his chili as very thick and complex in flavor, due in part to the addition of dark beer. Kansas is home to a growing number of microbreweries and brewpubs, so consider a dark Kansas beer when making this chili recipe.

"The recipe is published in the Schriner family cookbook that I gave my children when they left home," Dan says, "and it is made at my house every Halloween night." After trying many chili recipes over the years, Dan developed this one back in the 1980s and calls it "lucky" for two reasons: (1) Because the ingredients in this chili agree with his sensitive stomach, and (2) Because his kids like it. "They still come home for it!"—Dan Schriner, Lawrence

8 SERVINGS

2 tablespoons bacon drippings
2 onions, chopped
1 garlic clove, minced
3 tablespoons chili powder (Penzeys medium-hot preferred)
1 tablespoon ground cumin

3 pounds (85 percent lean) ground beef
1 (15-ounce) can tomato sauce
1 (12-ounce) bottle dark beer
1 jalapeño pepper, minced
2 whole bay leaves
1 teaspoon salt
1 (15-ounce) can black beans, drained and rinsed

Sharp cheddar cheese, shredded
Corn chips

In a large pot or Dutch oven, heat the bacon drippings over medium heat. Add the chopped onion and cook until lightly browned and tender, about 10 minutes. Add the garlic, chili powder, and cumin and cook for 1 minute more to allow the spices to "bloom."

Add the ground beef, breaking it up into small chunks. Cook until mostly browned, about 15 minutes. Stir in the tomato sauce and beer. Add the minced jalapeño pepper, bay leaves, and salt. Stir in the black beans. Bring the chili to a boil over medium-high heat. Reduce the heat to low and simmer uncovered for 1 hour, stirring every 10 minutes or so. Remove the bay leaves before serving. This is a very thick, rich chili, but if thinner chili is preferred, add more beer or water as it simmers.

Serve the chili with shredded cheddar cheese and corn chips.

The Chili Season

When the temperature drops and the skies are more often gray than blue, we reach for a warm coat and gloves, accepting that winter has arrived. Our appetites change, too. We begin to crave hearty, full-flavored dishes to push back against the cold. Heed the signal; it's time for chili.

Spice up your favorite meat, whether it's beef, chicken, turkey, pork, or venison, with toasted cumin seed, cinnamon, or clove to wake up your senses. Stir in some New Mexico red chile powder or chipotle peppers to add some smoky heat and take off the chill. Add beer or chocolate to pump up the flavors.

Southeast Kansans have a passion for serving cinnamon rolls with their chili, and the tradition also pops up in such places as Wichita and Kansas City, Kansas. Those in the western part of the state may prefer to serve tortillas with chili. And, for many Kansans, there is no shame in adding some pinto or black beans to the pot, regardless of what they claim is sacred in New Mexico. Simmer your own magical mix for a couple of hours and you are sure to find comfort for the chilly nights ahead.

Venison Chocolate Chili

For twenty-seven years, Christine Standard has been a volunteer for the Seward County Fire Department. Firefighters are known for their chili, and Christine's is likely to set off some alarms. She and her husband like to hunt, so deer meat, along with home-canned tomatoes from her garden, are used in her chocolate chili recipe. Christine says, "The chocolate does not make the chili sweet, it just enhances the flavor."

"I never dreamed that I would become a firefighter, but when they needed people for the fire department, I applied and was accepted into the department. In my opinion, firefighting is something that gets in your blood. Once you get into the profession, you are there for life! One of the best things about being on the department is that, while I often see people that are having one of the worst days of their lives, I have the opportunity to help them and hopefully make that worst day a little bit better. It is very rewarding!"—Christine Standard, Kismet

4 SERVINGS

1 pound ground venison (deer meat)

1 cup onion, chopped
2 garlic cloves, minced
2 tablespoons hot or mild chili powder
1 teaspoon ground cumin
1 teaspoon salt
½ teaspoon black pepper

1 (14.5-ounce) can diced tomatoes, undrained
1 cup water
1 ounce semisweet chocolate, coarsely chopped

Cheddar cheese, shredded (optional)
Sour cream (optional)

In a medium-size pot or Dutch oven, brown the ground venison over medium heat, breaking it up as it cooks. Drain off the fat, if needed.

Add the chopped onion and garlic to the meat and cook until tender, 3 to 5 minutes. Stir in the chili powder, cumin, salt, and pepper and cook for 1 to 2 minutes more.

Add the tomatoes, water, and chocolate and bring the mixture to a boil. Cover, reduce the heat to low, and simmer for 20 to 30 minutes, stirring occasionally. Taste and add more salt and pepper, if needed.

Ladle the chili into bowls and top with shredded cheese and sour cream, if desired.

Spicy Turkey Chili

For those who don't eat red meat, ground turkey makes a fine substitute for ground beef. In this chili recipe, cumin, cinnamon, clove, oregano, and tomatoes give the ground turkey big flavor. We add jalapeño peppers, chile powder, and chipotle peppers to pump up the heat. For a milder version, skip the jalapeños and use only one chipotle pepper.—Frank and Jayni

4 SERVINGS

1 tablespoon olive or canola oil
1 cup onion, chopped
2 garlic cloves, minced
2 jalapeño peppers, finely chopped
    (with or without seeds)
1 pound ground turkey

1½ teaspoons whole cumin seed
½ teaspoon cinnamon
½ teaspoon ground clove
1 tablespoon pure New Mexico
    red chile powder (mild or
    medium-hot)
½ teaspoon dried oregano
1 teaspoon salt
¼ teaspoon black pepper

1 (14.5-ounce) can fire-roasted
    diced tomatoes
1 (8-ounce) can tomato sauce
1½ cups water
1 (7-ounce) can chipotle peppers in
    adobo sauce
1 (15-ounce) can pinto beans,
    rinsed and drained

Sour cream
Corn or flour tortillas, warmed

Heat 1 tablespoon of oil in a Dutch oven over medium heat. Add the onion, garlic, and chopped jalapeño peppers and cook for 2 minutes. Add the ground turkey, breaking it up as it browns, about 10 minutes.

Coarsely crush the cumin seed in a mortar with pestle, or in a spice grinder. Add the crushed cumin seed, cinnamon, clove, chile powder, oregano, salt, and pepper to the browned turkey. Cook for 2 minutes to toast the spices, stirring frequently.

Add the tomatoes, tomato sauce, and 1½ cups of water to the turkey mixture. Wearing plastic gloves, remove two chipotle peppers from the can. Cut the peppers open, scrape out the seeds, and finely chop them. Add the peppers to the mixture along with 1 tablespoon of the adobo sauce from the can. Add more or less chipotle peppers and adobo sauce, depending on the desired level of hotness. Bring the turkey chili to a boil over medium heat. Partially cover the pot and reduce the heat to low. Simmer for about 1 hour, stirring occasionally, until the turkey is tender. Add the rinsed and drained pinto beans and continue cooking for 10 to 15 minutes more. Season with additional salt and pepper, if needed.

Top servings of the chili with a dollop of sour cream and serve with warmed corn or flour tortillas.

Chapter 3
Salads and Salad Meals

Offering to "bring a salad" may require you to do some explaining. Salads have evolved from the days of iceberg lettuce tossed with bottled dressing. Today a salad asks for some imagination. Fortunately, almost anything goes! Whether from greens to grains, or veggies to protein, salads are served as a first course, side dish, or can be substantial enough to be the entire meal.

Consider the greens. Though the crunch of iceberg lettuce is still a favorite, other lettuces such as romaine, butter, and microgreens have moved to center stage. Arugula is a peppery leaf featured in "Arugula, Blue Cheese, Walnuts, and Wine-Poached Pears with Pear Vinaigrette," and it makes a festive holiday salad. Slightly more exotic ingredients such as hearts of palm and fried shallot rings are tossed into "Pachamamas House Salad with White Balsamic Vinaigrette" for a fancy offering. Watch out: This side salad may steal the show.

As the weather warms up in the summer months, more substantial vegetables enter the bowl. "Zucchini and Tomato Salad" is perfect when these two prolific vegetables go gangbusters in the summer. "Watermelon and Cucumber Salad with Mint and Lime Dressing" tends to have a chilling effect on a warm summer evening.

A pair of chicken salads, "Chicken Salad with Grapes and Toasted Walnuts" and "Grilled Chicken Salad with Artichoke Hearts and Capers," are easy and satisfying lunch salads, and can always double as sandwiches.

Salads can shoulder an entire meal, and "Midwestern Steak and Vegetable Salad" builds on a foundation of lettuce with a bounty of Midwesterners' favorite vegetables topped with grilled steak. "Kale Salad with Grilled Chicken Breasts" may be just right for the diet conscious, and "Grilled Pork Tenderloin Salad with Barbecue Dressing" is bound to be a summertime family favorite.

Salads are always welcome at potlucks and picnics. Try this all-time favorite with a twist, "Grilled Sweet Corn and Black Bean Salad." Or, in the early spring, make colorful "Roasted Golden Beets with Butter and Balsamic Vinegar." "Quinoa Salad with Peaches, Mint, and Feta Cheese" gives the cook an opportunity to share a tasty and healthy offering.

Pachamamas House Salad with White Balsamic Vinaigrette

Chef Ken Baker's much-loved Pachamamas Restaurant and Star Bar in Lawrence served its final meal on February 14, 2015. Ken's popular house salad, made with local greens, marinated hearts of palm, toasted almonds, and crispy fried shallot rings, graced the menu for many years. To save time, prepare the vinaigrette, hearts of palm, and toasted almonds ahead of time.—Chef Ken Baker, Pachamamas Restaurant and Star Bar, Lawrence

6 SERVINGS

White Balsamic Vinaigrette:
1 tablespoon shallot, minced
½ teaspoon garlic, minced
1 tablespoon Dijon mustard
1 tablespoon sugar
1½ teaspoons fresh basil, chopped
1½ teaspoons fresh thyme, chopped
1½ teaspoons fresh oregano, chopped, or ½ teaspoon dried oregano
½ cup white balsamic vinegar
Salt and black pepper, to taste
½ cup extra-virgin olive oil
1 cup canola-olive oil blend

Marinated Hearts of Palm:
1 (14-ounce) can hearts of palm, drained
¼ cup olive oil
2 teaspoons shallot, minced
Zest of 1 lemon
Pinch of salt
Pinch of black pepper

Toasted Almonds:
½ cup sliced almonds

Fried Shallot Rings:
3 shallots, about 1 ounce each
½ cup buttermilk
1 cup rice flour
Peanut or canola oil, for deep frying
Salt, to taste

5 to 6 ounces mixed salad greens, rinsed and drained

White Balsamic Vinaigrette: Place the minced shallot and garlic in a bowl. Add the mustard, sugar, herbs, and vinegar and whisk to combine. Add salt and pepper to taste. Whisk in the extra-virgin olive oil and the canola-olive oil blend. Taste and add more salt and pepper, if needed. Let the vinaigrette stand at room temperature for at least 1 hour before using, or prepare it a day ahead and keep refrigerated until 1 hour before using. Makes about 2 cups.

Marinated Hearts of Palm: Slice the drained hearts of palm into ⅛-inch rounds and set aside. In a shallow bowl, add the olive oil, minced shallot, lemon zest, salt, and pepper. Add the sliced hearts of palm and stir gently to coat with the oil mixture. Let the marinated hearts of palm stand at room temperature for at

CONTINUED ➡

least 1 hour before using, or prepare them a day ahead and keep refrigerated until 1 hour before using.

Toasted Almonds: Spread out the sliced almonds on a baking sheet. Place them in a 350-degree oven for 3 minutes, turn them over, and cook for 3 minutes more, or until fragrant and lightly toasted. Transfer the almonds to a plate to cool. The almonds may be toasted a day ahead and stored in a covered container.

Fried Shallot Rings: Peel the shallots, thinly slice, and separate into rings. Pour the buttermilk into a shallow bowl. Place the shallot rings in the buttermilk briefly. Remove them with a slotted spoon, drain, and dust with rice flour. Pour the oil (about 2 or 3 inches deep) into a heavy-bottomed saucepan and heat over high heat. When the oil is hot, add the shallot rings in batches and fry until golden brown, about 1 minute. Remove them with a slotted spoon and drain on paper towels. Season with salt.

To assemble the salad, place the salad greens in a large salad bowl. Remove the sliced hearts of palm from the marinade (as many as desired) and add to the salad greens. Whisk the vinaigrette and drizzle as much as needed over the greens and toss gently to coat. Arrange the salads on six salad plates and garnish each with some of the toasted almonds and fried shallot rings.

Fig and Pear Salad with Sherry Vinaigrette

I put two fig tree starts in the ground one hot, dry August day but did not expect them to survive. After all, who grows figs in Kansas? To my delight, the starts grew into bush-like trees with exotic leaves, and eventually they began to bear fruit. What a happy surprise! Figs plucked off the tree taste wonderful and they are a nice embellishment to summer salads.

The fig starts came from a family farm in Arma, once owned by Italian immigrants. When the farm was sold a few years back, a friend of mine took starts from the fig trees, and that is how we acquired ours.

To plant a fig tree in your yard, choose a hearty variety that can withstand Kansas winters and be prepared to "winterize" it when cold weather arrives. An alternative is to plant the fig in a large planter that can be kept indoors during the winter months. I can't describe the joy of picking a few figs from our tree to dress up this salad.—Jayni

4 TO 6 SERVINGS

Sherry Vinaigrette:
3 tablespoons sherry vinegar
1 tablespoon shallot, finely
    chopped
2 teaspoons Dijon mustard
⅛ teaspoon salt
⅛ teaspoon black pepper
⅓ cup extra-virgin olive oil

1 medium head butter lettuce,
    rinsed and drained
1 or 2 ripe pears, peeled, cored, and
    diced
½ cup crumbled feta cheese
4 to 6 fresh figs, quartered

Sherry Vinaigrette: Pour the vinegar into a small bowl. Stir in the shallot, mustard, salt, and pepper. Whisk in the olive oil. Let the vinaigrette stand for at least 1 hour to allow the shallot to mellow.

Tear the lettuce leaves into a salad bowl. Add the diced pear and feta cheese. Whisk the vinaigrette and drizzle as much as needed over the salad. Toss gently to coat. Arrange the salad on four to six salad plates and surround by quartered figs.

Arugula, Blue Cheese, Walnuts, and Wine-Poached Pears with Pear Vinaigrette

Green salads needn't disappear from the menu in winter, and this one, featuring wine-poached pears and a pear vinaigrette, makes a festive salad to serve for a dinner party. A wide variety of pears are available in late summer through fall and winter, and most work well for poaching, as long as you choose ones that are less than ripe so they will stay firm while they cook. The contrast of the poached pears, with salty blue cheese, toasted walnuts, and peppery arugula, makes this salad a winner.—Frank and Jayni

4 TO 6 SERVINGS

Wine-Poached Pears:
2 firm pears (not quite ripe)
1 cup dry white wine
5 tablespoons sugar
2 teaspoons lemon juice

Pear Vinaigrette:
3 tablespoons pear syrup (made
    from the poaching liquid)
2 tablespoons white wine vinegar
⅛ teaspoon salt
⅛ teaspoon black pepper
¼ cup extra-virgin olive oil

½ cup walnuts
½ cup crumbled blue cheese

5 ounces arugula, rinsed and
    drained

Wine-Poached Pears: Peel the pears, cut them into quarters, and remove the stem and core. Set aside. Pour the wine, sugar, and lemon juice into a saucepan just large enough to hold the quartered pears in a single layer. Heat over medium heat, stirring, until the sugar dissolves. Add the pear quarters and reduce the heat to low. Cover and simmer for 20 to 25 minutes, turning two or three times, until the pears are tender. Using a slotted spoon, transfer the cooked pears to a plate to cool and reserve the pear liquid in the pan.

Pear Vinaigrette: To make pear syrup for the vinaigrette, simmer the reserved pear liquid over low heat, stirring occasionally, until reduced by about half and slightly syrupy, 8 to 10 minutes. Pour the syrup into a small container to cool. When cool, measure 3 tablespoons of the pear syrup and pour it into a small bowl. Whisk in the vinegar, salt, and pepper. Whisk in the olive oil.

Spread the walnuts on a baking sheet or in a pie plate. Place in a 325-degree oven for about 8 minutes, turning once, until lightly toasted. Cool the walnuts and coarsely chop. Let the crumbled blue cheese stand at room temperature for about 30 minutes before making the salad.

To assemble the salad, place the arugula in a large salad bowl. Whisk the vinaigrette and drizzle as much as desired over the arugula. Toss gently to combine. Add the crumbled blue cheese and toss again. Divide the salad among four to six salad plates. Garnish with pear quarters, or thinly slice or dice the pears and add to the salads. Top with the toasted walnuts.

Tomato and Avocado Salad with Lime Dressing

At the height of the tomato season, we look for interesting ways to take advantage of the summer's bounty. This salad pairs tomatoes with avocados, drizzled with lime dressing and showered with fresh cilantro for a colorful presentation.—Frank and Jayni

4 TO 6 SERVINGS

3 medium tomatoes
2 ripe avocados, pitted, peeled, and
    sliced

Lime Dressing:
2 tablespoons lime juice
1 small garlic clove, pressed or
    minced
¼ teaspoon salt
⅛ teaspoon black pepper
6 tablespoons olive oil

⅓ cup fresh cilantro leaves, snipped

Slice the tomatoes and arrange them on four to six salad plates. Tuck the avocado slices between the tomato slices.

Lime Dressing: Pour the lime juice into a small bowl. Add the garlic, salt, and black pepper. Whisk in the olive oil. Taste and add more lime juice or olive oil, if needed.

Using a large spoon, drizzle some of the lime dressing over each salad. Sprinkle each with snipped cilantro.

Tip: To snip the cilantro leaves, place the leaves in a measuring cup. Using the tips of kitchen shears, lower them into the cup and snip the leaves.

Zucchini and Tomato Salad

Zucchini and tomatoes are bountiful producers in the backyard garden, and cooks are constantly looking for new ways to use them up. We like this simple salad, which is a refreshing treat on a hot summer day.—Frank and Jayni

6 SERVINGS

2 medium, firm, ripe tomatoes
2 small, firm zucchini, about 4
    ounces each
¼ teaspoon garlic, minced or
    pressed
¼ teaspoon salt
¼ teaspoon black pepper
2 tablespoons extra-virgin olive oil

Cut the tomatoes in half, crosswise. Squeeze each half gently to remove most of the seeds. On a cutting board, cut the tomatoes into small dice, retaining the juice. Transfer the diced tomatoes and juice to a large bowl. Cut the zucchini into small dice and add to the tomatoes. Gently mix in the garlic, salt, and pepper. Stir in the olive oil. Cover and refrigerate for 2 hours to allow the flavors to blend.

Heirloom Tomatoes

Heirloom tomatoes are prized for their old-fashioned tomato flavor. An "heirloom" refers to a valued variety that seed savers have passed down through several generations because of special qualities and taste. Since the heirloom tomato's popularity took off in the 1990s, backyard gardeners have embraced them. For those who don't garden, a wide variety of heirloom tomatoes show up at most farmers' markets in mid- to late summer.

The color, shape, and variety of the heirloom tomato play a part in determining the flavor. The red tomatoes yield the rich, classic flavor that is absent in some of the newer varieties. Orange and yellow heirlooms tend to be sweeter and less acidic, the green varieties have a citrus profile, and the purple tomatoes possess a full-flavored, earthy quality. When several heirlooms are served together, their bright, bold colors, diverse flavors, and different shapes make a showy display. Look for names like "Brandywine," "Mortgage Lifter," "Hillbilly Potato Leaf," "Green Zebra," "Cherokee Purple," and "Black Krim." And this is only the beginning. There are countless varieties to choose from.

Heirloom Tomatoes and Goat Cheese with Herb and Garlic Vinaigrette

This summer recipe combines a colorful selection of heirloom tomatoes and vinaigrette made with fresh herbs and garlic. A garnish of crumbled goat cheese tops the tomatoes. The only accompaniment needed is a crusty baguette or a loaf of rustic bread to dip in the juices.—Frank and Jayni

6 TO 8 SERVINGS

Herb and Garlic Vinaigrette:
¼ cup red wine vinegar
1 small garlic clove, pressed
⅛ teaspoon salt
⅛ teaspoon black pepper
1 tablespoon fresh basil leaves, thinly sliced or chopped
1 teaspoon fresh lemon thyme, finely chopped
½ teaspoon fresh rosemary, finely chopped
6 tablespoons extra-virgin olive oil

2 pounds heirloom tomatoes, varieties of choice

1 ounce firm goat cheese, crumbled

Garlic and Herb Vinaigrette: In a small bowl, combine the red wine vinegar, garlic, salt, pepper, basil, lemon thyme, and rosemary. Whisk in the olive oil. Let stand for 15 minutes before using.

Slice the tomatoes about ⅜ inch thick. Arrange the slices in a large baking dish by overlapping them. Whisk the vinaigrette and pour it over the tomatoes. Let stand at room temperature for 30 minutes before serving.

When ready to serve, arrange some of the tomato slices on salad plates, spoon some of the vinaigrette over the tomatoes, and top with crumbled goat cheese.

Variation: Substitute crumbled feta cheese or miniature balls of fresh mozzarella for the goat cheese.

Organic
#3⁰⁰ lb

Watermelon and Cucumber Salad with Mint and Lime Dressing

Watermelon isn't just for a summer picnic anymore. Why not dress it up for dinner? Pair watermelon with crisp cucumber slices, mint, and feta cheese for a cool summer salad.—Frank

4 TO 6 SERVINGS

4 cups watermelon, seeded and
    chopped into 1-inch chunks
1 cucumber, about 4 ounces
    (peeled, if desired), cut into
    ¼-inch rounds
2 tablespoons fresh mint, finely
    chopped

Lime Dressing:
2 tablespoons fresh lime juice
¼ teaspoon salt
⅛ teaspoon black pepper
⅓ cup olive oil

4 to 6 large lettuce leaves
⅓ cup feta cheese, crumbled

Place the cut watermelon, cucumber slices, and chopped mint in a large bowl.

Lime Dressing: Pour the lime juice into a small bowl. Add the salt and pepper. Whisk in the olive oil.

Drizzle as much of the dressing as needed over the watermelon mixture and toss to coat.

Place the lettuce leaves on four to six salad plates. Spoon the salad onto the lettuce leaves. Sprinkle the crumbled feta over the salads.

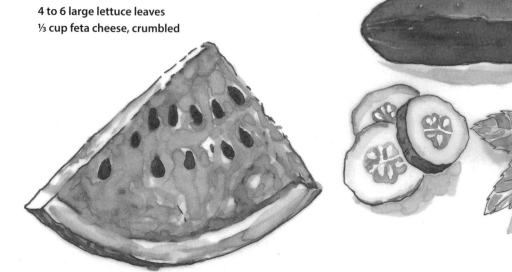

Roasted Golden Beets with Butter and Balsamic Vinegar

Fresh beets, simply roasted in the oven, are divine served as a small side salad. They have a wonderful flavor of their own and need no other seasoning than a bit of melted butter, a splash of white balsamic vinegar, and a sprinkle of salt and pepper.—Frank and Jayni

4 TO 6 SERVINGS

1 pound small to medium golden beets
Olive oil

1 tablespoon butter, cut into several pieces
1 tablespoon white balsamic vinegar
Salt and black pepper, to taste

Remove the tops and the roots from the beets. Rinse the beets well under cold running water. Pat dry and place on a large sheet of aluminum foil. Rub the beets with a small amount of olive oil. Enclose them in the foil to make a packet and seal tightly.

Place the foil packet in a small baking dish or pie plate. Place in a 375-degree oven and roast the beets for 45 minutes, to 1 hour 15 minutes (depending on the size), until tender-firm. Remove them from the oven and open the foil packet to allow them to cool. While the beets are still warm, remove the skins. Cool the beets to room temperature and slice them into thin slices or large cubes.

Place the sliced or cubed beets in a shallow microwave-safe bowl and dot with the butter. Place in a microwave oven and heat for 30 seconds to 1 minute on high power, until the butter is melted and the beets are warm. Toss gently to combine. Drizzle the beets with the white balsamic vinegar. Season with salt and pepper and toss again.

Arrange the sliced beets on a platter, or cubed beets in a shallow serving bowl. Serve warm or room temperature.

Variation: Use a combination of golden beets and Chioggia beets (deep pink-and-white striped beets) for added color.

Grilled Sweet Corn and Black Bean Salad

Summer, when Kansas sweet corn is at its peak, is the perfect time for making this colorful salad. "I make this recipe every year for my husband's July 4th birthday," Shari Paynter tells us. "Serve it as a salad or with a bowl of tortilla chips alongside for snacking. It's easy to make and can be prepared a day or two ahead of time."—Shari Paynter, Tonganoxie

8 SERVINGS

4 ears sweet corn, shucked
Olive or vegetable oil

2 (15.5-ounce) cans black beans, rinsed and drained
1 red bell pepper, seeded and thinly sliced or chopped
¼ cup red or mild yellow onion, chopped

Dressing:
3 to 4 tablespoons fresh-squeezed lime juice, to taste
3 tablespoons white vinegar
1 tablespoon honey or sugar
1 tablespoon fresh oregano, finely chopped, or 1 teaspoon dried oregano
¾ teaspoon salt
½ teaspoon black pepper
⅓ cup olive oil

Prepare a gas or charcoal grill for cooking over medium-high heat. Brush the ears of corn lightly with oil and place them on the grill for 5 to 10 minutes, turning occasionally, until some of the kernels begin to turn dark brown. Cool briefly. Cut the kernels off the cobs and measure 2 cups.

Place the grilled corn kernels in a large salad bowl. Add the black beans, red bell pepper, and onion.

Dressing: Pour the lime juice and vinegar into a small bowl. Add the honey or sugar, oregano, salt, and pepper. Whisk to dissolve the sugar, if using, and the salt. Whisk in the olive oil.

Pour the dressing over the salad and stir gently to coat all ingredients. Cover and refrigerate for several hours, or overnight, before serving. This salad keeps well for several days.

Option: The corn can be pan roasted over medium-high heat in a stainless steel or cast-iron skillet. Brush lightly with oil and cook for 5 to 10 minutes, turning occasionally, until some of the kernels begin to turn dark brown.

Are You a Locavore?

Are you concerned about where your food comes from? Do you seek out fresh, seasonal, locally grown produce, meats, and other foods? Chances are you are well on your way to becoming a locavore.

What is a locavore, exactly? The root of the term lies in the word "local." It means being conscious of the distance between where food is produced and where it is consumed. A locavore is a person who strives to eat foods grown and produced within a one hundred-mile radius, though the actual distance is determined by what is realistic for you.

It's not only about distance. It's also about economics and sustainability. Foods on North American plates may travel thousands of miles from farm to fork. Shipping foods over long distances requires more fuel for transportation (consider the air pollution), while buying products close to home supports local farmers and ranchers, builds community, and helps the local economy. Buying from local farmers allows them to experiment with new varieties of fruits and vegetables better suited to the climate and local environment. Building a local market for their meats allows ranchers to raise their animals in an environmentally sound way.

Buying locally ensures that foods will be fresher and more nutritious. Local produce doesn't have to stand up to the rigors of shipping. When grown nearby, melons are allowed more time to ripen on the vine, and corn tastes sweeter when picked the day you eat it. Compare a ripe tomato or a ripe peach found at a farmers' market to those shipped from far away. Does the flavor seem distant, or does it taste like home?

Becoming a locavore is not an all-or-nothing commitment. There are many ways you can start incorporating locavore practices into your lifestyle.

- Plant a small backyard garden. Your children can see where fruits and vegetables come from and experience the thrill of watching the garden grow.

- Shop at your local farmers' market and get to know who is growing your food. It is comforting to be acquainted with these folks to learn about the care taken to ensure the very best products.

- Sign up for a Community Supported Agriculture (CSA) program and enjoy the opportunity to sample a wide variety of local foods.

- Visit "you-pick" farms and pick, pluck, or dig your own fruits and vegetables at the height of their seasonal goodness.

- Many supermarkets now offer a whole foods section. Check it out and ask about the origins of the products. You may be surprised to find what local and organic products are available.

- Dine at restaurants that take pride in purchasing locally sourced foods. It's trending that many chefs seek out the best local products and often collaborate with their purveyors to grow and raise fruits, vegetables, and meats that inspire their creative menus.

Modern Potato Salad

"I learned to cook by osmosis from my French mother, and I grew a love of gardening from my American grandmother. I grow some of my own vegetables and fruits, and what I don't grow, I love to get at the local farmers' market. I try to use my own potatoes, peppers, onions, and parsley for this recipe. My family enjoys this potato salad with barbecue items such as hamburgers, chicken, and ribs."—Niki Schneider, Lawrence

8 SERVINGS

3 pounds medium-size red potatoes
2 tablespoons Champagne vinegar

Dressing:
1 teaspoon Dijon mustard
½ cup olive oil
¼ to ½ teaspoon salt, to taste
Black pepper, to taste

¾ to 1 cup red bell pepper, seeded and cut into small dice
2 celery ribs (about ¾ cup), cut into small dice
½ cup red onion, finely chopped
2 tablespoons capers, drained
¼ cup flat leaf parsley, chopped

Place the potatoes in a large pot, cover with water, and boil gently over medium-high heat just until they are tender. Drain and let cool slightly. Peel the potatoes, if desired, or leave the skins on if they are new potatoes or have very thin skins. Cut the potatoes into 1/2-inch chunks and place in a large bowl. Add the Champagne vinegar to the warm potatoes and toss gently to coat. Let cool completely.

Dressing: Place the Dijon mustard in a small bowl. Slowly whisk in the olive oil, then add the salt and pepper to taste.

Pour the dressing over the potatoes and gently toss to coat. Add the red pepper, celery, red onion, capers, and parsley and toss again.

Serve the potato salad at room temperature or slightly chilled.

Variation: If a less crunchy texture is preferred, sauté the chopped red bell pepper in a small amount of olive oil.

Potato Salad with Green Beans

The twist of adding garden-fresh, tender-crisp green beans to our favorite classic potato salad adds a mild crunch and a splash of color.—Frank and Jayni

6 TO 8 SERVINGS

6 ounces slender green beans, snapped in half

2 eggs

2 pounds Yukon Gold or red new potatoes
1 tablespoon coarse sea salt
2 tablespoons white wine vinegar

Dressing:
½ cup mayonnaise
1 tablespoon yellow mustard
1 teaspoon sugar

¼ cup mild red or yellow onion, finely chopped
½ cup celery, finely chopped

Bring a pot of water to a boil. Add the green beans and cook until tender-crisp, 2 to 3 minutes. Drain the beans and quickly transfer them to a bowl of ice water to cool. Drain well and set aside.

Place the eggs in a saucepan and cover with cold water. Bring to a boil over high heat, then cover the pan and remove it from the heat. Let the eggs stand in the hot water, covered, for 15 minutes. Pour off the hot water and run cold water in the pan until the eggs are cool. Peel the eggs and, when completely cooled, cut them into small dice and set aside.

Peel the potatoes and cut them into ¾-inch cubes. Place the potatoes in a Dutch oven or large pot and add enough water to cover by 1 or 2 inches. Add 1 tablespoon of coarse sea salt and bring to a boil over high heat. Reduce the heat to medium-high and cook the potato cubes until tender, but not falling apart. Drain the potatoes well and transfer them to a large serving bowl. Immediately pour the white wine vinegar over the hot potatoes and toss gently. Let the potatoes cool to warm or room temperature.

Dressing: Combine the mayonnaise, mustard, and sugar in a small bowl.

Add the cooked green beans, diced eggs, onion, and celery to the potatoes and toss to combine. Gently fold in the dressing. Cover the potato salad and chill for at least one hour before serving.

Quinoa Salad with Peaches, Mint, and Feta Cheese

Quinoa is prized for its nutritional value. Though it is actually a seed, quinoa is considered to be a whole grain and has become a popular ingredient for dishes typically based on grains.

We prefer the red quinoa for this salad because of its chewy texture and slightly earthy flavor. Make this salad in the summer when both fresh mint and peaches are in season. It is a great addition to any potluck dinner or picnic.—Frank and Jayni

8 TO 10 SERVINGS

1 cup red quinoa, rinsed
1¼ cups water
¼ teaspoon salt

3 tablespoons white balsamic vinegar
2 tablespoons olive oil
2 tablespoons fresh mint leaves, finely chopped
2 green onions, thinly sliced
2 medium peaches, pitted and chopped into ½-inch pieces
½ cup feta cheese, crumbled

Place the rinsed quinoa in a saucepan. Add the water and salt and bring to a boil over high heat. Stir, cover, and reduce the heat to low. Simmer for 13 to 15 minutes, or until all of the liquid is absorbed. Remove the pan from the heat and let stand, covered, for 10 minutes. Place the cooked quinoa in a large bowl and cool to room temperature. Cover and refrigerate, if not serving the salad within an hour.

If the quinoa has been refrigerated, set it out about 1 hour before adding the remaining ingredients. About 30 minutes prior to serving, add the white balsamic vinegar and olive oil to the quinoa and toss to combine. Add the chopped mint, green onion, peaches, and feta cheese, and toss gently.

Cranberry Fruit Salad

Toni Dixon's cranberry salad recipe was inspired by the old-fashioned fluffy concoction made with miniature marshmallows, whipped cream, and way too much sugar. "Over the years, we have made cranberry salad for every Thanksgiving and Christmas dinner, but we eliminated the marshmallows and whipped cream in exchange for fresh fruit and chopped nuts. It continues to be a family favorite, but it has evolved to fit our preferences for less sugar and fewer processed foods."—Toni Dixon, Lawrence

10 TO 12 SERVINGS

3 (12-ounce) packages fresh
　　cranberries, rinsed and drained
2 cups sugar

5 crisp apples
5 seedless oranges
2 cups red or black seedless grapes
2½ cups walnuts or pecans,
　　chopped

Place the cranberries in a food processor and pulse until coarsely chopped. Transfer the cranberry mixture to a large bowl or serving dish and stir in the sugar. Cover and refrigerate overnight.

The next day, core the apples (do not peel) and cut them into wedges. Peel the oranges and separate them into sections. Stem the grapes. Separately, place each fruit in the food processor and pulse until coarsely chopped. Add each chopped fruit to the cranberry and sugar mixture. Add the chopped walnuts or pecans.

The fruit salad can be served immediately, but for best results, refrigerate for several hours.

Option: The fruit salad can be added to yogurt or used as a topping on cereal.

Midwestern Steak and Vegetable Salad

On those warm Kansas evenings when we want something light, we often make a salad meal. More often than not, the ingredients will vary depending on what leftover vegetables may be discovered in the fridge to avoid heating up the kitchen. We find that it doesn't take much of each ingredient to build a satisfying salad meal. What ties the salad together is the sharp, coarse mustard vinaigrette drizzled over all. This recipe is our ideal combination of green beans, new potatoes, sweet corn, and cherry tomatoes, tossed with salad greens and topped with a few slices of medium-rare grilled steak.—Frank and Jayni

4 SERVINGS

2 (8- to 12-ounce) steaks of choice, grilled

Coarse Mustard Vinaigrette:
6 tablespoons red wine vinegar
4 teaspoons coarse mustard
¼ teaspoon salt
¼ teaspoon black pepper
⅔ cup extra-virgin olive oil

4 ounces green beans
8 ounces small new potatoes or fingerling potatoes

1 or 2 ears sweet corn

1 large head green leaf or romaine lettuce, rinsed and drained
4 ounces cherry tomatoes, halved
3 green onions, thinly sliced
2 tablespoons capers, rinsed and drained
¼ cup fresh tarragon leaves, finely chopped

Prepare a gas or charcoal grill for cooking over high heat. Grill the steaks to desired temperature. When ready to make the salad, cut the grilled steaks into thin slices or cubes.

Coarse Mustard Vinaigrette: Combine the red wine vinegar, mustard, salt, and pepper in a small bowl. Whisk in the olive oil.

Bring a large pot of water to a boil. Drop in the green beans and cook until tender crisp. Using a large slotted spoon, remove the beans from the pot (reserve the water) and submerge them in a bowl of ice water to stop the cooking process. When cool, remove and drain. Chop into 1-inch pieces. Return the pot of water to boiling and add the potatoes. Cook until tender, but still firm. Drain off the hot water and submerge the potatoes in ice water. When the potatoes are cool, remove and drain them. Remove the skins and slice, halve, or quarter the potatoes.

Trim the dried tassels off the ears of corn, but do not shuck them. Place the ears in a microwave oven and cook for 2 minutes on full power. Turn over and cook for 1 minute more, or to desired doneness. Let the ears rest in the microwave or on the counter for 3 to 5 minutes. Hold the warm ears with a tea towel or paper towels to shuck. (Grasping the leaves and silk together with your fingers as you shuck the ear will help to get all the silks off easily.) Cut the kernels off the cob using a sharp knife. You'll need 1 to 2 cups of kernels.

Tear or chop enough lettuce leaves for four large salads and place them in a large salad bowl. Add the green beans, potatoes, corn kernels, cherry tomatoes, green onion, capers, and tarragon. Whisk the vinaigrette and drizzle as much as needed over the salad mix. Toss to coat.

To assemble, divide the salad among four dinner plates. Arrange slices of steak alongside each salad, or, if the steak has been cubed, place it on top of the salads. Drizzle some of the remaining vinaigrette over the steak, or pass at the table.

Variation: In place of grilled steaks, sliced leftover tri-tip roast, standing rib roast, tenderloin, or flank steak may be used.

Pleasures of a Backyard Garden

In early March, if the weather cooperates, we wander out to our small backyard garden and, assured by the sun on our backs that all will work out well, poke some seeds into the cold, wet dirt. As our fear of frost diminishes, we plant more seeds, set out some herbs, and cheer when the first few spears of asparagus pierce the surface. Eventually, a few tomato plants will follow, which for us puts our "tiny farm" into full production.

It seems improbable that in just a few short months we will be plucking tender salad greens from the earth and tugging to convince slender French green beans and red, ripe tomatoes to let go of their vines. And that's just the beginning of the backyard bounty that will stretch into fall. For us, few endeavors are as rewarding as growing a backyard vegetable garden. We gaze from our deck over this small plot of earth and appreciate the colors, fragrance, and flavors it offers. It's a primal feeling of joy and well-being to harvest these jewels.

There are also practical reasons to grow your own. Foremost, of course, is to experience truly fresh vegetables at their peak of ripeness. It is an opportunity to ensure that what you eat is fresh, organic, and healthy, and for children to learn that nourishment comes from the earth and that a miracle and lifelong lessons are waiting outside your back door.

Though we love to garden, like most people, we don't have a lot of time to devote to it. The trick is to keep your garden small—just a row or two of your favorite vegetables and herbs. We plant vegetables that are hard to find or are expensive to buy. For us that means heirloom tomatoes, pencil-thin French green beans, a Provencal mix of salad greens, Shishito peppers, special varieties of garlic, and, of course, fresh herbs for cooking. We also maintain a small asparagus patch because it is "a gift that keeps on giving" year after year and requires very little attention. We skip squash, eggplant, potatoes, and cucumbers because they take up a lot of space and can be readily purchased at the farmers' market all summer long.

While Frank tills, weeds, and waters, I plant, pluck, and pull. I think I have the fun part, while Frank says his garden chores give him time to think. It is, however, an effort of two that gets the harvest from ground to mouth. As we walk from the garden to the kitchen with our bounty in hand, we taste, sniff, and discuss how these precious gifts will decorate our dinner plates.—Jayni

Grilled Pork Tenderloin Salad with Barbecue Dressing

By midsummer, when trucks appear at the farmers' market loaded with sweet corn, we've been cooking out on the grill more than in the kitchen. It seems only natural to put some of the vegetables for this salad meal on the grill, too. Once we grill the pork tenderloin, the sweet corn, and a big sweet onion, we arrange the meat and vegetables on a bed of lettuce topped with diced tomato. Pulling it all together is our favorite barbecue sauce whisked together with some mayonnaise and white wine vinegar. Whether it's smoky-hot or spicy-sweet, the barbecue sauce you choose influences the final outcome of this dressing.—Frank and Jayni

4 SERVINGS

1 pork tenderloin, 1¼- to 1½-pound
Olive oil
Salt and black pepper, to taste

1 large onion, sweet variety preferred
2 small to medium ears sweet corn, shucked
Vegetable oil

Barbecue Dressing
¼ cup barbecue sauce
½ cup mayonnaise
2 teaspoons white wine vinegar, or to taste

1 large head romaine lettuce, rinsed and drained
2 small to medium tomatoes, diced

Prepare a gas or charcoal grill for cooking over medium-high heat. Preheat a grill pan for grilling the vegetables. Brush the pork tenderloin with olive oil and season with salt and pepper. Place the tenderloin on the cooking grate and cover. Sear for 3 to 4 minutes, turning often, until browned on all sides. Place the tenderloin over indirect heat, or move to a cooler part of the grill and continue cooking for about 10 minutes more, until the meat registers 137 to 140 degrees for medium. Transfer the pork tenderloin to a platter, tent with aluminum foil, and let rest for 10 minutes before slicing.

CONTINUED ➡

Slice 1 medium onion into 4 thick slices, leaving the skin intact to help keep the slices together. Brush the onion slices and the shucked corn with vegetable oil and sprinkle with salt and pepper. Place the onion slices on the grill pan and the corn on the cooking grate. Grill the vegetables, turning occasionally, for 5 to 8 minutes or until lightly browned and tender. Remove the skins from the onions and set aside. Using a sharp knife, cut the corn kernels off the cobs.

Barbecue Dressing: In a small bowl, whisk together the barbecue sauce, mayonnaise, and white wine vinegar.

To assemble, tear or chop the lettuce leaves and place them on four dinner plates. Slice the pork tenderloin into thin slices and arrange a few slices alongside the lettuce and drizzle some of the barbecue dressing over the lettuce and pork. Place some of the grilled onion on each salad, sprinkle each with some of the corn kernels and diced tomato. Pass extra barbecue dressing at the table.

Chorizo-Stuffed Piquillo Peppers with Baby Arugula and Piquillo Pepper Vinaigrette

It is unlikely that you will find fresh piquillo peppers at a farmers' market. The pepper's tough skin and firm flesh lends it to roasting rather than eating fresh. This bright red Spanish pepper is usually found in jars, seeded, roasted, peeled, and ready to eat. Although there are other red peppers available, the piquillo pepper, because of its smoky, sweet, and spicy flavor, brings something more to the party. In this recipe, the peppers make a perfect pocket for stuffing spicy chorizo. Thanks to the influence of the Mexican community in Kansas, artisanal butcher shops, along with some grocery stores, make their own chorizo sausage.

We toss baby arugula with an easy-to-make piquillo pepper vinaigrette and tuck a pair of chorizo-stuffed peppers alongside each serving as a garnish. It makes a gorgeous salad meal fit for company.—Frank and Jayni

Piquillo Pepper Vinaigrette:

3 piquillo peppers from a 12-ounce jar of roasted piquillo peppers in water*

1 tablespoon shallot, chopped

1 garlic clove, minced

½ teaspoon smoked Spanish paprika

2 tablespoons red wine vinegar

⅛ teaspoon salt

⅛ teaspoon black pepper

¼ cup olive oil

8 ounces (2 links) fresh Mexican chorizo sausage

¼ cup onion, minced

½ cup cooked white rice

½ cup Manchego cheese, shredded

Salt and black pepper, to taste

10 to 12 piquillo peppers (from the same 12-ounce jar)

5 to 6 ounces baby arugula

⅓ cup shredded Manchego cheese, for garnish

Piquillo Pepper Vinaigrette: Place 3 peppers, shallot, garlic, smoked paprika, red wine vinegar, salt, and pepper in a blender. Purée until nearly smooth. With the blender running, pour the olive oil through the feed tube and blend until smooth. Pour the vinaigrette into a small bowl. Taste and adjust the seasoning, if needed. Let the vinaigrette stand at room temperature for at least 1 hour before serving to allow the flavors to develop.

Remove the chorizo sausage from the casings. Cook the sausage in a small skillet over medium heat, breaking it up as it cooks. Transfer the sausage to a bowl. Stir in the minced onion, cooked rice, and Manchego cheese. Season with salt and pepper and let the mixture cool to warm.

Remove 10 to 12 piquillo peppers from the jar and drain on paper towels. Using a small spoon or your fingers, gently press the sausage mixture into the peppers. Place them in a lightly oiled baking dish and bake, uncovered, in a 350-degree oven for 10 minutes, or until heated throughout. Remove the stuffed peppers from the oven and let cool for 5 minutes before serving.

To assemble the salads, put as much of the arugula as desired for four to six servings in a large salad bowl. Add 2 or 3 tablespoons of the vinaigrette and toss to coat the leaves. Arrange the arugula on four to six dinner plates. Garnish each salad with 2 or 3 stuffed piquillo peppers and a sprinkle of Manchego cheese. Pass the remaining vinaigrette at the table.

*Piquillo peppers can be purchased in the gourmet section of some large supermarkets, specialty stores, and online stores that sell Spanish products.

Kale Salad with Grilled Chicken Breasts

Kale, known for its health benefits, has become a popular garden green in recent years. We prefer lacinato kale, commonly called Tuscan or dinosaur kale, for making salads because of its earthy and delicate flavor. It is important to chop the kale into bite-size pieces, toss it with lemon juice and salt, and let it stand for a time to allow this firm, leafy green to soften before adding olive oil. To complete the salad, we like to load it up with tart, salty, and sweet flavors by adding dried tart cherries, crispy bacon, toasted pine nuts, and feta cheese. A grilled chicken breast, thinly sliced and fanned out alongside the kale, creates an enticing presentation for a healthy and satisfying salad meal.—Frank and Jayni

4 SERVINGS

1 pound (2 or 3) skinless, boneless chicken breasts

Marinade:
2 tablespoons lemon juice
¼ teaspoon garlic granules
½ teaspoon salt
¼ teaspoon black pepper
2 tablespoons olive oil

Kale Salad:
1 or 2 bunches (about 10 ounces total) lacinato kale
3 tablespoons lemon juice
¼ teaspoon salt

3 tablespoons pine nuts, toasted
3 bacon strips, chopped into ½-inch pieces

3 tablespoons extra-virgin olive oil
¼ cup dried tart cherries, coarsely chopped
⅓ cup feta cheese, crumbled

Pat the chicken breasts dry with paper towels, and place them in a shallow baking dish.

Marinade: In a small bowl, combine the lemon juice, garlic granules, salt, and pepper. Whisk in the olive oil. Pour the mixture over the chicken breasts and turn to coat. Marinate for 30 minutes at room temperature. Meanwhile, prepare the kale for the salad.

Kale Salad: Rinse the kale under cold running water. Drain well or spin in a salad spinner to remove the excess water. Using a sharp knife, remove the tough ribs from the leaves and discard. Chop the kale into bite-size pieces or thin strips and place in a large salad bowl. Add the lemon juice and salt and toss to coat thoroughly. Let the kale stand at room temperature for 30 minutes, tossing occasionally, to allow it to soften.

Toast the pine nuts by placing them in a small skillet over medium heat. Shake the pan gently until the nuts are fragrant and golden, 2 to 3 minutes. Pour the pine nuts onto a plate to cool. In the same skillet, cook the chopped bacon over medium heat, turning often, until crispy. Drain the bacon on paper towels.

After the chicken breasts have marinated for 30 minutes, prepare a gas or charcoal grill for cooking over high heat. Remove the chicken from the marinade, reserving the marinade. Place the chicken on the cooking grate and cover the grill. Cook for 4 to 5 minutes, turning a quarter turn after 2 minutes to mark the meat. When they are golden brown on the first side, spoon some of the remaining marinade over the tops of the chicken breasts. Turn them over, and place them over indirect medium heat for 5 to 10 minutes, until they register 160 degrees. Transfer the chicken breasts to a cutting board, tent with aluminum foil, and let rest for 10 minutes. Meanwhile, finish the salad.

Add the olive oil to the kale salad and toss to coat. Add the toasted pine nuts, bacon, dried cherries, and feta cheese, and toss to combine. Taste and add more oil, lemon, or salt, if needed.

Divide the salad among four dinner plates. Slice the grilled chicken breasts into thin slices and arrange them alongside each salad.

Chicken Salad with Grapes and Toasted Walnuts

Though chicken salad, in various forms, has graced the tables of potlucks and picnics for as long as most of us can remember, it never seems old-fashioned. In our version, sliced grapes add sweetness, and toasted walnuts and celery provide a satisfying crunch. Binding the salad together with mayonnaise, Greek yogurt, and Dijon mustard brightens the flavor. Serve the chicken salad on butter lettuce leaves for a light summer lunch or make sandwiches with whole wheat bread for a heartier meal.—Frank and Jayni

4 SERVINGS

1 pound skinless, boneless chicken breasts

Salt, to taste

⅓ cup walnut halves

¼ cup mayonnaise
2 tablespoons plain Greek yogurt
1 teaspoon Dijon mustard
⅓ cup celery, chopped
2 green onions, thinly sliced
½ cup small red seedless grapes, halved

Butter lettuce leaves
Whole wheat bread (optional)

Place the chicken breasts in a saucepan. Cover with 2 inches of water and bring to a boil over high heat. Cover, turn off the heat, and leave the pan on the warm burner. Let stand for 25 to 30 minutes, until the juices run clear when the chicken is pierced with a knife, or the internal temperature reaches 160 degrees.

Transfer the chicken breasts to a cutting board, tent with aluminum foil, and let them rest for 10 minutes. Cut the breasts into bite-size cubes and place them in a large bowl. Season lightly with salt and cool to room temperature.

Spread the walnuts out in a single layer on a baking sheet. Place them in a 325-degree oven for about 6 minutes, turning once after 3 minutes, until fragrant and lightly toasted. Cool the nuts and coarsely chop them. Set aside.

In a small bowl, combine the mayonnaise, yogurt, and Dijon mustard. Add the mixture to the chicken and mix to combine. Fold in the chopped celery, green onions, halved grapes, and toasted nuts. Cover and refrigerate for at least 2 hours before serving.

Serve the chicken salad on lettuce leaves, or as sandwiches on whole wheat bread topped with lettuce leaves.

Grilled Chicken Salad with Artichoke Hearts and Capers

Grilling the chicken breasts for this salad adds a mild smoky dimension when combined with artichoke hearts, green onions, capers, and Parmesan cheese. A creamy lemon dressing binds the salad. Serve it on romaine lettuce leaves, or on ciabatta rolls for sandwiches.—Frank and Jayni

4 SERVINGS

1 pound skinless, boneless chicken
    breasts
1 tablespoon olive oil
1 tablespoon lemon juice
Salt and black pepper, to taste

Lemon-Mayonnaise Dressing:
6 tablespoons mayonnaise
1 tablespoon plain Greek yogurt
1 teaspoon lemon zest
2 teaspoons lemon juice
½ teaspoon garlic granules or
    powder

1 (14-ounce) can quartered artichoke
    hearts, drained (measure ¾ cup
    artichoke hearts for recipe)
3 green onions, thinly sliced
2 tablespoons capers, rinsed and
    drained
2 tablespoons grated Parmesan
    cheese
Romaine lettuce leaves, chopped
Ciabatta rolls (optional)

Place the chicken breasts in a shallow baking pan. Drizzle them with the olive oil and lemon juice, turning to coat. Season with salt and pepper. Marinate the chicken breasts at room temperature for about 15 minutes, turning once.

Prepare a gas or charcoal grill for cooking over medium-high heat. Remove the chicken breasts from the marinade and place them on the cooking grate. Cover and cook the breasts for 4 to 5 minutes, turning them a quarter turn after 2 minutes of cooking to make crosshatched grill marks. When they are nicely browned, turn the breasts over and cook for 4 to 5 minutes more, again turning a quarter turn after 2 minutes. If the chicken breasts are not done after 8 to 10 minutes, move them to indirect heat, or a cooler part of the grill, to finish cooking.

Transfer the chicken breasts to a cutting board, tent with aluminum foil, and let them rest for 10 minutes. Cut the breasts into bite-size cubes and place them in a large bowl. Cool to room temperature.

Lemon-Mayonnaise Dressing: In a small bowl, combine the mayonnaise, yogurt, lemon zest, lemon juice, and garlic granules. Add the dressing to the chicken and mix to combine.

Fold in ¾ cup of the artichoke hearts, green onion, capers, and grated cheese. Cover and refrigerate for at least 2 hours before serving. Serve the chicken salad on chopped romaine lettuce leaves, or as sandwiches on ciabatta rolls topped with lettuce leaves.

Chapter 4
Vegetables

We've all heard the command, "Eat your vegetables!" But we're adults now, so there's no need for coaxing. The benefits are clearly healthful, and the variety alone is seductive. On Saturday morning almost anywhere in Kansas, the farmers' market is jam-packed with friendly vendors enticing the shoppers with a variety of seasonal temptations. The vegetables nearly sell themselves. "Behold my vivid color!" a yellow squash may boast. Or, a tomato counsels, "Ripeness is fleeting; better buy me today."

The staples are all there. A pickup bed is loaded with sweet corn. There are piles of big leafy cabbage heads, potatoes with the fragrance of fresh earth, and bright red, juicy tomatoes. Step out of your comfort zone and try some kale, Brussels sprouts, shiitake mushrooms, or microgreens. Shopping-in-the-season is the very definition of a farmers' market. It's easy to pick a winner and it's good family fun.

Not willing to play the market? Some enterprising farmers have thought of that. You can join a CSA (Community Supported Agriculture) program where you'll receive a weekly "surprise package" filled with produce of the moment. The reward may be that you've found a new favorite vegetable to prepare.

Perhaps it's time to get serious and take life into your own hands—plant a backyard garden. The joy of growing your own comes from picking and eating the freshest vegetables possible. And, as many schools know, gardens are better than books when it comes to discovering some of life's lessons. Along with nature and nutrition, kids learn to share in the garden chores and develop the patience and care necessary to help vegetables grow.

In this chapter, you will find a variety of vegetable preparations. There are recipes for vegetables that are served nearly naked, such as "Grilled Asparagus" and "Winter Veggie Roast." For something with a little more complexity, try "Sweet Corn with Shallot and Tarragon," "Brussels Sprouts with Pancetta and Lemon," and "Green Beans with Shiitake Mushrooms and Bacon." Or, if you prefer a rich vegetable dish, "Zucchini Gratin" and "Fresh Garden Ratatouille" may be just for you.

Sweet Corn with Shallot and Tarragon

Sweet corn appears at farmers' markets and in local grocery stores from mid-July through August. Kansans love their corn, and talk abounds of who has the sweetest variety. Corn tastes sweeter when freshly picked, so plan to cook it soon after purchase.

We no longer bother with a pot of boiling water to cook the corn. Simply put it in the microwave, up to three ears at a time, shucks and all. In just three to four minutes you will have perfectly cooked sweet corn, ready to serve solo or with butter, shallot, and fresh tarragon, as in the following recipe.—Frank and Jayni

4 TO 6 SERVINGS

3 medium to large ears sweet corn

2 tablespoons butter
2 tablespoons shallot, finely chopped
1 tablespoon fresh tarragon leaves, finely chopped
Salt and black pepper, to taste

Trim the dried tassels off the ears of corn, but do not shuck them. Place the ears in a microwave oven and cook on full power for 2 minutes. Turn the ears over and cook for 1 to 2 minutes more, to desired doneness. Let the ears rest for 3 to 5 minutes in the microwave or on the countertop. Hold the warm ears with a tea towel or paper towels to shuck. Grasping the leaves and silks together with your fingers as you shuck them will help to get all the silks off easily. Cut the kernels off the cobs using a sharp knife and place them in a bowl.

Heat the butter in a large saucepan over low heat. Add the chopped shallot and cook until tender, but not browned, about 5 minutes. Add the corn kernels and chopped tarragon. Toss together and warm over low heat for about 1 minute. Season with salt and pepper.

Glazed Carrots with Thyme

Carrots taste best when they are locally grown and freshly harvested in the early summer. This recipe calls for cooking the carrots in beef broth, but chicken or vegetable broth can be substituted, depending on the main dish you'd like to pair them with. Try using rosemary in place of the thyme, if the notion fits. —Frank and Jayni

4 TO 6 SERVINGS

1 pound carrots
Salt and black pepper, to taste
1 cup beef broth
2 tablespoons butter, diced
4 sprigs fresh thyme

Peel or scrub the carrots. Leave slender ones whole and cut thicker ones in half, lengthwise, so they will cook more evenly. Put the carrots in a large braising or sauté pan. Season them with salt and pepper. Pour in the beef broth. Scatter the diced butter and herb sprigs over the carrots. Bring to a boil over medium-high heat. Cover the pan and cook the carrots for about 4 minutes, just until they begin to soften. Uncover, reduce the heat to medium, and continue cooking for 8 to 10 minutes more, shaking the pan occasionally, until the broth evaporates and the carrots are lightly browned and glazed. Reduce the heat to low, if necessary, to prevent the carrots from burning.

Growing Food, Growing Health: A School Garden Story in Lawrence

The last head of lettuce came out of the ground at West Middle School in December, but for the Growing Food, Growing Health crew, the garden season is never truly over. It is a continuous cycle of planning, growing, reflecting, and then starting all over. The big difference is that in winter we're not weeding, so we have just a little more breathing room.

It has become a meaningful wrap-up ritual to gather our outgoing Student Gardeners together at the end of the year to share a meal while we share our thoughts and experiences about the past season. While these young people are learning how to grow beautiful vegetables, they are also growing their minds and their lives. This is evident on a daily basis in the garden, where time and time again we are lifted up by the wisdom and humor of these extraordinary young people. But when we are gathered together for the final garden reflection, their insights are, well—amazing.

In early March, we'll launch another season by digging around in our low tunnels to see if any of our carrots overwintered. Some of our current Student Gardeners will return as Mentor Gardeners. We'll plant the first seeds of the season. It will eventually get hot again, and we'll eat popsicles to cool down. More children and youth will connect with the food on their plates and learn to love veggies, and that will remind us of why we started this wonderful project and joined this hopeful movement in the first place.

As the school garden movement continues to blossom around our state, we're encouraged by the unique and varied projects sprouting up all over Kansas. Building these gardens on school grounds does more than produce a few tomatoes and heads of lettuce. It helps the kids build a more robust relationship with fruits and vegetables.

Garden projects such as the one at West Middle School in Lawrence, Central Plains' garden in Bushton, and all of the dozens of projects in between are shining examples of a hopeful aspect of our local food system. We're proud to be in such great company in such a great state.—Nancy O'Connor, executive director, Community Mercantile Education Foundation, Lawrence

Sautéed Zucchini with Tomato

This easy, simple vegetable side dish asks for only a couple of small zucchini, a tomato, and some seasonings. It is a versatile accompaniment when grilling or sautéing fish fillets, chicken breasts, or steaks. Cutting the zucchini into little barrel shapes is important so that they brown quickly yet remain firm inside. It's better to hedge on the side of undercooking, since you will return the zucchini to the skillet in the final step before serving. —Frank

4 SERVINGS

2 tablespoons olive oil
2 zucchini (about 6 ounces each), sliced into ¾-inch rounds (barrel shapes)
1 garlic clove, minced
1 large tomato, chopped
1 tablespoon fresh lemon thyme, chopped
Salt and black pepper, to taste

Heat the olive oil in a 10-inch skillet or sauté pan over medium-high heat. Stand the zucchini barrels on a cut end and let brown before turning once. Brown the other end, then transfer to a small bowl with a slotted spoon, leaving the oil in the skillet. Add the garlic to the remaining oil and cook for about 10 seconds. Add the chopped tomato and simmer over medium heat until it breaks down and some of the liquid is reduced. Return the zucchini to the skillet, sprinkle with lemon thyme, and simmer for about 1 minute to reheat. Season with salt and pepper.

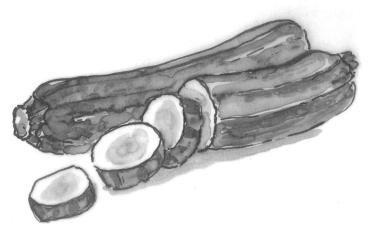

Grilled Eggplant with Herbs

Eggplant doesn't need much enhancement, just a generous drizzle of olive oil, some fresh herbs, and a little salt to make it a tasty side vegetable. We've found that the quickest way to prepare eggplant is to grill it over high heat—conveniently at the same time we happen to be grilling lamb or beef. Choose slender, firm eggplants free of blemishes and soft spots for this recipe.—Jayni and Frank

4 TO 6 SERVINGS

2 slender eggplants, about 6 ounces each
Olive oil
Salt, to taste
1 tablespoon fresh parsley, finely chopped
1 tablespoon fresh rosemary, finely chopped
1 tablespoon fresh lemon thyme, finely chopped

Remove the stems and cut the eggplants into ½-inch-thick slices. Place the eggplant slices on a baking sheet. Brush the slices with olive oil, sprinkle with salt and half of the chopped herbs. Turn the slices over and repeat.

Prepare a gas or charcoal grill for cooking over high heat. Place a large grill pan on the cooking grate to preheat.

When the grill is hot, place the eggplant slices in a single layer on the grill pan. Cook for 3 to 5 minutes on each side, until tender and golden, turning once or twice during cooking.

Transfer the eggplant slices to a warm platter and serve immediately.

Fresh Garden Ratatouille

"I first made ratatouille as a teenager, and it is still one of my favorite things to cook. This recipe is my own version and can be modified and adapted to suit individual needs and tastes. Use whatever happens to be growing in the garden, is available at your local farmers' market, or is on the grocery store shelves," says Gesine Janzen.

Gesine says her ratatouille is delicious served with a baguette, noodles, or polenta. If you like cheese, top it with grated Parmesan, Romano, or fresh mozzarella slices.—Janzen Family Farms, Newton

6 TO 8 SERVINGS

¼ cup olive oil
1 large onion, chopped
4 garlic cloves, minced
2 red bell peppers, seeded and
    chopped into medium chunks
1 large (peeled or unpeeled)
    eggplant, chopped
Salt and black pepper, to taste
2 small zucchini, halved and sliced
4 large fresh tomatoes, or 1
    14.5-ounce can plum tomatoes,
    chopped
½ teaspoon dried oregano

Fresh basil leaves, torn or thinly
    sliced, to taste
½ cup black olives of choice, pitted
    and sliced in half (optional)

Grated Parmesan or Romano
    cheese, or fresh mozzarella
    cheese, sliced (optional)

Heat the olive oil in a large saucepan over medium heat. Add the onion and garlic and sauté until softened. Add the red bell peppers and eggplant and cook until lightly browned. Season the vegetables with salt and pepper. Stir in the zucchini, tomatoes, and oregano. Cover the pan and reduce the heat to low. Simmer the mixture for about 20 minutes, stirring occasionally.

When the vegetables cook down and become tender and saucy, add the fresh basil and olives, if using. Taste and season with additional salt and pepper, if needed.

Top each serving of ratatouille with grated Parmesan or Romano cheese, or slices of fresh mozzarella cheese, if desired. Serve warm or room temperature.

Eggplant Stacks

There are many ways to make ratatouille, the classic French vegetable dish composed of eggplant, tomatoes, onion, garlic, and sometimes other vegetables. We make individual stacks with the browned eggplant slices, onion with garlic and herbs, and roasted red pepper slices. Tomato halves are placed on top before the stacks roast in a hot oven until the vegetables are caramelized. Eggplant stacks make a delicious side whether served warm, room temperature, or chilled.—Frank and Jayni

4 SERVINGS

2 eggplants, about 1 pound each
Salt

4 to 8 tablespoons olive oil, divided
1 large onion, thinly sliced into
    half-rounds
3 to 4 garlic cloves, cut into thin
    slivers
2 tablespoons Italian parsley,
    chopped
1 tablespoon fresh thyme, chopped
1 tablespoon fresh rosemary,
    chopped

1 large red bell pepper, roasted*
2 medium ripe tomatoes (about 5
    ounces each), halved
Olive oil
Salt and black pepper

Slice the eggplant into ½-inch-thick slices of equal size (the slices should be 2½ to 3 inches across). You will need 12 equal slices. Reserve any remaining eggplant for another use. Sprinkle the slices lightly with salt on both sides and place them on paper towels to drain. After about 20 minutes, pat dry with paper towels to remove as much moisture as possible. While draining the eggplant, cook the onion and garlic.

Heat 1 to 2 tablespoons of the olive oil in a nonstick skillet over medium-low heat. Add the sliced onion and cook until lightly

CONTINUED ➡

browned, stirring occasionally. Add the garlic slivers during the last 2 to 3 minutes of cooking. Off heat, stir in the herbs and transfer the mixture to a bowl.

Heat 2 tablespoons of olive oil in the same skillet over medium-high heat. Add the drained eggplant slices and brown quickly on both sides. Add more oil as needed.

Brush ½ teaspoon of olive oil in the bottom of an 8- or 9-inch baking dish. Place four browned eggplant slices in the baking dish, sides not touching. Place a piece of roasted red pepper on each eggplant slice. Stack another slice of eggplant on top. Place some of the cooked onion and herb mixture on each stack. Cover with another slice of eggplant. Place a tomato half cut side down on the top of each stack. Brush the tops of the tomatoes with a small amount of olive oil and sprinkle with salt and pepper.

Bake the eggplant stacks, uncovered, in a 400-degree oven for 50 to 60 minutes, until the tomatoes are charred and wrinkled and the eggplant is caramelized.

*To roast the red bell pepper, slice the pepper in half and remove the stem and seeds. Press the pepper halves gently to flatten slightly. Lay them cut side down on a foil-lined baking sheet and place about 6 inches under the oven broiler. Broil until the skins are wrinkled and slightly charred. Transfer the pepper to a plastic or paper bag, seal the bag, and let the pepper "sweat" for 20 to 30 minutes. Peel the pepper and cut four pieces to fit on the eggplant slices.

Cultivating Value from the Land

A short drive down a gravel country road will take you to Pendleton's Kaw Valley Country Market, just east of downtown Lawrence. As you approach the farm in early spring, you'll see asparagus spears springing up from what appears to be a barren field. You can purchase them in the country market or walk out to the field and pick the spears yourself.

John Pendleton's father, Albert, farmed their land in the Kaw River Valley before John and Karen took over in 1980. At first they raised cattle, corn, and soybeans on the land, but the couple imagined growing something different. As they searched for a new crop, they became interested in alternative farming, diversification, and value-added products. They soon realized food trends were moving toward a healthier diet of less meat, less fat, and more vegetables, so they decided to grow asparagus. They chose asparagus because it is a perennial that has the protection of being in the ground until the weather is right for the spears to come up. It is easy to manage, has no pests or predators, and doesn't need watering. And, as the Pendleton's patrons will tell you, it's such fun to pick!

Over time, the popularity of the asparagus farm has sprouted in many directions. The Pendletons have added tomatoes, peppers, eggplants, and other vegetables to the mix. You can "dig your own" sweet potatoes and "pick your own" sugar snap peas. Produce, herbs, and fresh eggs can be purchased at their country market as well as at the Lawrence Farmers' Market and through their Community Supported Agriculture (CSA) Program.

A large variety of cut flowers and bedding plants for the flower and vegetable garden are also available in the spring.

Activities on the farm were a part of the Pendletons' vision from the start. They participate in the Kaw Valley Farm Tour every fall and invite school groups to visit the farm to learn about growing vegetables. The kids walk through the butterfly garden and participate in many other farm activities. The Pendletons have cultivated a loyal following. John tells us that the secret to their success is having customers who embrace the farm as their own. He says, "People take ownership of what we do. And in exchange, we get to know them well over time. We hear about their families—the births, deaths, and vacations. They treasure the connection to the farm and to the land, just as we do."

"The entire business is directed by our customers," Karen adds. "It's important to watch the trends. For instance, young people are now more interested in planting vegetables instead of flowers. They see it as a moral issue and they want to be good stewards of the land. They want

their children to understand where their food comes from."

The Pendletons used to place an ad in the local newspaper to alert people about upcoming crops and events at the farm. Now it's all done through social media. Through Facebook, Twitter, and email, customers can tap into what's happening on the farm in an instant.

Over the years, with all the changes on the farm, the Pendletons have raised three children: Liz, Margaret, and Will. Though they are all grown with lives of their own, they occasionally help out on the farm.

John and Karen Pendleton's warmth and friendliness toward their customers, and their enthusiasm for growing healthy foods and respecting the land, make them stars in Douglas County.

Grilled Asparagus

One of the easiest vegetables to grow in a backyard garden is asparagus. We put in an asparagus patch several years ago, and what a pleasure it is to snap these seasonal beauties from the earth each spring! Asparagus is perennial, has no pests, and the rabbits and deer won't eat it.

We use asparagus in many ways—in salads and soups, and simply boiled, steamed, or pan-sautéed. Our favorite preparation is to grill the spears with a splash of olive oil, salt, and pepper and serve it as the vegetable side to almost any meal.—Frank and Jayni

6 TO 8 SERVINGS

1½ to 2 pounds asparagus spears

Olive oil
Salt and black pepper, to taste

Lemon wedges

Snap off the tough ends of the asparagus spears. Rinse the spears in cold running water and drain well.

Place the asparagus spears in a shallow baking dish or on a tray, drizzle them with a small amount of olive oil, and toss to coat. Season the spears with salt and black pepper.

Prepare a gas or charcoal grill for cooking over high heat. Preheat a grill pan large enough to hold the asparagus on the cooking grate.

When the grill is hot, transfer the asparagus spears to the grill pan. Cook for 3 to 5 minutes, turning occasionally with grilling tongs, until tender-crisp and lightly charred.

Transfer the spears to a warm platter and serve with lemon wedges.

Brussels Sprouts with Pancetta and Lemon

Brussels sprouts are available throughout most of the year, though their peak season runs from September through February. John Bellome says, "Not everyone likes this overlooked vegetable, especially children." John tames the taste of Brussels sprouts by briefly cooking them in boiling water before pan-sautéing them. When purchasing Brussels sprouts, choose ones of equal size to ensure even cooking. Smaller sprouts tend to be sweeter tasting and more tender than larger ones. The sprouts should be bright green, compact, and free of blemishes.—John Bellome, Lawrence

4 TO 6 SERVINGS

1 pound Brussels sprouts, rinsed, trimmed, and halved lengthwise

1 tablespoon olive oil
⅓ cup (about 1½ to 2 ounces) cubed pancetta
1 tablespoon butter
1 tablespoon lemon juice, or to taste
1½ teaspoons lemon zest
Salt and black pepper, to taste

Bring a pot of water to a boil over high heat. Add the Brussels sprouts and boil for 2 minutes or until tender-crisp. Drain well and set aside.

Heat the olive oil in a nonstick skillet over medium heat. Add the pancetta cubes and cook until crisp. Remove the pancetta from the skillet and drain on paper towels. Add the butter to the skillet drippings. When the butter is melted, add the sprouts and sauté until lightly browned, 2 to 4 minutes. Stir in the lemon juice and zest. Season with salt and pepper and add the pancetta. Serve warm.

Variation: Bacon may be used in place of pancetta.

Braised Brussels Sprouts

Eat your Brussels sprouts—they're good for you! These little sprouts that resemble tiny heads of cabbage pack a lot of protein, fiber, vitamins, and antioxidants. We like to brown Brussels sprouts in butter, then quick-braise them in white wine and chicken broth. The tender, glazed sprouts go well with roasted or grilled meats.—Frank and Jayni

4 TO 6 SERVINGS

1 pound Brussels sprouts

4 tablespoons butter, divided
⅓ cup dry white wine
½ cup chicken broth
Salt and black pepper, to taste

Trim the Brussels sprouts and remove any damaged leaves. Rinse well and pat dry with paper towels. Cut in half, lengthwise.

Heat 3 tablespoons of butter in a large braising or sauté pan over medium-high heat. Place the sprouts cut side down in the pan and cook for 2 to 3 minutes, until browned. Turn the sprouts over and add the wine and chicken broth. When the liquid comes to a simmer, cover the pan with a lid and reduce the heat to medium-low. Braise the sprouts for 5 minutes. Remove the lid and raise the heat to medium-high. Add the remaining table-spoon of butter. Continue cooking the Brussels sprouts, turning them occasionally, until most of the liquid is absorbed. The sprouts should be tender and lightly glazed. Season with salt and pepper.

Roasted Brussels Sprouts with Bacon and Apples

"Germans love their roast meats and vegetables. At Beethoven's #9 we offer this roasted Brussels sprouts dish as a vegetable of the day, and our guests love it. We serve it with stuffed pork loin, schnitzel, and other meat dishes."—Chef Linzi Weilert, Beethoven's #9, Paola

10 TO 12 SERVINGS

2 pounds Brussels sprouts

8 ounces good-quality bacon, chopped

¼ cup butter
2 Granny Smith apples, cored and cubed
2 to 3 tablespoons lemon juice
Salt and black pepper, to taste

Rinse, trim, and cut the Brussels sprouts in half. Small sprouts may be left whole. Bring a pot of salted water to a boil. Blanch the Brussels sprouts in the boiling water for 1 to 2 minutes, until bright green. Drain and transfer them to a bowl of ice water to cool. Drain well.

In a large skillet, cook the chopped bacon over medium heat. Add the Brussels sprouts to the skillet, shake the pan to coat them with the drippings, and set aside.

In a separate skillet, melt the butter over medium-low heat and add the cubed apples. Poach the apples for about 3 minutes, turning frequently. Add the apples to the bacon and sprouts. Sprinkle the mixture with the lemon juice and season with salt and pepper.

Transfer the Brussels sprouts mixture to a large baking dish or sheet pan. Roast, uncovered, in a 350-degree oven for 20 minutes, stir, and roast for 10 to 20 minutes more. The sprouts should be fork tender but still hold their shape.

Green Beans with Shiitake Mushrooms and Bacon

In early summer, tender green beans are prolific and fun to pluck from the vines in our backyard garden. Though tradition suggests cooking them with a piece of ham and new potatoes, we like the contemporary combination of smoky bacon and shiitake mushrooms to underpin their flavor with a rich, earthy broth. As a variation, add new potatoes for a heartier side serving or as a "summer stew."—Frank and Jayni

6 SERVINGS

3 bacon strips, chopped
1 cup onion, chopped
2 ounces shiitake mushrooms, cleaned, stemmed, and thinly sliced
1 large garlic clove, minced

1 pound green beans, trimmed and broken in half
4 cups hot water
1 teaspoon salt
¼ teaspoon black pepper

Fry the chopped bacon in a large pot or Dutch oven over medium heat. Using a slotted spoon, remove the bacon pieces, reserving the drippings in the pot. Set the bacon aside. Add the chopped onion and mushrooms to the pot and cook over medium-low heat to soften, about 3 minutes. Add the garlic and cook for 1 minute more.

Add the green beans, water, salt, pepper, and reserved bacon to the pot. Bring the mixture to a boil over high heat, reduce the heat to medium-low, and simmer for 25 to 30 minutes, or until the beans are tender. Taste and season with additional salt and pepper, if needed.

Variation: Peel 1 pound of small new potatoes. After the green beans have cooked for 10 minutes, add the potatoes to the green beans along with 1 extra cup of hot water. Cook until the green beans and potatoes are both tender, 15 to 20 minutes more.

Kale with Garlic and Shallot

Kale is good for you! This cruciferous vegetable is high in antioxidants and packed with fiber, vitamins, minerals, and calcium. Due to the rising popularity of kale, you may find several varieties at farmers' markets, as well as in supermarkets. We like common curly green kale for this recipe because of its hardy texture and robust flavor.—Frank and Jayni

4 TO 6 SERVINGS

1 pound curly green kale

3 tablespoons butter
2 garlic cloves, minced
2 tablespoons shallot, finely
    chopped
1 cup chicken broth
Salt and black pepper, to taste

Thoroughly rinse the kale in cold water. Cut or tear the leaves from the tough stems and discard the stems. Bring a large pot of water to a boil over high heat. Add the kale leaves and boil for about 6 minutes, until fairly tender. Drain the kale in a wire-mesh strainer and run cold water over it to cool. Press out the excess water with the back of a large spoon or your hands. Place the kale on a cutting surface and chop into small pieces.

Heat the butter in the pot over medium-low heat. Add the garlic and shallot and cook, stirring frequently, for about 3 minutes, until tender. Add the chopped kale and cook for 1 minute. Stir in the chicken broth and simmer over low heat for about 8 minutes, stirring occasionally, until all the liquid has been absorbed. Season the kale with salt and pepper.

Mushrooms in Red Wine with Rosemary

Mushrooms cooked in red wine add a touch of elegance to the plate. Serve them as a side to grilled or roasted chicken, or spoon them on top of grilled steaks.—Frank and Jayni

4 SERVINGS

8 ounces small cremini
    mushrooms, cleaned and
    trimmed

2 tablespoons butter
1 tablespoon olive oil
2 tablespoons shallot, finely
    chopped
1 tablespoon fresh
    rosemary, finely
    chopped
½ cup dry red wine
Salt and black pepper,
    to taste

If the mushrooms are small (about ¼ ounce each), leave them whole. If larger, slice them in half or into several slices. Set aside.

Heat the butter and oil over medium heat in a sauté pan or skillet. Add the chopped shallot and cook for 1 minute, stirring constantly. Add the mushrooms and rosemary. Stir or shake the pan frequently until the mushrooms soften, 4 to 5 minutes. Pour in the wine and when it begins to boil, reduce the heat to medium-low. Let the mixture simmer, stirring occasionally, until the wine is absorbed and the mushrooms are glazed and tender, about 5 to 8 minutes. Season with salt and pepper.

Roasted Butternut Squash, Apples, and Walnuts

We like to prepare this recipe in late summer and fall when both butternut squash and apples are at their best. Roasting brings out the richness of the squash, while the apples add a sweet-tart flavor to the dish. Scattering rosemary sprigs across the squash and apples provides an herbal embellishment, and sprinkling walnuts over the top during the last few minutes of cooking adds just the right crunch.

This dish signals to us that it is time to transfer a rosemary plant from the garden to the kitchen garden window so that we can extend summer's freshness into the winter months.—Frank and Jayni

6 TO 8 SERVINGS

2 pounds butternut squash
5 tablespoons olive oil, divided
Salt and black pepper, to taste
2 medium tart red apples, such as
    Jonathans

4 to 6 sprigs fresh rosemary

½ cup walnuts, coarsely chopped

Peel the butternut squash using a sharp, sturdy vegetable peeler. Cut the squash in half, crosswise, to separate the neck from the base. Scrape out the seeds from the base. Cut the squash into ½- to ¾-inch pieces and place them in a large bowl. Add 2 to 3 tablespoons of olive oil and toss to coat. Season the squash with salt and pepper. Core the apples (do not peel) and cut them into ½- to ¾-inch pieces. Place them in a separate bowl, add 2 tablespoons of olive oil and toss to coat. Season the apples with salt and pepper.

Place the squash in one side of a large sheet pan. Place the apples in the other side. The apples will cook quicker and need to be removed from the pan before the squash is done. Divide the rosemary into small sprigs, or chop it, and scatter over the squash and apples.

Roast the squash and apples in a 400-degree oven for 15 minutes. Turn both over, keeping them separated. Roast for 5 minutes more. Check the apples and, if they are tender, remove them from the pan. Continue roasting the squash for 10 to 15 minutes more, turning once or twice, until tender and lightly browned. Return the apples to the sheet pan and combine with the squash. Top with the chopped walnuts and roast for about 3 minutes to toast the walnuts and reheat the apples.

Roasted Vegetables

When the bounty of summer vegetables becomes a fading memory and spring's emergence is too far away to imagine, it's time to embrace cool-season and winter vegetables. Don't consider these hardy fellows second choice. Roasting vegetables warms the kitchen as well as the soul. Winter squash, Brussels sprouts, beets, carrots, and other cold weather favorites such as parsnips, turnips, and rutabagas release their sweetness and comforting aroma when roasted at a moderately high temperature with just a splash of olive oil and a few sprigs of fresh herbs. Roast these full-flavored beauties separately or tossed together. They pair well with roast pork, beef, or chicken.

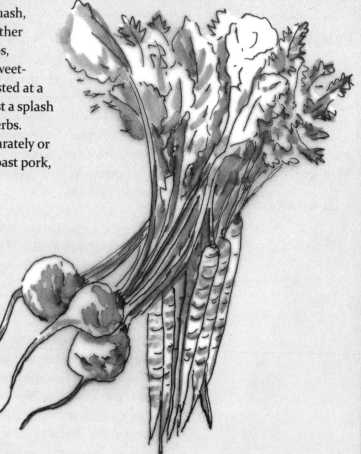

Winter Veggie Roast

Delicata squash is considered a winter squash, but it is actually a cousin to summer squash varieties. It has a pretty yellow exterior with green stripes and, because of its ridges, looks attractive when sliced into half rounds. Its thin skin is edible so there's no need to peel it. The creamy yellow-orange flesh tastes similar to acorn squash and sweet potatoes.

Dorothy Hoyt-Reed likes to roast the delicata squash along with Brussels sprouts, carrots, and onions that have been tossed in a spicy olive oil mixture. "During the Holiday Farmers' Market in Lawrence, I bought a winter squash I had never cooked before called delicata. It is now my favorite squash, and I plan on growing some in my own garden."—Dorothy Hoyt-Reed, Lawrence

6 SERVINGS

1 pound (1 or 2 small) delicata squash
1 pound Brussels sprouts, rinsed and halved lengthwise
5 baby carrots or 3 medium carrots, peeled and sliced thinly
½ medium onion, coarsely chopped

3 tablespoons garlic-infused olive oil
1 to 2 teaspoons garlic powder, to taste
½ to 1 teaspoon cayenne pepper, to taste
½ teaspoon salt
1 teaspoon black pepper

Wash the delicata squash and remove any damaged spots (do not peel). Cut the squash in half, lengthwise. Scrape out the seeds. Place the squash halves cut side down on a cutting surface. Cut each half crosswise into ½-inch slices, then into smaller pieces if desired. Place the squash in a large bowl. Prepare the remaining vegetables as directed and add them to the bowl.

In a small bowl, combine the garlic-infused olive oil, garlic powder, cayenne, salt, and pepper. Pour the mixture over the vegetables and toss to coat.

Brush a large sheet pan lightly with olive oil. Transfer the vegetables to the pan. Using a rubber spatula, scrape any remaining oil and spices in the bowl onto the vegetables. Roast in a 400-degree oven for 10 minutes. Turn the vegetables over and continue roasting for 10 minutes more or until the vegetables are tender and caramelized around the edges.

Roasted Beets and Carrots

In early summer, farmers' markets are overflowing with tender beets and carrots, and roasting them brings out their natural sweetness. Serve these roasted roots as a colorful side dish to any meal, or toss them with vinegar and olive oil and use as a garnish on a green salad.—Frank and Jayni

6 SERVINGS

3 medium (about 1 pound) red
    beets

1 pound medium carrots

¼ cup olive oil, divided
4 garlic cloves, peeled and smashed
2 teaspoons fresh rosemary or
    tarragon, chopped
2 teaspoons fresh thyme, chopped
2 teaspoons fresh sage, chopped
Salt and black pepper, to taste

Fresh rosemary, thyme, or sage
    sprigs, for garnish

Trim the tops of the beets and rinse them well under cold running water. Pat the beets dry with paper towels and wrap them together in a large piece of aluminum foil. Place them in a shallow baking pan and roast in a 400-degree oven until tender-firm, about 1 hour to 1 hour and 15 minutes, depending on size. Open the foil and cool the beets until they can be handled. Peel and cut them into 1- to 1½-inch pieces and place them in a mixing bowl.

Peel the carrots and slice them on the diagonal into ¾- to 1-inch-thick slices. Place the carrot slices in a separate bowl to avoid the beets discoloring them.

Drizzle the vegetables in each bowl with 2 tablespoons of olive oil. Add 2 smashed garlic cloves and half of the chopped herbs to each bowl. Season each with salt and pepper and toss to combine.

Place the beets in a medium-sized sheet pan lined with aluminum foil, if desired, to prevent staining the pan. Place the carrots in a separate medium-sized sheet pan. Roast the vegetables in a 400-degree oven for 20 minutes, turn them over, and roast for 15 to 20 minutes more, until tender.

To serve, place the beets on a serving platter. Scatter the carrots over the top. Garnish with fresh herb sprigs.

Beets and Greens

Cooks recognize the nutrient-rich health benefits of leafy greens and are including them more often on the menu. The beauty of beets is that both the beetroot and the leafy green foliage are edible and nicely complement each other. Beets arrive in the spring at farmers' markets, and they are best when freshly harvested.—Frank and Jayni

4 SERVINGS

2 bunches beets with green tops

Olive oil

2 to 3 tablespoons olive oil
1 large garlic clove, minced
Salt and black pepper, to taste

Red wine vinegar

Remove the green tops from both bunches of beets and reserve them. Trim the remaining stems to within ½ inch of the beets. Choose two or three small to medium beets for the recipe. Leave the roots intact to prevent bleeding while roasting. Reserve the remaining beets for another use.

Rinse the beets well and pat dry with paper towels. Place them on a piece of heavy-duty aluminum foil and coat with a small amount of olive oil. Roast them in a 400-degree oven for 40 to 50 minutes, until tender but still firm, depending on the size of the beets. Cool the beets to warm, remove the remaining stems and roots, and peel them. Do this while they are warm for easier peeling. Slice the beets into thin matchsticks or small dice and set aside.

Remove and discard the tough stems from the beet greens. Rinse the trimmed greens well in cold running water, spin them in a salad spinner to remove the excess water or pat dry with paper towels. Tear or chop the greens into several pieces.

Heat the olive oil in a large skillet over medium heat. Add the garlic and cook for about 30 seconds. Add the beet greens and sauté until they are wilted and tender, 2 to 3 minutes. Add the beets and cook for 1 minute more. Season with salt and pepper.

Serve the beets and greens with a splash of red wine vinegar.

Hippie Lasagne

"My favorite wedding gift from thirty-two years ago was a recipe box full of handwritten recipe cards collected by my sister from friends and family. The original version of this favorite dish, a baked noodle-less vegetable lasagne, came from friends of my husband's family who lived in Lawrence in the early 1970s. I think of those tumultuous times on the KU campus and realize this was real hippie food! It is a very tasty recipe. Peace and Love."—Marianne Wille, Lawrence

8 SERVINGS

2 pounds (about 4 medium) zucchini, cut in half lengthwise and then sliced into 1-inch pieces
1 pound Japanese eggplant, ends trimmed, cut into 1-inch pieces
5 tablespoons extra-virgin olive oil, divided
½ teaspoon sea salt
½ teaspoon freshly ground black pepper

1 onion, finely chopped
1 red or green bell pepper, medium dice
8 ounces fresh button mushrooms, sliced
3 garlic cloves, minced
2 teaspoons dried oregano
2 teaspoons dried basil
8-ounce can tomato sauce

10 ounces fresh spinach, stemmed and rinsed

1 (15-ounce) carton whole milk ricotta cheese
8 ounces mozzarella cheese, shredded

Parmesan cheese, grated

In a large bowl, toss the zucchini and eggplant with 3 tablespoons of olive oil, then add the sea salt and black pepper. Spread the zucchini and eggplant out in a single layer in a 13 × 18-inch rimmed baking sheet. Roast the vegetables in a 400-degree oven until they are golden brown, about 35 to 45 minutes, turning them over with a wide spatula after 20 to 25 minutes. When done, set aside to cool in the pan.

While the zucchini and eggplant are roasting, warm the remaining 2 tablespoons of olive oil over medium heat in a large sauté pan or skillet. Add the onion, green or red pepper, and mushrooms and sauté for 6 to 7 minutes, or until the onion and mushrooms begin to soften. Add the garlic and cook for 3 to 5 minutes more. Add the oregano and basil. Stir in the tomato sauce to deglaze the pan and simmer for 3 to 5 minutes. Transfer the mixture to a large bowl to cool. Add the roasted eggplant and zucchini and stir to coat with the sauce.

Put the spinach, still wet from rinsing, into a nonstick sauté pan or skillet over medium heat. Cover and wilt the spinach, 2 to 3 minutes. Transfer the spinach to a strainer to cool, then squeeze out any excess liquid. Roughly chop the spinach leaves and set aside.

Spoon half of the vegetable and tomato mixture into a 13 × 9-inch baking dish. Layer with half of the ricotta cheese by dropping it onto the vegetables in small dollops, half of the spinach, and half of the shredded mozzarella. Repeat with a second layer of the same.

Bake uncovered in a 375-degree oven until the lasagne is bubbly and the mozzarella is light gold, about 35 minutes. Let rest for about 10 minutes before cutting. Top servings with grated Parmesan cheese.

Summer Veggies Baked in Phyllo Pastry

"I like to make this vegetable casserole at the end of summer when the zucchini, eggplants, peppers, garlic, and basil are ready and waiting! This dish serves a lot of people, so invite over a bunch of good friends and serve it with a big green salad and your favorite rice dish."—Patty Boyer, Lawrence

10 TO 12 SERVINGS

1 (16-ounce) package frozen phyllo dough (phyllo pastry sheets)

4 medium zucchini, diced into ¼-inch pieces

2 small eggplants, diced into ¼-inch pieces

2 bell peppers (red, orange, or yellow), seeded and diced into ¼-inch pieces

3 tablespoons olive oil

3 eggs, beaten

⅓ cup pesto, homemade or bottled

1½ cups Swiss cheese, shredded

Salt and black pepper, to taste

½ cup (1 stick) butter

½ cup olive oil

CONTINUED ➡

Set out the frozen phyllo dough on the counter to thaw quickly if using right away, or thaw slowly in the refrigerator.

Prepare the vegetables as directed. In a large skillet, heat the olive oil over medium heat. Add the diced zucchini, eggplant, and peppers and sauté until almost tender. Cool slightly, then add the beaten eggs, pesto, and Swiss cheese. Season the mixture with salt and pepper and set aside.

Unroll one roll of phyllo dough and cover it with plastic wrap to keep it from drying out while using.

Heat the butter and olive oil in a small saucepan over low heat. Cut one roll of the phyllo sheets to fit a 13 × 9-inch baking dish. Using two sheets of phyllo at a time (one on top of the other), place them in the baking dish. Brush the top sheet generously with the butter and oil mixture. Continue adding two sheets of phyllo at a time to the casserole, basting the top sheet, until the roll of phyllo is used up. Pour the vegetable mixture into the baking dish. Cut the second roll of phyllo sheets to fit the baking dish. Continue layering as before, using up the second roll to cover the vegetables.

With a sharp knife, cut the casserole (all the way through) into a diamond pattern before baking. This will make it easier to serve after baking. Bake the casserole in a 350-degree oven for 50 minutes.

Baked Tomatoes Stuffed with Bulgur Wheat, Basil, Olives, and Feta Cheese

These baked, stuffed tomatoes can accompany any main course. As an alternative, serve them as a warm starter or chilled with a soup or sandwich as part of a light lunch. Make this recipe during the summer when fresh tomatoes are at their very best.—Frank and Jayni

6 SERVINGS

½ cup bulgur wheat, fine or
    medium grain
1 tablespoon lemon juice
Water

⅓ cup fresh basil leaves, thinly
    sliced
1 medium tomato, cut into small
    dice
12 pitted Kalamata olives, halved or
    quartered
½ cup crumbled feta cheese
Salt and black pepper, to taste

6 ripe tomatoes, 4 or 5 ounces each
Salt

Olive oil

Place the bulgur wheat in a wire-mesh strainer and rinse under cold running water. Drain well and place in a medium bowl. Pour 1 tablespoon of lemon juice into a 1-cup measure and add enough water to make ½ cup. Pour the lemon juice and water over the bulgur and let stand for 40 to 60 minutes, or until the liquid is absorbed and the bulgur has softened. Stir two to three times while the mixture stands.

Once the bulgur has softened, stir in the basil, diced tomato, olives, and feta cheese. Season the mixture with salt and pepper.

Cut the tops off the tomatoes using a small, serrated knife. Cut out the core and, using a spoon, carefully hollow out the inside of the tomatoes, leaving the walls about ½ inch thick. Sprinkle the insides of the tomatoes with salt, turn them upside down on a plate or tray, and let drain for about 10 minutes.

Stuff 2 to 3 tablespoons of the bulgur mixture into each tomato, piling it high on top. Place the tomatoes in a baking dish and drizzle the tops lightly with olive oil.

Bake the tomatoes in a 375-degree oven for 20 to 25 minutes, until they soften and the filling is hot. Avoid overbaking the tomatoes because they can split or collapse. Let stand for 10 minutes before serving.

Zucchini-Corn Casserole

"Who doesn't have too much zucchini in their garden?" asks Sharyna Reece, of Reece's Cafe. "We grill it, fry it, bake brownies and cake with it, and use it to make our 'Zucchini-Corn Casserole.' There are many, many variations on this recipe. Garlic, onion, cilantro, chicken, or brisket can be added for a spin on this wonderful, summertime bounty!"

At Reece's Cafe, dishes are made to order, utilizing the highest-quality and the freshest ingredients. The cafe is located in Alden, a small community tucked away in Rice County, southwest of Lyons and northwest of Sterling. "Although we're off the beaten path, we strive to be a pleasant destination dining experience for the central Kansas region, and we plan to continue welcoming our loyal customers for years to come!"—Sharyna Reece, Reece's Cafe, Alden

12 TO 16 SERVINGS

8 cups zucchini, shredded

2 cups sweet corn kernels, cut from the cob or canned

4 eggs, slightly beaten

1 cup half and half

1 teaspoon salt

1 teaspoon liquid smoke

2 teaspoons Mrs. Dash Original Blend seasoning

2 tablespoons barbecue sauce

½ cup bacon bits

3 cups room temperature shredded cheddar or pepper jack cheese, or a combination of both

Place the shredded zucchini and corn kernels in a large bowl.

In a separate bowl, combine the eggs, half and half, salt, liquid smoke, Mrs. Dash seasoning, barbecue sauce, and bacon bits. Pour the mixture into the zucchini and corn mixture and mix well. Transfer the mixture into an 11 × 15-inch baking pan, coated with butter or nonstick cooking spray.

Bake the casserole, uncovered, in a 350-degree oven for 45 minutes, or until the eggs are set and an inserted toothpick comes out clean. Remove the casserole from the oven and sprinkle the cheese on top immediately. Let stand for 10 minutes before serving.

Zucchini Gratin

We are always looking for new ways to prepare zucchini during the summer months. This rich zucchini casserole made with eggs, cream, and cheese and topped with buttered breadcrumbs travels well to a potluck dinner or can be served alongside any main course in place of potatoes.
—Frank and Jayni

8 SERVINGS

2 tablespoons olive oil
¾ cup onion, finely chopped
1 pound small, firm zucchini (combination of green and yellow), sliced into ¼-inch rounds
Salt, to taste

2 eggs
½ cup heavy cream
⅓ cup half and half
1 teaspoon fresh lemon thyme, chopped
¼ teaspoon salt
⅛ teaspoon black pepper
½ cup Gruyère cheese, shredded

1½ cups fresh breadcrumbs
2 tablespoons butter, melted

Heat 2 tablespoons of olive oil in a large skillet over medium-low heat. Add the onion and cook about 3 minutes to soften. Add the zucchini rounds and cook partially to soften, about 5 minutes. Season the mixture lightly with salt. Transfer the zucchini and onion to an 8- or 9-inch baking dish.

Whisk the eggs, cream, and half and half together in a medium bowl. Whisk in the lemon thyme, salt, and pepper and pour the mixture over the zucchini and onion. Sprinkle the cheese evenly over the top.

Place the fresh breadcrumbs in a bowl, drizzle with the melted butter, and toss to coat. Sprinkle the buttered breadcrumbs evenly over the cheese. Bake the gratin in a 375-degree oven for 30 to 35 minutes, until the topping is golden brown.

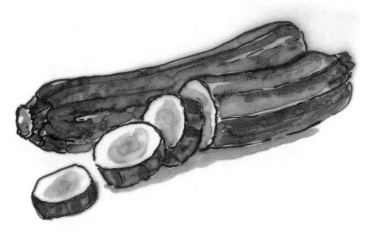

Chapter 5
Starch Sides and Mains

Here in cattle country, some of our favorite Kansas dishes contain more starch than protein. Though beef and pork tend to be the stars on the plate, potatoes, grains, pasta, and beans are a cast of characters prepared to provide a supporting role. After all, what's a steak without a potato? Though these sidekicks may be humble and modest, don't be surprised if they steal the show. These fellows may look plain but if you dress them up, they can even become the main dish.

So if the parson happens to drop by for dinner, you can quickly elevate a weekday sautéed chicken breast to its Sunday best simply by serving "Boiled Potatoes with Dill, Sour Cream, and Lemon Zest" alongside. For something with a little more flair, try "Cheddar and Chive Mashed Potatoes" or fix some "Spicy Oven Fries" to spark up a meal.

If you're a fan of grains, pair "Kansas Wheat Pilaf with Black Walnuts and Sunflower Seeds" with any main course. "Bulgur Pilaf with Butternut Squash, Pistachios, and Golden Raisins" is the perfect fit for an autumn meal. And, if the meal is a potluck or picnic, "Chipotle Baked Beans" makes a spicy side to hamburgers and hot dogs.

Of course, starch mains can stand up all by themselves. The bold yellow backdrop of saffron rice underpins the peppers and spicy Italian sausage in the full-flavored "Kansas Paella." Consider, too, the contrast provided by the potatoes against an earthy mix of wild mushrooms, asparagus, and bacon in "Brown Butter-Glazed New Potatoes, Morel Mushrooms, Asparagus, and Crispy Bacon."

Try your hand at making fresh pasta—along with some family memories—with the savory richness of "Fresh Pappardelle with Cremini, Shiitake, and Porcini Mushroom Sauce." No one expects a meatball to go it alone. We offer meatballs poached in a spicy tomato sauce and gently tossed with a family favorite, spaghetti. For a taste of Kansas, "Bison Bolognese" is a sure winner when entertaining friends. Once you taste the Midwestern classic "Chicken and Homemade Noodles," you'll understand why so many say they crave the noodles as much as they do the chicken.

Cheddar and Chive Mashed Potatoes

Who doesn't love mashed potatoes? This popular preparation for spuds is a favorite side dish of Midwesterners. Around our house, potatoes are common but prepared uncommonly. We like to pump up the flavor by adding a local farmhouse cheddar and some chives fresh from the garden. These potatoes go especially well with grilled steaks or fried chicken.—Frank and Jayni

6 TO 8 SERVINGS

1½ pounds Yukon Gold potatoes
2 teaspoons salt

3 tablespoons butter, room temperature
½ cup shredded sharp cheddar cheese, room temperature
½ cup hot milk
1 tablespoon fresh chives, finely chopped, plus extra for garnish
Salt and black pepper, to taste

Peel the potatoes, cut them into 1½- to 2-inch chunks, and place them in a large pot or Dutch oven. Add cold water to cover by about 2 inches and stir in the salt. Bring to a boil over high heat and cook the potatoes until they are very tender.

Pour the potatoes and water through a strainer to drain and return the potatoes to the warm pot. Using a potato masher, mash the hot potatoes immediately, until no lumps remain. Add the butter and blend into the potatoes with a rubber spatula. Stir in the shredded cheese. Slowly add as much of the hot milk as needed to achieve the desired consistency. Stir in 1 tablespoon of chopped chives. Taste and season with salt and pepper. Cover the pot and keep the mashed potatoes warm until ready to serve. Sprinkle with extra chives to garnish.

Potato Gratin with Apples and Walnuts

This rich potato gratin makes the perfect side to beef tenderloin filets, pork roast, or leg of lamb. We like to serve it for special meals, especially during the holiday season.—Frank and Jayni

4 TO 6 SERVINGS

1 teaspoon butter, softened
1 to 1¼ pounds medium-size russet
    or Yukon Gold potatoes, peeled
    and thinly sliced
1 small tart red apple, cored and
    sliced into thin wedges
Salt and white pepper, to taste

1 cup heavy cream
¾ cup half and half

1 cup Gruyère cheese, shredded
¼ cup walnuts, coarsely chopped
1 tablespoon fresh parsley,
    chopped

Butter a 13 × 9-inch baking dish. Fan the potato slices out in the dish, overlapping them. Tuck the apple slices in between every three or four potato slices. Season with salt and white pepper.

Combine the heavy cream and half and half in a glass measuring cup and heat to very warm (not boiling) in a microwave oven. Pour the cream evenly over the potatoes and apples.

Bake uncovered in a 375-degree oven for 12 to 15 minutes, until the cream begins to simmer and the potatoes are beginning to soften. If the potatoes and apple wedges appear a bit dry, spoon some of the cream in the baking dish over them. Sprinkle the cheese over the top and continue baking the gratin for 15 to 20 minutes more, or until the potatoes are tender and most of the cream is absorbed. During the last 5 minutes of baking, scatter the chopped walnuts over the top of the potatoes. Remove the gratin from the oven and immediately sprinkle with chopped parsley.

Onion-Smothered Potatoes and Carrots

One of our weeknight kitchen tricks is to start cooking the side dish before we've nailed down just how we're going to prepare the main course. Sliced potatoes and carrots, smothered with onions and sprinkled with fresh dill, can bake slowly in the oven—no attention required—to buy us some time. This warm, fragrant, and buttery vegetable combo goes great with pan-fried pork chops, chicken breasts, or fish fillets. It also works well to tuck it into the oven to bake alongside our favorite meatloaf.—Frank and Jayni

6 SERVINGS

1 pound potatoes, peeled and
    sliced into ¼-inch rounds
4 medium carrots, peeled and
    sliced into ¼-inch diagonal
    slices
1 large onion, halved and thinly
    sliced
2 tablespoons butter
2 tablespoons olive oil
Salt and black pepper, to taste
1 tablespoon fresh chopped dill, or
    1 teaspoon dried dill

Prepare the vegetables as directed. Melt the butter and combine it with the olive oil in a measuring cup or small container. Place half of the potatoes in the bottom of a lightly oiled 9-inch baking dish. Add half of the sliced carrots and top with half of the onion. Sprinkle the vegetables with salt and pepper and drizzle with half of the butter and olive oil mixture. Sprinkle half of the dill over the top. Repeat with the remaining ingredients.

Cover the baking dish tightly with aluminum foil and place in a 350-degree oven for 1 hour, or until the vegetables are very tender.

Roasted Potato Wedges with Rosemary

When Jayni cooks the main course, my job is to make a side, and I often go to my favorite potato recipe. These oven-fried potato wedges can complement a steak or saddle up next to a burger. Yukon Golds are my choice for this recipe because they come out of the oven firm and golden, almost like thick French fries. Roasting them with a sprinkle of fresh rosemary from the herb garden fills the kitchen with a wonderful aroma.—Frank

4 TO 6 SERVINGS

1½ pounds medium-sized Yukon
    Gold potatoes
3 tablespoons olive oil
Salt and black pepper, to taste
2 tablespoons fresh rosemary,
    finely chopped

Peel the potatoes and cut each into approximately eight thick wedges. Place them in a wide, shallow bowl. Drizzle the olive oil over the potatoes and, using your hands, toss to coat them with the oil. Season with salt and pepper, add the rosemary, and toss again.

Spread out the potatoes in a single layer on a jellyroll pan or large, shallow baking pan. Roast in a 400-degree oven until the wedges are browned on the underside, about 12 minutes. Turn them over with tongs or a metal spatula and return them to the oven. Roast until the potato wedges are lightly browned on top and tender on the inside, about 6 to 8 minutes more.

Roasted Fingerling Potatoes with Rosemary and Thyme

Fingerling potatoes are little, elongated potatoes with a finger-like appearance. They come in many colors, but for roasting we prefer the white- or yellow-fleshed varieties for their sweet, buttery flesh. Roasting fingerlings enhances the texture, and sprinkling a bit of rosemary and thyme over the top intensifies their earthy flavor.—Frank and Jayni

4 SERVINGS

8 ounces fingerling potatoes, rinsed and dried
1 tablespoon butter, melted
1 tablespoon olive oil
Salt and black pepper, to taste
1½ teaspoons fresh rosemary, chopped
1½ teaspoons fresh thyme, chopped

Place the fingerling potatoes in a shallow baking dish or pie plate. Drizzle with melted butter and olive oil and sprinkle with salt and pepper. Toss to coat the potatoes. Sprinkle the chopped rosemary and thyme over the top.

Roast the potatoes in a 375-degree oven for 15 minutes, turn them over, and roast for 15 minutes more, or until tender.

Spicy Oven Fries

When you want French fries without the fuss of deep-frying, try potato sticks tossed in a spicy mix and roasted in a hot oven. They taste great with a burger or steak. —Jayni and Frank

4 SERVINGS

Seasoning Mix:
2 teaspoons chili powder
1 teaspoon smoked Spanish paprika
1 teaspoon garlic granules
1 teaspoon onion granules
¾ teaspoon salt
¼ teaspoon black pepper
½ teaspoon Tabasco Chipotle Pepper Sauce
3 tablespoons olive oil

1 pound potatoes, russet or Yukon Gold

2 tablespoons olive oil

Preheat the oven to 400 degrees. Position an oven rack to the lowest rung of the oven.

Seasoning Mix: In a wide, shallow bowl large enough to hold the potato sticks, combine the chili powder, smoked paprika, garlic granules, onion granules, salt, and pepper. Add the Tabasco Chipotle Pepper Sauce and whisk in the olive oil.

Peel the potatoes and cut them into ½-inch sticks. Transfer the potato sticks to the seasoning mix and toss to coat them on all sides.

Brush 2 tablespoons of olive oil over the bottom of a medium-sized, rimmed sheet pan. Place the potato sticks in a single layer in the pan and place the pan on the lowest rack in the oven.

Roast the potatoes for 10 minutes. Turn them over with a metal spatula or tongs and cook for 5 minutes, turn again and cook for 2 to 5 minutes more, until the potatoes are browned on the outside and tender on the inside.

Boiled Potatoes with Dill, Sour Cream, and Lemon Zest

We've grown to appreciate the simple way of making this comforting potato side dish. Boiling the potatoes takes about the same amount of time as sautéing chicken breasts or fish fillets, both good choices to pair with the potatoes. Once you stir in the sour cream, butter, and seasonings, the potatoes will wait patiently, warm in the pot, until you are ready to serve them up. —Frank and Jayni

4 SERVINGS

1 pound Yukon Gold potatoes
2 teaspoons kosher salt

3 tablespoons butter, melted
3 tablespoons sour cream
1 tablespoon fresh dill, chopped, or
**   1 teaspoon dried dill**
1 teaspoon lemon zest
Salt and black pepper, to taste

Peel the potatoes and cut them into 1-inch dice. Place them in a pot, cover with cold water by about 2 inches, and add the kosher salt. Bring the water to a boil over medium-high heat and cook the potatoes until tender, but still firm.

Over the sink, pour the cooked potatoes into a wire-mesh strainer to drain the water, then return them to the warm pot. Add the melted butter, sour cream, dill, and lemon zest, then turn gently to coat the potatoes. Season with salt and pepper.

Loaded Sweet Potatoes

"I love roasted sweet potatoes, and so I make a meal out of them by loading them up with a mixture of sautéed spinach, chopped bacon, dried fruits, candied pecans, and cilantro. I like to put goat cheese crumbles on top and add a sprinkle of ground cinnamon."—Angela Finch, Lawrence

4 SERVINGS

4 medium-size sweet potatoes
    (about 8 ounces each), rinsed
    and dried
Olive oil
Sea salt

Filling:
4 bacon strips
1 large bunch fresh spinach,
    stemmed, rinsed, and drained
3 garlic cloves, minced
¼ cup dried peaches, chopped
¼ cup dried cherries
¼ cup candied pecans, chopped
2 tablespoons fresh cilantro leaves,
    chopped

¼ cup goat cheese crumbles
Ground cinnamon

Pierce the sweet potatoes a few times with a knife. Rub a small amount of olive oil over each sweet potato and sprinkle them with sea salt. Place them on a foil-lined baking sheet and roast in a 400-degree oven for 50 to 60 minutes, or until tender. Let cool for 5 to 10 minutes before filling.

Filling: Cook the bacon strips in a large skillet over medium heat until brown and crispy. Remove them from the skillet and drain on paper towels. Chop the bacon into bite-size pieces and reserve. Pour off and discard all but 1 tablespoon of the bacon drippings from the skillet. Add the spinach and garlic to the skillet and sauté over medium heat for 2 to 3 minutes, until the spinach is wilted. Add the peaches, cherries, pecans, cilantro, and reserved bacon. Toss to combine.

Slice each sweet potato down the center, about halfway through the flesh. Pinch the ends to open the potato, revealing the flesh. Using a fork, gently break up the cooked flesh. Generously load each sweet potato with the filling.

To serve, garnish each sweet potato with 1 tablespoon of goat cheese crumbles and top with a sprinkle of ground cinnamon.

Deluxe Sweet Potatoes

If you think your dinner guests are ready to break from tradition this holiday season, serve this rich but "not-so-sweet" sweet potato recipe for Thanksgiving dinner. It can be made the day before and finished in the oven just before serving.—Frank and Jayni

8 TO 10 SERVINGS

2 pounds sweet potatoes

2 tablespoons butter, softened
3 tablespoons cream cheese, softened
2 tablespoons sour cream
Salt and white pepper, to taste

1 tablespoon butter
2 tablespoons maple syrup
2 tablespoons walnuts, coarsely chopped

Wash the sweet potatoes and pat dry with paper towels. Place them on a baking sheet and bake in a 400-degree oven for 50 to 60 minutes, or until tender. Cool briefly, then peel while still very warm.

Place the potatoes in a large mixing bowl and mash them with a potato masher. Using an electric mixer, blend in the butter, cream cheese, and sour cream. Beat until light and fluffy. Blend in salt and white pepper, to taste.

Butter a 9-inch baking dish and scrape the potato mixture into the dish. Using the back of a large spoon, smooth the potatoes evenly in the pan. Cover and refrigerate for at least 8 hours, or overnight.

Dot the sweet potatoes with 1 tablespoon of butter and bake in a 350-degree oven for 20 to 25 minutes, until heated throughout. Drizzle maple syrup over the top, sprinkle with walnuts, and bake for 10 minutes more.

Chestnut Cornbread Dressing

"Chestnut dressing is as traditional as turkey for the holidays. Prepare this chestnut dressing, or use your own favorite dressing recipe and simply add some cooked chestnuts to it. Serve the dressing as a side dish, or use it to stuff the turkey before roasting."—Debbie Milks and Charlie Novo-Gradac, Chestnut Charlie's, Lawrence

10 TO 12 SERVINGS

1 to 1½ pounds (2 cups peeled) chestnuts, peeled and coarsely chopped

3 to 4 tablespoons butter, to taste
1½ cups onion, chopped
2 cups celery, chopped

10 cups coarsely crumbled home-made unsweetened cornbread, or packaged cornbread stuffing
2 tablespoons fresh sage leaves, finely chopped, or 1 teaspoon ground sage
1 cup chopped apple, dried cranberries, or dried cherries
1 to 1½ cups chicken or turkey broth
Salt and black pepper, to taste

Roasting and Peeling Chestnuts: Using a sharp knife or chestnut knife, make an incision about ⅛ inch deep through the shell around half the circumference of each nut. Place the chestnuts in a covered pan or baking dish and bake in a 375-degree oven for about 20 minutes, or until the nuts are tender. The cooking time depends on the moisture content (freshness) and size of the chestnuts. Taste for desired doneness. Peel the roasted chestnuts while warm or they will be difficult to peel. Coarsely chop them and measure 2 cups. Set aside.

Cornbread Dressing: Melt the butter in a Dutch oven over medium-low heat. Add the onion and celery and cook until tender. Do not brown.

Off heat, add the crumbled cornbread (or packaged cornbread stuffing). Add the sage, chopped apple or dried fruit, and chestnuts. Toss to combine. Stir in as much of the chicken or turkey broth as needed to moisten the crumbs, taking care not to make the dressing too wet. Season the dressing with salt and pepper.

Spoon the dressing into a greased 13 × 9-inch baking dish. Cover and bake in a 325-degree oven for 30 minutes.

Variation: Substitute ½ cup of apple juice for some of the chicken or turkey broth.

Chestnut Charlie's: Growing Chestnuts in Kansas

"Head north out of downtown Lawrence, just past Teepee Junction, and you'll see a grove of trees to the east," the directions say. It's easy to spot, since most trees in the Kaw River valley have been removed to facilitate farming. But this isn't just any grove of trees. It's actually a twenty-acre chestnut plantation—Chestnut Charlie's. Charlie NovoGradac and Debbie Milks have been growing chestnuts on their land since 1995. Their plantation became certified organic in 1998. Of the few growers in Kansas, Chestnut Charlie's is the largest producer.

Charlie and Debbie returned home to Kansas after living in the western Pacific for many years. Charlie has always been driven to plant trees that produce food. Whether the problem is erosion, declining water quality, dead zones, or global warming, trees are part of the solution. They learned that the American chestnut forests were no more. Though chestnuts were a popular folk food, the well-loved trees had been wiped out long ago by a chestnut blight that began in 1904. Most of the chestnuts consumed in North America are imported and their quality suffers after being shipped from overseas. Charlie and Debbie decided to join the movement to restore the trees and make fresh chestnuts available.

"The more we learn about modern petrochemical-based agriculture, the more convinced I am that tree crops offer a lifesaving, sustainable path to the future," Charlie tells us. Selecting among the American-Chinese hybrids with names like Luvall's Monster, Sleeping Giant, Revival, Peach, and Gideon, Charlie and Debbie established their plantation and now produce more than twenty thousand pounds of chestnuts every year. And the number continues to grow.

The fruit of a chestnut tree is contained in a bright green, spiny cupule the size of a baseball, called a burr. Each burr contains approximately three chestnuts. Between the middle of September through the middle of October when the chestnuts ripen, the burr splits open and the chestnuts fall to the ground or the entire burr falls off the tree. Charlie and Debbie, along with their pickers, pick up the chestnuts by hand and, using heavy work gloves, remove any chestnuts still trapped inside the burrs. The chestnuts are then placed in a tank of water and the "floaters," which are damaged chestnuts, are discarded. The good chestnuts are washed several times, inspected for flaws, graded by size, and stored in a high-humidity cooler to retain their freshness until sold. Thanks to the popular Christmas song, most people think of roasting chestnuts for a holiday treat. They are actually available fresh beginning in the middle of September, shortly after they are harvested. When Chestnut Charlie's first started marketing them, most Kansans weren't familiar with chestnuts or had little knowledge of what to do with them. Charlie and Debbie discovered that Asians and Europeans are by far the largest consumers of chestnuts.

"I like to think of them as potatoes that grow on trees," Charlie jokes. The chestnut, unlike most nuts, has almost no fat but is high in complex carbohydrates and only a third of the calories found in peanuts and cashews. After a few days of curing, some of the starch in the chestnuts turns into sugar. Roasting and other cooking methods bring out their sweetness. Chestnuts taste great when added to soups, stir-fries, and vegetable dishes. "Chestnut Cornbread Stuffing," found in this chapter, is a tasty way to use them at holiday time. Debbie says that roasting chestnuts and serving them warm in the shells is probably the easiest way to get acquainted with them. Europeans pair them with a glass of red wine or Port. It's easy to imagine that the conviviality of shelling warm chestnuts with wine may cause diners to break into song.

"What gives me the greatest pleasure," Debbie says, "is when some of our Asian and European customers come out to pick chestnuts. They tell us, sometimes with tears in their eyes, that the experience stirs up childhood memories of harvesting chestnuts in their home country."

Kansas Wheat Pilaf with Black Walnuts and Sunflower Seeds

Wheat berries, which are whole wheat kernels, have a chewy texture and robust flavor. They are packed with protein, fiber, and iron, making them a nutritious addition to your diet. Wheat berries are delicious prepared as a pilaf and pair nicely with roast chicken or pork.

Sarah Andersen Higgins likes to use black walnuts in her wheat pilaf. "Black walnuts were available from the trees by our house on our farm in my childhood," she says. "My mother used them in cookies and cakes. They are delicious in applications where one would use other nuts, such as pecans or English walnuts."—Sarah Andersen Higgins, Lawrence

4 TO 6 SERVINGS

1 cup hard red winter wheat berries (whole kernel red winter wheat)
2 cups homemade chicken broth, or low-sodium canned chicken broth
½ teaspoon salt

2 tablespoons butter, or 1 tablespoon butter plus 1 tablespoon olive oil
⅓ cup celery, finely chopped
¼ cup shallot, finely chopped
¼ teaspoon dried thyme
½ teaspoon freshly ground black pepper

2 tablespoons black walnuts, coarsely chopped
2 tablespoons raw, unsalted sunflower seed kernels

Place the wheat berries in a saucepan. Add the chicken broth and salt and bring to a boil over high heat. Cover, reduce the heat to low, and cook the wheat berries for 45 to 60 minutes, until tender, but still chewy. Drain off any extra liquid. Cover and set aside.

Melt the butter, or the butter and oil combination, in a small saucepan over low heat. Add the chopped celery and shallot and cook until softened, 5 to 8 minutes. Stir the mixture into the wheat pilaf along with the thyme and black pepper.

Toast the chopped black walnuts and sunflower seeds over low heat in a small stainless steel skillet, stirring often, until lightly toasted and fragrant, 2 to 3 minutes.

Stir the walnuts and sunflower seeds into the wheat pilaf and serve immediately.

Bulgur Pilaf with Butternut Squash, Pistachios, and Golden Raisins

"For more than twenty years, the Education and Outreach Department at The Merc Co-op in Lawrence has gone out into the community to teach people about healthy eating and sustainable lifestyles. In 2002, in addition to our normal roster of classes, we began offering a series of classes taught by local chefs. One of our first chef presenters was Paige Vandegrift. With training that included stints in England and France, as well as area restaurants, Paige was an immediate draw. She is still with us today and remains one of our most popular presenters.

"Paige developed this grain salad for the annual Kaw Valley Farm Tour several years ago. She has since incorporated her recipe into her normal rotation of classes. Paige says that it is a perfect recipe for a light autumn meal, or as an unusual addition to your Thanksgiving spread."—Nancy O'Connor, The Merc Co-op, Lawrence

4 TO 5 SERVINGS

2- to 2½-pound (5 cups) butternut squash, peeled, seeded, and cut in ¾-inch dice
3 to 4 tablespoons olive oil, divided
Salt and black pepper, to taste

1 cup onion, diced
Kosher salt
1 large garlic clove, minced
1 teaspoon ground cumin
Pinch of cayenne pepper
1 cup (6 ounces) medium bulgur, rinsed and drained
1¼ cups water
½ cup golden raisins

¼ cup fresh mint, cut into thin strips
2 tablespoons fresh flat leaf parsley, minced
½ cup shelled and toasted pistachios*, coarsely chopped

Place the diced squash in a bowl. Toss the squash with 1 to 2 tablespoons of olive oil and season with salt and pepper. Spread it in a single layer on a baking sheet and bake in a 425-degree oven until tender and caramelized, 20 to 30 minutes. Stir halfway through to encourage even browning.

Warm 2 tablespoons of olive oil over medium heat in a medium-sized saucepan with a tight-fitting lid. Add the onion along with a pinch of kosher salt, cover, and "sweat" until tender and translucent. Lower the heat, if necessary, to prevent the onions from caramelizing. Add the garlic, cumin, and cayenne pepper and cook until fragrant, about 1 minute. Increase the heat to medium-high and add the drained bulgur along with a generous pinch of salt. Continue to cook for 1 minute. Add the water and bring the mixture to a boil. Reduce the heat to low, cover, and cook until the bulgur is tender, 12 to 15 minutes. Remove the pan from the heat and scatter the raisins over the surface of the bulgur. Cover and let stand for 5 minutes.

Transfer the bulgur to a large bowl. Add the mint, parsley, toasted pistachios, and the roasted squash. Toss until all ingredients are well combined. Serve the pilaf warm or room temperature.

* Toasted Pistachios: Spread the pistachios on a small baking sheet and place in a 350-degree oven. Bake until tinged with color and fragrant, about 5 minutes.

Variation: To make a more substantial pilaf to be served as an entrée, add one (15-ounce) can of drained and rinsed chickpeas.

Chipotle Baked Beans

Baked beans never go out of style! They continue to be a family favorite at potlucks and picnics. These days, we prefer them not so sweet, made with a vinegar-based barbecue sauce and some chipotle chile powder to jazz them up.—Frank and Jayni

10 TO 12 SERVINGS

6 bacon strips, diced

1 medium onion, cut into ¼-inch dice

1 medium green bell pepper, seeded and cut into ½-inch dice

1 (15-ounce) can black beans

1 (16-ounce) can dark red kidney beans

1 (28-ounce) can pork and beans, undrained

½ cup barbecue sauce

3 or 4 tablespoons brown sugar, to taste

1 teaspoon chipotle chile powder, or more to taste

1 teaspoon smoked Spanish paprika

CONTINUED ➡

Brown the diced bacon in a large skillet over medium heat. Remove the cooked bacon with a slotted spoon and reserve, leaving the drippings in the skillet.

Add the diced onion to the drippings and cook until softened, about 5 minutes. Add the green pepper and continue cooking until the onion is golden and caramelized and the green pepper is tender, about 8 minutes more. Remove the skillet from the heat.

Pour the black beans and kidney beans through a wire-mesh strainer to drain. Rinse them in the strainer under cold running water and drain well. Place the drained beans in a large bowl. Stir in the can of pork and beans (undrained), barbecue sauce, brown sugar, chipotle chile powder, and smoked Spanish paprika. Add the bacon, cooked onion, and green pepper and stir gently to combine.

Pour the bean mixture into a 13 × 9-inch baking dish. Cover with aluminum foil and bake in a 350-degree oven until hot and bubbly, 45 minutes to 1 hour.

Brown Butter-Glazed New Potatoes, Morel Mushrooms, Asparagus, and Crispy Bacon

Because mushroom lovers prize the morel for its delicious taste, they are always looking for new ways to use them in a recipe. Sautéed morels, paired with new potatoes and asparagus, and topped with crispy bacon and a brown butter glaze, is a celebration of spring at our house. Serve as a light main dish with a salad.—Frank and Jayni

4 TO 6 SERVINGS

4 to 6 ounces fresh morel mushrooms

1 pound small red new potatoes
Salt and black pepper, to taste

3 tablespoons unsalted butter, divided

4 to 5 ounces fresh asparagus spears

3 bacon strips

To clean the morel mushrooms, trim the bottoms of the stems, if needed. Slice the morels in half lengthwise. Rinse them under cold running water. Prepare a bowl of cold, salted water. Add the mushrooms and let stand for 5 to 10 minutes to remove bugs and dirt. Drain and repeat several times until the mushrooms are clean. Give them a final rinse in plain, cold water. Drain the mushrooms on paper towels while preparing the remaining ingredients.

Rinse the potatoes, place them in a pot, and cover them with water. Boil the potatoes over medium-high heat until tender-firm. Drain and cool briefly. Cut them in halves or quarters and place them in a large serving bowl. Season with salt and pepper.

Melt 1 tablespoon of the unsalted butter in a skillet or sauté pan over medium heat. Add the morels and cook until tender, 2 to 3 minutes on each side. Transfer the morels to the bowl of potatoes.

Snap the tough ends off the asparagus spears and cut them into 1-inch pieces. Place them in a shallow, microwave-safe container and sprinkle with a tablespoon of water. Microwave the spears on high power for 1 minute, or until tender-crisp, shaking the container after 30 seconds. Add the asparagus to the potatoes.

Fry the bacon in a small skillet over medium to medium-low heat, until crispy. Drain on paper towels, crumble, and reserve.

To make the brown butter glaze, melt the remaining 2 tablespoons of unsalted butter in a small saucepan over medium heat until it begins to foam. Stir constantly until the butter becomes a rich golden brown color and gives off a nutty aroma, 3 to 4 minutes. Immediately pour the browned butter over the potato mixture and toss gently to combine. Add the crumbled bacon and toss again. Season with additional salt and pepper, if needed. Serve warm or room temperature.

Variation: 4 ounces of lightly cooked sugar snap peas or regular peas (fresh or frozen) may be used in place of the asparagus spears.

The Elusive Morel Mushroom

The search for the highly prized morel mushroom is a spring ritual for mushroom lovers in Kansas. This much-sought-after wild mushroom pops up in wooded areas, by creek beds, in old apple orchards, near dead and dying trees, and sometimes in places you least expect, like your own backyard.

Experienced 'shroomers search their secret spots each spring when the ground is damp and the weather begins to warm up, in hope of finding the elusive morel. Tales abound of hunters wandering into a meadow covered with morels, finding giant morels over a foot tall, or coming home with a "gunnysack full."

Kansas hunters search for other mushroom varieties too—chanterelle, black trumpet, oyster, and maitake (hen-of-the-woods)—but the morel seems to be the favorite, partly because it is easily recognizable and is admired for its rich, earthy, and nutty flavor. For those reluctant to tramp around in the woods and risk ticks and snakes, mushroom farmers grow some equally delicious varieties such as oyster and shiitake mushrooms. They can be purchased at some farmers' markets and grocery stores.

Some mushrooms found in Kansas can be toxic, so hunters should practice caution when searching for edible mushrooms. Beginners should consider joining a local mycology group devoted to mushroom hunting, use a field guide, or consult with experienced hunters before consuming your find. As the saying goes, "When in doubt, throw it out."

A popular way to prepare morels is to simply dust them with flour or coat them with a light breading and deep-fry until golden brown. Sautéing morels in butter is another delicious way to enjoy them. Add morels to a pizza, a sauce, or use them in a recipe like "Brown Butter-Glazed New Potatoes, Morel Mushrooms, Asparagus, and Crispy Bacon."

Kansas Paella

"For several years on New Year's Eve, I make what we've come to call Kansas Paella. I have adapted the Spanish version of paella to Kansas ingredients, such as using Italian sausage that we purchase from Kroeger's Country Meats in Lecompton. It is basically a stir-fry of sausage and vegetables served over saffron rice. Now that I am retired, when I make it in the summer, the zucchini and sweet peppers are from my own garden."—Dorothy Hoyt-Reed, Lawrence

4 SERVINGS

Saffron Rice:
2 pinches saffron threads, or ⅟₁₆ teaspoon preground saffron
¼ cup hot water
1 tablespoon extra-virgin olive oil
½ cup yellow onion, finely chopped
2 cups white basmati rice, rinsed if desired
3¾ cups chicken broth
1 teaspoon garlic, minced, or more, to taste
1 teaspoon salt

½ cup red bell pepper, julienned
½ cup green bell pepper, julienned
1 small broccoli crown, chopped
1 small zucchini, chopped
1 small yellow squash, chopped
½ cup portobello mushroom, chopped or sliced
2 to 4 tablespoons roasted garlic, chopped, or fresh garlic, chopped, to taste
½ cup onion, chopped

3 tablespoons garlic-infused extra-virgin olive oil
8 ounces hot Italian sausage
8 ounces shrimp, shelled and deveined
1 teaspoon salt
1 teaspoon black pepper
½ to 1 teaspoon garlic powder, to taste
½ to 1 teaspoon cayenne pepper, to taste

Saffron Rice: Take one pinch of saffron threads and grind them into powder in a small mortar with a pestle. Pour ¼ cup of hot water into the mortar and add the remaining pinch of saffron, or place preground saffron in a small bowl and add the hot water. Let the saffron soak for 5 minutes. In a large, heavy pot or saucepan, heat 1 tablespoon of extra-virgin olive oil over medium-low heat. Add the onion and sauté until tender, about 8 to 10 minutes. Add the rice and sauté for 1 minute more, coating the rice with oil. Pour the soaked saffron and liquid over the rice. Add the chicken broth, garlic, and salt to the pot. Bring to a boil, stir, and cover the pot. Reduce the heat to low and cook for 20 minutes, or until

CONTINUED ➡

the rice is tender and the liquid is absorbed. Keep the pot covered until ready to use. Fluff the rice with a fork before serving.

Prepare all the vegetables as directed. Put the peppers and broccoli in one bowl, squash and mushrooms in a second bowl, and roasted garlic and onion in another bowl.

Heat 3 tablespoons of garlic-infused olive oil over high heat in a cast iron or stainless steel skillet or wok. Add the Italian sausage and stir to break it up as it browns, about 3 minutes. The sausage should be partially cooked. Add the prepared peppers and broccoli and sauté for about 2 minutes. Add the shrimp, squash, and mushrooms, then the salt, pepper, garlic powder, and cayenne pepper, and sauté for about 3 minutes. When the shrimp begins to turn pink, add the roasted garlic and onion. Cook, stirring often, until the onion is just cooked, 2 to 3 minutes. By now all the sausage, vegetables, and shrimp should be thoroughly cooked.

To serve, spoon about 1/2 cup of the saffron rice on each of four dinner plates and top with the sausage and vegetable mixture. Or, serve family style, with saffron rice in one bowl and the sausage and vegetable mixture in a separate bowl.

Tip: As a nod to Spain, add a teaspoon of smoked Spanish paprika to the mixture when adding the other spices.

Fresh Pappardelle with Cremini, Shiitake, and Porcini Mushroom Sauce

Many meals in our kitchen are a team effort, and this one has become a favorite. When the tasks are divvied up, we get to the table sooner. I mix up the pasta dough ahead of time, and when I'm ready to make the noodles, Jayni prepares the mushroom sauce. I roll out the pasta and cut it into wide, rustic noodles called pappardelle. The three varieties of mushrooms create a complex and earthy sauce, and the fresh pasta seems to complement the texture of the mushrooms. Together, they create a comforting and satisfying meal. —Frank

4 SERVINGS

Fresh Pappardelle:
1½ to 2½ cups all-purpose flour, unsifted
3 large eggs

Mushroom Sauce:
½ ounce dried porcini mushrooms
1½ cups chicken broth

8 ounces cremini mushrooms
5 ounces shiitake mushrooms

4 tablespoons butter, divided
¼ cup shallot, finely chopped
2 garlic cloves, minced
¾ cup dry white wine

1 tablespoon fresh chopped thyme, or 1 teaspoon dried thyme
2 teaspoons fresh marjoram, chopped, or ½ teaspoon dried marjoram
Salt and black pepper, to taste

⅓ cup Parmigiano-Reggiano cheese, grated, plus extra for garnish

Fresh Pappardelle: On a clean, smooth countertop, make a pile with 1½ cups of the flour. Make a well in the center of the flour and add the eggs. With a fork, gently beat the eggs, incorporating the flour as you stir, until a stiff paste forms. Using your hands, continue to incorporate as much of the flour as possible, adding more, if necessary, to create a stiff ball of dough. Include as much of the sticky dough as possible from the countertop and your hands as you work. Ideally, the countertop will be clean when the dough is ready to knead.

Flour the countertop and begin kneading the dough by pushing it down and away with the heel of your right hand in the direction of your left and then, using your left hand, push it back toward the right. These short back-and-forth strokes should turn the dough on itself and keep it in a compact mass. Continue to add small amounts of flour as needed to make kneading and handling less sticky. After about 7 minutes of this 10-minute process, the dough should become very firm and not sticky.

CONTINUED ➡

Continue to knead the dough until it is uniformly smooth. Wrap the dough in plastic wrap or let rest in a covered bowl for about 20 minutes.

Avoid frustration by preparing a place to set the pasta sheets *before* you begin the final stage of stretching and cutting the pasta. Use a pasta rack to hang the pasta, or dust a couple of large tea towels with flour and drape them over the backs of two chairs.

Divide the dough into three equal parts. Starting with the widest setting, pass a portion of dough through the machine a few times. Square it up each time by folding it onto itself in order to make it a uniform rectangle. Repeat with the remaining portions. Then pass each portion of pasta through the machine, once for each setting, until you reach the thinnest width (#6). As the pasta gets thinner, it also gets longer, so, after setting #5, cut its length in half and hang each sheet on the drying rack as you work.

Before cutting the sheets into noodles, the pasta should be dry on the surface but still supple. To avoid the noodles sticking to one another, lightly dust the sheets with flour or let the pasta dry longer. For pappardelle, lay each sheet on a cutting board and, using a small knife, cut each sheet into lengths about 8 to 10 inches long, roll or gently fold each cut sheet onto itself and cut it into ¾-inch-wide noodles. Unfurl each noodle and hang it on the rack while cutting the remaining dough.

To cook the pappardelle, bring a large pot of water to a boil and add 1 tablespoon of salt. Drop the fresh pappardelle into the pot. When the water returns to a boil, the pasta will float to the top. Check for doneness. It only takes a minute or two for the pasta to cook. Drain the pappardelle well, and return to the warm pot. Warm the mushroom sauce, if needed, and pour it over the pappardelle. Toss, add ⅓ cup Parmigiano-Reggiano cheese, and toss again.

Divide the pasta among four pasta bowls. Garnish with extra cheese, if desired.

Mushroom Sauce: Place the dried porcini mushrooms in a bowl. In a small saucepan, bring the chicken broth to a boil and pour it over the mushrooms. Let stand for at least 15 minutes. Pour the mushrooms and broth through a wire-mesh strainer, reserving the broth. Chop the mushrooms and reserve.

Clean the fresh cremini and shiitake mushrooms. Thinly slice the cremini mushrooms. Stem the shiitake and thinly slice them. Set aside.

Heat 1 tablespoon of the butter in a large skillet or braising pan over low heat. Add the chopped shallot and cook for 3 minutes, until tender but not browned. Add the garlic and cook for 2 minutes more. Pour in the white wine, raise the heat to medium, and simmer until reduced by half. Add 1 tablespoon of the butter and, when melted, add the cremini and shiitake mushrooms. Cook them over medium heat, stirring often, until tender.

Add the chopped porcini mushrooms to the skillet and cook for 1 minute. Pour in the reserved broth, add the herbs, and simmer the mixture for 2 to 3 minutes over medium heat to reduce the liquid slightly. Off heat, stir in the remaining 2 tablespoons of butter and season with salt and pepper. Set aside.

Variation: 1 (16-ounce) package dried pappardelle or fettuccine may be used in place of the fresh pappardelle.

Summer's End Pasta

"We always celebrate with this pasta dish when the tomatoes are at their peak quality in August, knowing that this year's season of delicious tomatoes is nearing its end. I use plum tomatoes, such as Roma or San Marzano, but any meaty tomato can be used."—Shirley Domer, Baldwin City

4 SERVINGS

8 to 10 garden-ripened Roma or
    other plum tomatoes, peeled
    and diced
2 garlic cloves, minced
¼ cup olive oil, or more to taste
Salt and black pepper, to taste
    (optional)

2 sweet Italian sausage links (op-
    tional)
1 tablespoon olive oil

8 ounces (about 2 heaping cups)
    dried whole wheat penne

Fresh basil leaves
Parmesan cheese, grated

Place the diced tomatoes and garlic in a large, nonreactive bowl (glass, stainless, or glazed ceramic) and stir in ¼ cup of olive oil, or more to taste. Season with salt and pepper, if using. Let stand at room temperature for two or three hours to marinate.

Cut 2 sweet Italian sausage links, if using, into bite-size slices. Heat 1 tablespoon of olive oil in a skillet over medium-low heat. Add the sausage and turn occasionally until browned and cooked through. Drain the sausage on paper towels.

Bring a large pot of salted water to a boil over high heat. Add the whole wheat penne to the boiling water. When the water returns to the boil, cook the pasta for 10 to 14 minutes, depending on the firmness or softness desired. When the pasta is done, drain the water and immediately pour the hot pasta into the marinating tomatoes. Add the sausage, if using, and toss to combine.

Snip fresh basil leaves over the pasta mixture and generously sprinkle it with the grated Parmesan cheese. Toss and add more basil, olive oil, or Parmesan cheese, to taste.

Sowing Seeds of the Future

Wes Jackson grew up on a farm in the Kansas River valley near Topeka. He earned a BA in biology at Kansas Wesleyan College, an MA in botany at the University of Kansas, and, after receiving his doctorate in genetics at North Carolina State University, established one of the first environmental studies programs at California State University, Sacramento. He returned to Kansas in 1976 to co-found The Land Institute, located southeast of Salina.

"The idea was that students were to spend half their time reading and thinking and the other half hands-on. In 1977, we set out to solve the ten thousand-year-old problem of agriculture," Wes Jackson tells us in his affable way. The ideal agricultural model, he came to realize, was not far from his childhood home: the Kansas prairie.

"The Land Institute believes that to save soil from erosion without fossil fuels or chemicals, we must grow food in partnership with nature, by planting perennial grains in mixtures that can help build and protect soil," Wes says. "As we say at the Institute, we are dependent on our soil. It is everyone's future."

The Land Institute is a science-based organization whose work is dedicated to advancing perennial grain crops grown in mixtures or as polycultures. Wes said the breeding to develop perennial-based grains would likely take fifty to one hundred years, and now reports that their research is ahead of schedule. Kernza, the Institute's first perennial, is a domesticated form of wheatgrass and a distant relative of wheat. The name of the new grain combines the word "kernel" with the word "Konza," derived from the Kansa natives and referring to the Konza Prairie, located near Manhattan. Kernza is low in gluten and is suitable for making pancakes, waffles, and muffins. It can be mixed with whole wheat flour to make bread. It is also being used to make beer and whiskey.

For those who want to learn more about The Land Institute, the Prairie Festival is held at the institute the last full weekend in September. The event starts with a bonfire and a barn dance on Friday night. Saturday is devoted to presentations by well-known speakers, among them, biologists, environmentalists, entomologists, scientists, and Land Institute staff. "The event is sort of an intellectual hootenanny," Wes says. The evening features a local foods dinner and entertainment. On the menu are bison stew, Kernza bread, and ice cream. Sunday events begin with a morning prairie walk, followed by more presentations, and ending with a talk by Wes Jackson.

Before stepping down as president of The Land Institute on June 30, 2016, Wes stated, "The Institute is turning forty years old and I'm turning eighty. I thought that was an auspicious multiplier. I'll step down as president, but will continue this work with the Institute developing an ecospheric studies curriculum and continue to promote natural systems agriculture."

Wes Jackson is a tireless evangelist with a new vision for agriculture. He was named Pew Scholar in

Bison Bolognese

"As a child I spent my free time staring up at my parents in the kitchen as they were cooking. My mother would take on the most difficult recipes in her Junior League cookbooks while my father would go all-in with his attempts to create something original. It is from these two amazing cooks that my love of food and creativity was forged.

"This recipe is an example of how you can take a classic recipe like Bolognese sauce and not only put your spin on it but also feature local ingredients. Take your time when you make this recipe to allow the flavors to develop. Your house will smell awesome! It's the perfect meal when it's too chilly to go out and you want some good comfort food."—Chef-Owner T. K. Peterson, Merchants Pub & Plate, Lawrence

4 SERVINGS

½ cup yellow onion, chopped
¼ cup fennel bulb, chopped
½ cup carrot, peeled and chopped
⅓ cup celery, chopped
4 garlic cloves

2 tablespoons olive oil
1 pound ground bison
3 bacon strips, chopped into small pieces
Salt and pepper, to taste

¼ cup tomato paste
2 cups dry red wine
1 sprig fresh thyme
1 bay leaf
5 to 6 cups hot (low-sodium) chicken broth

1 pound dried pappardelle, tagliatelle, or rigatoni
Parmigiano-Reggiano cheese, grated

CONTINUED ➡

Place the chopped onion, fennel, carrot, celery, and garlic cloves in a food processer or blender and purée until smooth. Set aside.

In a large rondeau or Dutch oven, heat 2 tablespoons of olive oil over medium-high heat. Add the ground bison and chopped bacon and season generously with salt and pepper. Cook until browned, 8 to 10 minutes. Add the puréed vegetables and continue to cook until the mixture is well browned, about 10 minutes.

Stir in the tomato paste and red wine and cook the mixture until the liquid is absorbed. Add the thyme sprig, the bay leaf, and enough of the hot chicken broth to cover the meat. Reduce the heat to low and simmer gently until the broth is absorbed, stirring occasionally. Add more broth to cover the meat and reduce again. Continue the process, simmering for 1 to 1½ hours, or more, until the bison is tender. Taste and add more salt and pepper, if needed. After the last addition of broth, reduce the Bolognese sauce only partially, so that it will nicely coat the pasta. Remove the bay leaf.

When the sauce is ready, cook the pasta in a large pot of boiling, salted water. Drain off the water and toss the pasta with the Bolognese. Garnish each serving with grated Parmigiano-Reggiano cheese and serve immediately.

Spaghetti and Meatballs

When it comes to making the classic Italian dish spaghetti and meatballs, we were inspired by recipes sent to us for our first Kansas cookbook from the southeast region of Kansas, known for the Italian immigrants who came in the 1870s to work the coal, lead, and zinc mines. We like to simmer the meatballs in a tomato sauce to keep them tender while their flavors meld. If there are leftovers, we tuck the meatballs, a spoonful of sauce, a slice of provolone, and grated Parmesan cheese into an Italian-style roll or baguette. Wrap each sandwich in aluminum foil and bake in a 400-degree oven until heated throughout.—Frank and Jayni

6 TO 8 SERVINGS

Meatballs:
1 cup fresh breadcrumbs
½ cup milk

2 tablespoons olive oil
1 cup onion, finely chopped
2 garlic cloves, minced

2 eggs
¼ teaspoon hot pepper sauce
½ cup Pecorino Romano or
    Parmigiano-Reggiano cheese,
    grated
3 tablespoons fresh flat leaf parsley,
    chopped
1 teaspoon dried oregano
1 teaspoon fennel seed, coarsely
    crushed
1¼ teaspoons salt
1 teaspoon black pepper
1 pound ground beef
1 pound ground pork

Tomato Sauce:
2 tablespoons olive oil
2 to 3 garlic cloves, minced
¼ teaspoon crushed red pepper
3 (14-ounce) cans chopped toma-
    toes
¼ cup tomato paste
¼ cup dry red wine
¼ cup water
1 teaspoon dried oregano
1 teaspoon dried basil
1 bay leaf
1 teaspoon sugar
Salt and black pepper, to taste

1½ to 2 pounds dried spaghetti
Kosher or sea salt

Grated Pecorino Romano or
    Parmigiano-Reggiano cheese,
    for garnish

CONTINUED

Meatballs: Place the breadcrumbs in a large bowl. Pour the milk over them and soak for 20 minutes.

Heat the olive oil in a skillet over medium heat. Add the onion and cook until tender, but not browned, 5 to 8 minutes. Add the garlic and cook for 1 to 2 minutes more. Cool briefly.

Add the eggs, cooked onion, and garlic to the soaked breadcrumbs and combine. Stir in the hot pepper sauce, grated cheese, parsley, oregano, crushed fennel seed, salt, and pepper. Mix well. Crumble the ground beef and pork into the breadcrumb and egg mixture. Mix until all ingredients are combined.

Spray a large rimmed sheet pan with cooking spray. Form the meat mixture into meatballs about 1½ inches in diameter. Place them on the sheet pan (bake in two batches, if needed). Bake in a 450-degree oven for 10 minutes, turn the meatballs over with a metal spatula or tongs, and bake for 5 minutes more. While the meatballs bake, prepare the sauce.

Tomato Sauce: Pour the olive oil into a Dutch oven and heat over medium-low heat. Add the garlic and cook for 1 to 2 minutes. Do not brown. Add the crushed red pepper and cook for a few more seconds. Pour the tomatoes into the pot. Add the tomato paste, red wine, water, oregano, basil, bay leaf, and sugar. Season with salt and pepper. Bring the sauce to a simmer over medium-low heat. Add the cooked meatballs, partially cover the pot, and maintain a gentle simmer for 30 minutes. Discard the bay leaf before serving.

Cook the spaghetti in a pot of boiling, salted water until tender, but still firm. Pour the cooked pasta through a strainer and return it to the warm pot. Ladle some of the sauce over the pasta and stir to coat. Add as many of the meatballs and as much sauce as desired and toss gently.

Serve the spaghetti and meatballs in pasta bowls. Top with a generous sprinkle of Pecorino Romano or Parmigiano-Reggiano cheese.

Chicken and Homemade Noodles

Along with beef and pork, Dale Family Farms in Protection raises free-range poultry, so chicken is often on the menu. A warm bowl of chicken and noodles is classic comfort food and never goes out of style with the Dale family. Andi Dale lets her slow cooker simmer a whole bird. And because she doesn't have to tend the pot, there is plenty of time to mix up the dough, roll it out, and cut the noodles. To make it easy, Andi recommends using a pizza cutter. Though making noodles takes a little more time, their rustic, handmade appearance makes this dish the picture of home cooking. It's sure to make some family memories.—Andi Dale, Dale Family Farms, Protection

6 SERVINGS

1 whole chicken, 3½ to 4 pounds
Salt and black pepper
1 celery rib
1 carrot, peeled
½ medium onion
1 fresh rosemary sprig
2 fresh thyme sprigs
2 fresh parsley sprigs
1 large garlic clove, smashed
 2 quarts (8 cups) water

Homemade Noodles:
2 eggs, slightly beaten
1½ cups all-purpose flour
½ teaspoon salt
2 to 5 tablespoons milk

3 to 4 tablespoons all-purpose
   flour, for thickening broth

Pat the exterior of the chicken dry with paper towels. Season with salt and black pepper and set aside. Cut the celery rib and carrot into three or four pieces. Cut the onion into large dice. Put the vegetables in a 7-quart slow cooker and place the chicken on top. Tie the rosemary, thyme, and parsley sprigs together with kitchen twine. Place in the slow cooker along with the smashed garlic clove. Pour in the water. Cover with the lid and set on the slow cooker on high for 6 hours, or low for 8 hours. The chicken is done when it is very tender and falling off the bone.

Remove the chicken from the slow cooker and cool briefly. Remove the meat and discard the skin and bones. Cut the meat into bite-size pieces or shred the meat using two forks. Strain the broth through a wire-mesh strainer. Pour the broth into a fat separator, or skim with a large spoon to remove the fat. Discard the onion, celery, herbs, and garlic. Reserve the carrot, if desired, and chop it into small pieces (to be added to the broth later). If a thickened broth is preferred, measure 1 cup of the chicken broth and set aside.

Homemade Noodles: In a large bowl, combine the eggs with the flour and salt. Add the milk a tablespoon at a time, until a stiff

CONTINUED ➡

dough is formed. Knead briefly, just until the dough is smooth. Divide the dough into two equal portions and roll out to about ⅛-inch thickness on a lightly floured surface. Let stand for 20 minutes. Cut the dough into narrow strips, about ¼ inch wide, using a pizza cutter or sharp knife. Spread the noodles out and let them dry before cooking, 1 to 2 hours.

Pour the chicken broth into a large pot or Dutch oven and add the chopped carrot, if using. Bring the broth to a boil over high heat. Add the noodles and cook until tender, about 10 to 20 minutes. To thicken the broth, whisk 3 to 4 tablespoons of flour into the reserved 1 cup of chicken broth. Stir in as much of the broth and flour mixture as needed to achieve the desired thickness. Add the chicken pieces and heat for about 2 minutes. Season with additional salt and pepper, if needed.

Chapter 6
Red Meats

Kansans love beef. The state has some of the best grazing land in the nation, and its ranches, both large and small, are typically family operations responsible for raising a large percentage of the cattle for the nation. Consumers can choose from naturally raised grain-finished or grass-finished, certified organic, or traditionally raised beef. Ground beef is the favorite choice, followed by steak.

No matter which cut you prefer, this chapter provides some creative ways to prepare beef. Though some purists prefer their steak unadorned, we tempt you with "Grilled Chile Steak," a grilled steak of choice rubbed with a spice blend including chile powder and smoked paprika. If you like sauce on your steak, try "Grilled Strip Steaks with Bourbon Mushroom Sauce." There are new twists on some old Kansas favorites, such as "Pot Roast with Mushrooms" and "Pressure Cooker Brisket Sloppy Joes." And, of course, you'll find several new ideas for economical cuts of beef such as recipes for "Grass-Fed Beef and Bacon Meatloaf," "Ground Beef-Stuffed Yellow Squash with Tomato-Oregano Topping," and "Beef Heart Tacos with Spicy Salsa."

Pork is at home on the range, too. Kansas has more than a thousand pig farms, and nearly all of them are family owned. Modern pork is tender and juicy, and its appealing flavor provides a backdrop for some delicious enhancements. For cooks with more time on their hands, consider "Slow-Cooked Pork Chops with Madeira and Dried Cherry Sauce" or "Slow-Baked Baby Back Ribs with Fennel Seed Spice Rub and Peach Jam Glaze." As an alternative, "Pork Chops with Whole Grain Mustard Pan Sauce" provides a quick, but still special, main course to serve on weeknights.

Other red meats such as lamb and goat are growing in popularity with consumers, and small farmers in Kansas are working to meet the demand. Herb-coated "Grilled Lamb Chops" are easy and elegant enough for company. "Farmer Debbie's Shepherd's Pie" is a family comfort dish made with ground lamb, and should there be any leftovers from "Grill-Roasted Leg of Lamb with Mint Chimichurri Sauce," you're in luck! "Lamb Hash" is a delicious skillet dish for a weeknight supper. Goat meat is increasingly available from small farmers, and we include a few recipes to acquaint you with this tasty meat, such as "Grilled Tequila-Lime Goat Chops," "Grilled Rack of Goat," and "Jamaican-Style Goat."

Red meats aren't limited to this chapter. You'll find other recipes with meat as an ingredient woven throughout the book. Take a look in Chapter 1, "Starters and Small Plates"; Chapter 2, "Soups, Stews, and Chili"; and Chapter 3, "Salads and Salad Meals" for other dishes that include red meat.

Grilled Strip Steaks with Bourbon Mushroom Sauce

Even the purist who refuses to sauce his steak will welcome this embellishment of sliced mushrooms steeped in bourbon. Though any bourbon will do, I prefer to use a bourbon made by Union Horse Distilling Co. in Lenexa.—Frank

SERVES 4

2 strip steaks (10 to 12 ounces each), 1 to 1¼ inch thick

Salt and black pepper, to taste

Bourbon Mushroom Sauce:

8 ounces medium-size button mushrooms

4 tablespoons unsalted butter, divided

¼ cup onion, finely chopped

1 clove garlic, minced

¼ cup molasses

¼ cup bourbon

½ cup chicken broth

1½ tablespoons balsamic vinegar

Season the steaks with salt and pepper and set them aside while the grill heats up. Prepare and measure all the ingredients for the bourbon mushroom sauce in advance.

Prepare a gas or charcoal grill for cooking over high heat. Place the steaks on the cooking grate and cover. Sear for 3 to 5 minutes, turning a quarter turn after the first 2 minutes to mark the meat. When the steaks are well browned on the first side, turn them over, cover, and cook for 3 to 5 minutes more, until the meat registers 130 to 135 degrees for medium-rare. Transfer the steaks to a cutting board, tent with aluminum foil, and let them rest for about 10 minutes before serving. Meanwhile, make the mushroom sauce.

Bourbon Mushroom Sauce: Clean the mushrooms, trim the stems, and cut them into ⅛-inch-thick slices. Set aside. In a large nonstick skillet over medium heat, melt 3 tablespoons of the butter, reserving 1 tablespoon to finish the sauce. Add the chopped onion and cook until soft, about 2 minutes. Add the garlic and cook for 30 seconds more. Add the mushrooms, stirring and tossing until they are soft, release their juices, and are nicely browned.

Raise the heat to medium-high, stir in the molasses, bourbon, and chicken broth and allow the sauce to reduce until lightly thickened, 4 to 6 minutes. Remove the skillet from the heat and stir in the balsamic vinegar. To finish the sauce, stir in the

CONTINUED ➡

reserved tablespoon of butter, letting it melt slowly and thicken the sauce. Makes about 1 cup of sauce.

Just before serving, slice the steaks into ¼- to ½-inch-thick slices and arrange a portion on each of four dinner plates. Spoon the sauce over the steak slices and serve immediately.

Tip: The bourbon mushroom sauce can be made in advance and kept warm, but not hot, until ready to serve. If the sauce becomes too hot the butter emulsion will break.

Distilling Kansas Spirits

The family-owned Union Horse Distilling Co. in Lenexa was founded in 2010 and is operated by three brothers and a sister. Patrick Garcia is the master distiller, Damian is the director of marketing, Eric is the general manager, and Mary Garcia Gallagher is the director of special events. For a long time, the four siblings discussed starting a business together and wanted to do something that would be creative and fun. Damian Garcia tells us, "At the time the discussion began, the craft spirits trend was just beginning across the country with a little more than two hundred craft distilleries opening in the United States. So after much research and intense discussion, we decided to try our hand at making spirits." To date, Kansas is home to several other distilleries, including Good Spirits Distilling in Olathe, Wheat State Distilling in Wichita, and High Plains Inc. in Atchison.

Union Horse Distilling Co. is a craft distillery. Damian explains, "A craft distillery, or microdistillery, is a small operation that creates spirits in single small batches, as compared to the large big-brand distillers, who produce spirits in large quantities. As a hands-on operation, we are involved in every aspect of the production process—grain sourcing, milling, mashing, fermenting, distillation, barreling, and finally, bottling. But, we have more freedom to experiment in the creative process than the bigger producers because we are not tied to a single recipe that has been passed down from generation to generation."

The Garcia family focuses on making bourbon and rye whiskey, though they also produce two clear liquors—vodka and white whiskey. By law, bourbon must be made with a mash consisting of at least 51 percent corn, and rye whiskey must be made with at least 51 percent rye. Other grains—wheat and barley—round out the mix.

As master distiller, Patrick Garcia enjoys the thrill of making spirits. "Basically, I'm a cook who turns grains into alcohol. Because the whiskey has to sit in barrels for so long before you can consume it, it has to be a labor of love."

Making a distilled liquor begins with the grains. The grain mixture is ground, combined with water, and cooked in the mash cooker, which turns the starch in the grains to sugar. The process takes eight to ten hours. The cooked mash is cooled and transferred to the fermenter where yeast is added. The fermentation process takes five to six days. Next, the mixture, now called distillers' beer, is pumped into the still where the alcohol is vaporized, then condensed, and the resulting alcohol is collected and distilled again to remove impurities and raise the alcohol content. The alcohol is adjusted with water and put into barrels to mature. Both bourbon and rye whiskey must be aged in new American oak barrels. And finally, the whiskey is filtered and bottled for consumption.

The whiskey movement is growing, and more craft distilleries, like Union Horse Distilling Co., are making whiskey with a handcrafted taste. "It's great to produce a local product that is beginning to be appreciated around the nation," Patrick tells us. "We sell our whiskey in six states now and we are growing." When asked if anything humorous ever happens at the distillery, he recalls when a distilling tank overflowed and created a sticky mess to clean up: "It's funny now, but not at the time!"

How should one enjoy bourbon or rye? Patrick thinks it is best to appreciate the flavor by drinking it straight, although it's acceptable to add an ice cube or a few drops of water, as some people prefer. "The glass is important too," he says. "I like a Glencairn whiskey glass. It is bell-shaped at the bottom and fluted at the top. It's essential that you take in the aroma of the whiskey as you sip it. It's part of the experience, and the special glass helps with that." Brother Damian adds, "Most of us here at the distillery enjoy our whiskey neat—without ice—because we don't like diluting it. We definitely love drinking it by itself but, coming from the Kansas City area, we love our bourbon with barbecue!"

Grilled Chile Steak

A spicy rub is an easy way to jazz up steak. Pure red chile powder provides heat and spice, brown sugar adds a bit of sweetness, and Spanish paprika ties it all together with a smoky aroma and flavor. Choose flank, rib eye, or strip steaks for the best results. Serve the steak with your favorite potato and vegetable sides or slice the meat and drape over salad greens with some grilled vegetables for a salad meal.—Frank and Jayni

4 SERVINGS

1 flank steak (1½ pounds), or
    2 rib eye or strip steaks
    (12 ounces each)
Olive oil

Chile Rub:
1 tablespoon pure red chile powder,
    hot or mild
1 tablespoon brown sugar
1 teaspoon smoked Spanish
    paprika
¼ teaspoon garlic granules
1½ teaspoons salt
¼ teaspoon black pepper

Trim excess fat from the steak of choice and place on a piece of plastic wrap. Drizzle with a small amount of olive oil to coat the meat.

Chile Rub: In a small container, combine the chile powder, brown sugar, smoked Spanish paprika, garlic granules, salt, and pepper.

Sprinkle about 1 tablespoon of the chile rub over one side of the flank steak, or 2 teaspoons of the rub, if using rib eye or strip steaks. Using your fingers, rub it into the meat. Turn the meat over and repeat. Wrap in plastic wrap and refrigerate for several hours, or overnight. Take the steak out of the refrigerator about 30 minutes before cooking.

Prepare a gas or charcoal grill for cooking over high heat. Place the steak on the cooking grate and sear for 3 to 5 minutes, turning a quarter turn after the first 2 minutes to mark the meat. Turn the steak over and place over indirect medium heat, or move to a cooler part of the grill. Cover and cook for 3 to 5 minutes more, until the meat registers 130 to 135 degrees for medium-rare, or to desired doneness.

Transfer the steak to a cutting board or platter, tent with aluminum foil, and let rest for 5 minutes before carving. If cooking flank steak, cut across the grain into thin slices. For rib eye or strip steaks, cut each in half or into thick slices to serve.

Grilled Flank Steak with Chimichurri Sauce and Farro Pilaf

Kansas meets Argentina when spice-rubbed flank steak is topped with the famous Argentinian chimichurri sauce. The thin slices of steak lie over a warm broth of farro and vegetables to create a hearty meal-in-one. —Frank and Jayni

4 TO 6 SERVINGS

1 flank steak (1 to 1½ pounds)
Olive oil

Rub:
1 tablespoon brown sugar
1 tablespoon smoked Spanish
    paprika
⅛ teaspoon garlic powder or
    granules
1 teaspoon salt
¼ teaspoon black pepper

Chimichurri Sauce:
3 tablespoons red wine vinegar
1 teaspoon dried oregano
1 teaspoon fresh thyme, chopped,
    or ¼ teaspoon dried thyme
¼ teaspoon crushed red pepper
1 large garlic clove, minced
¼ teaspoon salt
⅛ teaspoon black pepper
½ cup extra-virgin olive oil
1 cup fresh flat-leaf parsley, rinsed,
    stemmed, and minced

Farro Pilaf:
1 cup farro (semi-pearled)
2 tablespoons olive oil
1 small (1 cup) red bell pepper,
    seeded and diced
½ cup onion, finely chopped
1 garlic clove, minced
2½ cups low-sodium chicken or
    vegetable broth
½ cup fresh, frozen, or canned
    yellow corn kernels
¼ teaspoon salt

1 large tomato, chopped

Place the flank steak on a piece of plastic wrap and brush lightly with olive oil.

Rub: Combine the brown sugar, smoked paprika, garlic powder or granules, salt, and pepper in a small bowl. Rub about half of the mixture into each side of the flank steak. Wrap in the plastic wrap and refrigerate for at least 3 hours, or overnight.

Chimichurri Sauce: Place the red wine vinegar, oregano, thyme, crushed red pepper, garlic, salt, and pepper in a medium bowl. Whisk in the olive oil. Stir in the minced parsley. Taste and

CONTINUED ➡

adjust seasonings, if needed. Let stand for at least 1 hour to allow the flavors to blend.

Farro Pilaf: Place the farro in a strainer and rinse under cold running water. Drain well and let dry. Heat the oil in a saucepan over medium-low heat. Add the red pepper and onion and cook until tender-crisp, 3 to 5 minutes. Add the garlic and cook for 1 minute. Raise the heat to medium and stir in the farro. Toast, stirring often, for about 3 minutes. Add the broth, corn kernels, and salt. Raise the heat to high. When the mixture comes to a boil, partially cover the pan with a lid and reduce the heat to low. Simmer the farro for about 20 minutes or until tender to the bite, but still chewy. (The pilaf should have a brothy consistency.) Cover until ready to serve.

To grill the flank steak, let the steak stand at room temperature for 30 minutes before grilling. Prepare a gas or charcoal grill for cooking over high heat. Place the steak on the cooking grate and sear for 3 to 5 minutes, turning a quarter turn after the first 2 minutes to mark the meat. Turn the steak over and place it over medium indirect heat or move it to a cooler part of the grill. Cover and cook for 4 to 6 minutes more, until the meat registers 130 to 135 degrees for medium-rare. Transfer the steak to a cutting board, tent with aluminum foil, and let rest for 5 minutes before carving. Slice the flank steak across the grain into thin slices.

To serve, place a generous scoop of the farro pilaf along with some of the pan broth in the center of each dinner plate. Arrange slices of flank steak over the pilaf. Whisk the chimichurri sauce and spoon some over the steak. Garnish each serving with chopped tomato.

Grilled Beef Tenderloin Filets with Shallot and Rosemary Butter

For beef tenderloin, the most highly prized cut of beef, a marinade or rub could unintentionally divert your attention from its tenderness and full beef flavor. We think it's best to serve the filets with a subtle and complementary embellishment, such as a flavored butter. In this recipe, the filets are grill-smoked with pecan wood chips and then, just before serving, topped with a flavorful shallot and rosemary butter.—Frank and Jayni

4 SERVINGS

Shallot and Rosemary Butter:
¼ cup butter, softened
2 tablespoons shallot, finely chopped
2 teaspoons fresh rosemary, finely chopped

1 cup pecan wood smoking chips

4 beef tenderloin filets (6 ounces each)
Olive oil
Salt and black pepper, to taste

Shallot and Rosemary Butter: Place the butter in a small bowl. Add the chopped shallot and rosemary and mix well. If made ahead, cover and refrigerate. Set out to soften at room temperature for 1 to 2 hours before using.

Place the smoking chips in a container and cover with water. Let soak for 30 minutes before using.

If the tenderloin filets are uneven, tie kitchen twine firmly around the circumference of each and pat them into shape. Rub the steaks lightly with olive oil, season them with salt and pepper, and let stand at room temperature for 15 to 30 minutes before grilling.

CONTINUED ➡

Prepare a gas or charcoal grill for cooking over high heat. Drain the soaked pecan wood smoking chips. If using a gas grill, place the wood chips in the smoker box. If using a charcoal grill, wrap the chips in aluminum foil. Seal tightly to make a foil packet and poke a few holes in the foil to allow the smoke to escape. Place the packet directly on the hot coals.

When the grill is hot and the wood chips begin to smoke, place the steaks on the cooking grate and cover. Sear for 4 to 5 minutes, turning a quarter turn after the first 2 minutes to mark the meat. Turn the steaks over and place over indirect medium heat, or move to a cooler part of the grill. Cover and cook for 4 to 5 minutes more, until the meat registers 130 to 135 degrees for medium-rare.

Transfer the steaks to a warm platter and immediately top each steak with about 1 tablespoon of the shallot and rosemary butter. Tent the filets with aluminum foil and let rest for 5 to 10 minutes before serving.

Grilled Beef Tenderloin Filets with Red Wine Sauce

Beef tenderloin filets are the most tender steaks, and they have great beef flavor. Caramelizing the exterior on the grill is special enough, but because the filets are expensive, a red wine sauce can elevate them to special occasion status. Beef tenderloin is very lean, so serve the filets rare to medium-rare for the best flavor.—Frank and Jayni

4 SERVINGS

4 beef tenderloin filets (6 ounces each)
Olive oil
Salt and black pepper, to taste

Red Wine Sauce:
1 tablespoon unsalted butter
¼ cup shallot, finely chopped
½ cup dry red wine
½ cup low-sodium chicken broth
1 tablespoon balsamic vinegar
1 sprig fresh rosemary
2 sprigs fresh thyme
2 tablespoons chilled unsalted butter, diced
Salt and black pepper, to taste

Fresh rosemary and thyme sprigs, for garnish

If the tenderloin filets are uneven, tie kitchen twine firmly around the circumference of each, and pat them into shape. Rub the steaks lightly with olive oil, season them with salt and pepper, and let stand at room temperature for 15 to 30 minutes before grilling.

Prepare a gas or charcoal grill for cooking over high heat. Place the steaks on the cooking grate and cover. Sear for 4 to 5 minutes, turning a quarter turn after the first 2 minutes to mark the meat. Turn the steaks over and place over indirect medium heat or move to a cooler part of the grill. Cover and cook for 4 to 5 minutes more, until the meat registers 130 to 135 degrees for medium-rare.

Transfer the steaks to a warm platter and tent with aluminum foil. Let rest for 5 to 10 minutes before serving. Meanwhile, prepare the wine sauce.

Red Wine Sauce: Heat 1 tablespoon butter in a small saucepan over medium-low heat. Add the chopped shallot and cook until softened, about 3 minutes. Add the red wine, chicken broth, balsamic vinegar, rosemary, and thyme. Raise the heat to medium-high and boil gently until the liquid is reduced to ¼ cup. Strain out the shallots and herbs and return the sauce to a clean saucepan. Add the accumulated juices from the grilled steaks to the sauce. Return to simmering, remove the pan from the heat, and quickly whisk in the 2 tablespoons of diced butter, a few pieces at a time. Season the sauce with salt and pepper, if desired.

To serve, spoon some of the wine sauce over each filet. Garnish with fresh rosemary and thyme sprigs.

Grilled Beef Tri-Tip

The tri-tip roast is a small, boneless cut of beef from the bottom sirloin. This often overlooked roast is tender, fine grained, and full flavored. We like to grill a tri-tip when we're having company for dinner. If we have leftovers, we use them to make a steak salad or sandwiches.—Frank and Jayni

4 TO 6 SERVINGS

1 beef tri-tip roast (1½ to 2 pounds)
1 tablespoon olive oil

Rub:
1 teaspoon salt
½ teaspoon black pepper
¼ teaspoon garlic granules
¼ teaspoon onion granules
1 tablespoon fresh rosemary, minced
1 tablespoon fresh thyme, minced

Trim most of the fat from the tri-tip roast. Rub or brush the meat with olive oil.

Rub: Combine the salt, pepper, garlic, and onion granules in a small container. Combine the minced herbs in a separate container. Rub the spice mixture evenly into the meat. Press the herbs into the meat. Wrap the tri-tip in plastic wrap and refrigerate for 3 hours or more before grilling. Take the tri-tip roast out of the refrigerator about 30 minutes before cooking.

Prepare a gas or charcoal grill for cooking over high heat. Place the tri-tip roast on the cooking grate and brown quickly on both sides. Place the roast over indirect medium heat, or move to a cooler part of the grill. Cover and cook for 20 to 30 minutes, until the meat registers 130 to 135 degrees for medium-rare.

Transfer the roast to a cutting board and tent with aluminum foil. Let rest for 10 to 15 minutes before carving. Slice the tri-tip roast across the grain into thin slices.

Oven-Roasted Rib Eye Steaks with Brandy-Mustard Sauce

No need to fire up your grill for this steak recipe—you won't miss it. Just quickly brown the steaks on the stovetop and place them into a hot oven to finish the cooking. Use the pan drippings to make a luxurious sauce with brandy, Dijon mustard, and fresh herbs. Whisk in butter at the end for a velvety smooth finish.—Frank and Jayni

4 SERVINGS

2 rib eye steaks (12 ounces each),
    1 inch thick
Salt and black pepper, to taste
1 tablespoon olive oil

Brandy-Mustard Sauce:
¼ cup shallot, minced
⅓ cup brandy
1 cup beef broth
1 teaspoon fresh rosemary,
    chopped
1 teaspoon fresh thyme, chopped
1 tablespoon red wine vinegar
1 tablespoon brown sugar
1 tablespoon Dijon mustard
2 tablespoons cold butter, cut into
    small cubes

Preheat the oven to 500 degrees. Trim the excess fat from the steaks and season them with salt and pepper. Heat a stainless steel (oven-safe) skillet just large enough to hold the two steaks over medium-high heat. When the skillet is very hot, add the olive oil, then immediately place the steaks in the skillet, sides not touching. Brown for 1 to 2 minutes, or until the steaks release naturally from the hot skillet. Turn the steak over and place the skillet in the preheated oven. Cook the steaks for 4 to 5 minutes, or until the meat registers 130 to 135 degrees for medium-rare. Remove the steaks from the oven and slide a handle cover over the skillet handle to prevent burning your hands. Transfer the steaks to a cutting board, reserving the pan drippings in the skillet. Tent the steaks with aluminum foil and let rest for about 10 minutes while preparing the sauce.

Brandy-Mustard Sauce: Place the skillet over medium-low heat and add the shallots to the pan drippings. Cook the shallots until softened, 2 to 3 minutes. Add the brandy, beef broth, rosemary, and thyme. Raise the heat to medium-high and boil the liquid until it is reduced to about ⅓ cup, stirring occasionally. Pour the sauce through a wire-mesh strainer into a glass measure or small bowl. Discard the shallot and herbs and return the sauce to the skillet. Stir in the vinegar, brown sugar, and Dijon mustard. Simmer over medium heat, stirring, for about 1 minute more. Remove the skillet from the heat and quickly whisk in the butter, a few pieces at a time, until melted.

CONTINUED ➡

To serve, cut the steaks in half, or thinly slice them, and arrange on four dinner plates. Spoon some of the sauce over each serving.

What's Happening in Kansas?

Just talk to Marci Penner and she will tell you, as she bubbles over with enthusiasm, where to find just about anything. She knows where to find the best restaurants, who is growing the best produce, where little-known attractions are located, and what is new and interesting to see in any given place—if that place is in Kansas. What Marci won't tell you, perhaps due to modesty, is that she is the authority on what's happening all over the state. Marci has assumed the responsibility to make sure all Kansans and tourists alike develop a deep appreciation of what this state has to offer.

Apparently, there were plenty of things going on in Kansas, but folks needed a little help to find them. So in 1990, Marci and her late father, Mil Penner, coauthored their first Kansas guidebook, *Kansas Weekend Guide*. The Penners decided to have a book-signing party on their farm near Inman and invited representatives of the places featured in the guidebook to come and present their information and exhibits. They set up a tent large enough for the exhibitors, but as luck would have it, that November day was cold, and the rain soon turned into snow. It didn't seem to dampen the interest in Kansas, however, when a thousand people showed up!

The following year, the event became the Kansas Sampler Festival and was held on the Penners' farm for seven years. The project was so successful that they formed the Kansas Sampler Foundation in 1993. "The foundation was formed because there wasn't any system in place to help people get to know the towns in Kansas," explains Marci. "We care about community sustainability and educating the public." Marci is currently the executive director of the nonprofit Kansas Sampler Foundation. WenDee LaPlant is the assistant director and festival overseer, and Kim Clark is the bookkeeper.

For Marci Penner, this was just the beginning. In order to turn the guidebooks into action, in 1994 Marci and her network started the Kansas Explorers Club. Its purpose is to inspire, educate, and encourage the exploration and appreciation of Kansas—and have fun doing it!

In 1998, the Kansas Sampler Festival went on the road to expose more people to the festival's exhibitors. "We realize that the festival is a joyful and positive way of bringing Kansans together and sharing what our state has to offer," says Marci. "It gives small towns a chance to be involved, too." Pratt was the first town chosen to host the festival, and as it continues to move around the state, other towns and cities compete to host it. The festival showcases more than 150 communities and attractions so the public can learn about the attractions to visit, explore cultural heritages, and buy products made in Kansas. The festival is held the first full weekend in May and stays in the chosen town for two consecutive years. Eventually, the Kansas Sampler Festival will come to an end, and Marci Penner will launch the next great idea to promote the state of Kansas.

In 2011, Marci wrote an award-winning book, *The 8 Wonders of Kansas Guidebook*. The book, filled with 800 beautiful photos by Harland J. Schuster of the 216 entries, serves as both a travel guide and coffee table book.

"Through our Explorers Club, we try to create an audience for smaller towns and help them to recognize what they have to offer from an explorer's point of view," Marci tell us. "Club members receive a newsletter and e-blasts to provide information that will make you want to jump in your car and head down Kansas roads!" So, what are you waiting for? Let's go Kansas!

Peruvian Stir-Fried Beef (Lomo Saltado)

Janzen Family Farms is a diversified livestock and grain operation that utilizes sustainable practices, including organic crop production. They raise a herd of about forty head of 100 percent grass-fed Angus beef.

"People rave about the flavor of the beef without anything at all—just a little salt. My sense is that it comes from the prairie grasses that nourish the animals. But you can't put any of that into a recipe," Kristi Bahrenburg Janzen says. To showcase their beef, Kristi shares this Peruvian preparation of sirloin steak. The family is always on the lookout for interesting flavors and techniques, and this recipe comes from Peruvian friends.—Janzen Family Farms, Newton

4 SERVINGS

1 pound sirloin steak, grass-fed
    beef preferred
Salt and black pepper, to taste
2 teaspoons ground cumin, or
    1 tablespoon cumin seed,
    coarsely ground

1 small onion, thinly sliced
1 tablespoon apple cider vinegar

3 tablespoons olive, vegetable, or
    canola oil, divided
1 red bell pepper, seeded and cut in
    thin strips
1 green bell pepper, seeded and cut
    in thin strips
1 tomato, cut into thin wedges

Cooked rice

Remove the bone and trim the fat from the steak. Cut it into ½-inch strips and place in a shallow bowl. Season with salt and pepper. Sprinkle the cumin over the meat and toss to coat. If using coarsely ground cumin seed, gently press the cumin into the meat using your fingers. Set aside.

Put the onion slices in a bowl. Add the apple cider vinegar and toss together. Let stand for 10 to 15 minutes.

Heat 1 tablespoon of the oil in a large skillet over medium-high heat. Add the onion and stir-fry until soft and translucent, 3 to 5 minutes. Lower the heat if necessary to prevent burning. Add the peppers and tomato and stir-fry until the peppers are tender, but still firm.

In a separate skillet, heat the remaining 2 tablespoons of oil over high heat. A fast, very hot stir-fry will sear the strips on the outside and keep the inside tender. Add the beef strips and stir-fry for 3 to 5 minutes, or to desired doneness. Take care not to overcook or burn the steak.

Combine the steak and vegetables and serve on a platter. Accompany with hot, cooked rice.

Sauerbraten

After Kansas was opened for settlement, Germans were the largest group of Europeans to settle here. Their food traditions remain strong throughout the state and are often exemplified in the form of restaurants, festivals, and celebrations of German heritage. Sauerbraten is a German specialty and a popular dish at Beethoven's #9, a German restaurant in Paola. Jeanie Clerico owns the restaurant with her daughter, Chef Linzi Weilert.

"The key to good sauerbraten is taking the time to marinate the sirloin for at least four hours, or up to two days. The result is tender meat that is full of flavor."—Jeanie Clerico, Beethoven's #9, Paola

12 TO 15 SERVINGS

4 to 5 pounds top sirloin
5 tablespoons spicy mustard

1 large onion, diced
5 bay leaves
5 whole cloves
2 teaspoons salt
2 teaspoons whole peppercorns
2½ cups distilled white vinegar
2½ cups water, or dry red wine

5 tablespoons butter
5 tablespoons all-purpose flour
Salt and black pepper, to taste

Place the sirloin on a cutting board and cut into 8-ounce chunks. Slather the pieces on both sides with the spicy mustard. Set aside.

Place the diced onion in a large baking dish. Add the bay leaves, cloves, salt, and peppercorns. Place the chunks of sirloin on top. Pour the vinegar and water (or red wine) into the baking dish. Cover and marinate the beef in the refrigerator for a minimum of 4 hours, or up to 2 days.

Take the meat out of the refrigerator about 1 hour before baking. Cover the baking dish with aluminum foil and bake the sirloin in a 350-degree oven for 1 hour. Remove the baking dish from the oven, leave covered, and allow the meat to cool in the liquid.

To make the gravy, remove the meat from the cooking liquid, transfer to a baking dish, and keep warm. Pour the cooking liquid through a strainer into a saucepan. Reduce the liquid by half over medium-high heat. Set aside.

In another saucepan, melt the butter over medium heat. Stir in the flour and cook, stirring, until the mixture begins to color. Slowly whisk in the reduced cooking liquid until the desired

CONTINUED ➡

thickness is reached. Simmer the gravy for a minute or two over low heat and season with salt and pepper.

To serve, slice the sauerbraten into ¼-inch-thick slices and top with the gravy.

Kansas-Style Beef and Chicken Tagine

George Laughead began cooking with exotic spices when he was a newlywed student at the University of Kansas in the early 1970s. He likes the flavors of Morocco and, though a tagine such as this is usually cooked in a special tagine cooking pot, he cooks it in a Dutch oven. George has also tailored his recipe to suit Kansans' tastes by using a combination of beef short ribs and chicken.

"If you make apple pies or gingerbread, you'll have the spices needed for a great tagine."
—George Laughead, Dodge City

4 TO 6 SERVINGS

2½ to 3 pounds bone-in short ribs or 1½ to 2 pounds boneless beef short ribs
6 to 8 chicken legs
Salt

3 tablespoons olive oil, divided
1 large onion, chopped
1 garlic clove, chopped
1 teaspoon ginger paste, or 2 teaspoons fresh ginger, chopped

Spice Blend:
¾ teaspoon ground allspice
½ teaspoon black pepper
½ teaspoon ground cumin
½ teaspoon ground cinnamon
½ teaspoon ground ginger
¼ teaspoon ground cloves
¼ teaspoon turmeric

4 or 5 medium carrots
6 sun-dried tomatoes, halved, sliced, or chopped
¼ cup golden raisins
½ preserved lemon,* sliced, or zest of 1 lemon plus 1 tablespoon lemon juice
1 tablespoon fresh thyme, chopped, or 1 teaspoon dried thyme
1 tablespoon honey

Cooked couscous or rice, or rustic-style bread

If using large bone-in beef short ribs, remove the bone and cut the meat in half. If using boneless short ribs, leave whole or cut in half. Remove excess fat from the meat. Salt the short ribs and chicken legs and set aside. Preheat the oven to 400 degrees.

Heat 2 tablespoons of the olive oil in large Dutch oven over medium-high heat. Add the short ribs and brown on all sides, 8 to 10 minutes. Transfer the short ribs to a large platter. Add the remaining tablespoon of oil to the pot and brown the chicken legs on all sides, about 8 minutes. Lower the heat if necessary to prevent burning. Transfer the chicken legs to the platter, reserving the drippings in the pot. Add the onion, garlic, and ginger paste or fresh ginger to the drippings in the pot. Sauté over medium heat until the onion is tender, about 5 minutes. While the onion mixture is cooking, combine the spices.

Spice Blend: In a small bowl, combine the allspice, pepper, cumin, cinnamon, ginger, cloves, and turmeric. Add half of the spice mixture to the onion mixture during the last minute or so of cooking.

Arrange the beef short ribs around the inside edge of the pot on top of the onion mixture. Place the chicken legs in the pot with the meaty ends of the legs in the center, like spokes on a wheel. Sprinkle the remaining spice mixture over the meat pieces.

Peel the carrots and cut them in half crosswise, then slice each carrot piece in half lengthwise. Add the carrot pieces to the pot, placing them like spokes on a wheel over the meat. Scatter the sun-dried tomato pieces, raisins, and preserved lemon slices or lemon zest and juice over the contents of the pot. Sprinkle with thyme and drizzle the honey over top.

Seal the Dutch oven tightly with aluminum foil and place the lid on top. Place the Dutch oven in the 400-degree oven and immediately reduce the temperature to 350 degrees. Cook for 2 hours. Do not open the pot before then. The meat should be very tender when done. Place the lid back on the pot and let rest for 15 minutes.

Serve the tagine on plates over hot couscous or rice, or in a bowl with rustic-style bread.

* Preserved lemons can be found in stores that carry Moroccan or Middle Eastern products. To prepare the preserved lemon for cooking, rinse the lemon under cold, running water to remove some of the salt. Cut the lemon in half, and reserve one half for another use. Remove the pulp from the remaining half and rinse the lemon peel. Pat the peel dry with paper towels and cut into six pieces.

Pot Roast with Mushrooms

A pot roast slowly simmering for Sunday lunch is a Midwestern tradition. I've enhanced this much-loved classic dish by adding fresh cremini mushrooms and dried porcinis, along with some herbs, red wine, and beef broth. For convenience, it cooks slowly in the oven rather than on the stovetop. The result is a tender roast with a generous amount of rich mushroom gravy to serve over mashed potatoes and perhaps some roasted root vegetables.—Frank

6 SERVINGS

2½- to 3-pound beef chuck roast
Salt and black pepper, to taste
2 tablespoons olive oil

1 medium onion, sliced into ¼-inch
    half rounds
2 garlic cloves, chopped
½ ounce dried porcini mushrooms,
    broken into small pieces
8 ounces cremini mushrooms,
    whole, halved, or quartered,
    depending on size
¾ cup beef broth
¾ cup dry red wine
6 to 8 sprigs fresh thyme, bundled
    together with kitchen twine
1 bay leaf

2 tablespoons all-purpose flour

Place the chuck roast on a plastic cutting board and pat dry with paper towels. Season both sides with salt and pepper. Heat the olive oil over medium-high heat in a Dutch oven, or other large pot. Add the roast and brown, 3 to 4 minutes each side. Transfer the roast to a cutting board or platter. Pour off the fat, if desired.

Put the onion, garlic, and mushrooms, both dried and fresh, in the Dutch oven. Pour in the beef broth and wine, and simmer over medium heat for about 2 minutes, scraping up the browned bits. Tuck in the thyme bundle and bay leaf. Place the roast on top. Cover the pot with a lid and place in a 325-degree oven. Cook the roast for 2 hours 30 minutes to 2 hours 45 minutes, until tender. Baste the roast with the juices after 1 hour of cooking.

Transfer the roast to a warm platter. Remove the mushrooms and onion with a slotted spoon and place them around the roast. Discard the thyme bundle and bay leaf. Tent the roast, mushrooms, and onion with aluminum foil.

To make the gravy, pour the pan juices through a strainer into a fat separator and let stand for 5 to 10 minutes. Pour off the defatted juices and set aside, reserving 2 tablespoons of the fat. Pour the reserved fat (or 2 substitute tablespoons of olive oil) into the Dutch oven or a saucepan, and heat over medium heat. Add the flour and stir for about 2 minutes, until it turns a medium brown color. Slowly add the defatted juices, stirring or whisking until well combined. Let the gravy simmer over low heat until lightly thickened, about 2 minutes. Season the gravy with salt and pepper, to taste.

Serve the gravy over the pot roast and mushrooms.

Pressure Cooker Brisket Sloppy Joes

This modern version of the ever-popular sloppy joe sandwich substitutes brisket for ground beef, and pressure-cooks it in a tasty sweet-sour tomato sauce. Serve the brisket in the traditional way on hamburger buns or pile the meat onto open-faced, crusty French rolls.—Frank and Jayni

8 TO 12 SERVINGS

2- to 2½-pound beef brisket (flat piece)
Salt and black pepper, to taste
1 tablespoon vegetable oil
½ medium onion, sliced ¼-inch thick

1 (15-ounce) can tomato sauce
¼ cup brown sugar
2 tablespoons tomato paste
1 teaspoon dry mustard
1 tablespoon Worcestershire sauce
1 tablespoon red wine vinegar
1 teaspoon chili powder blend
½ teaspoon garlic powder or granules
½ teaspoon onion powder or granules
¼ teaspoon salt
⅛ teaspoon black pepper

2 tablespoons vegetable oil
1 cup onion, cut into ½-inch dice
1 cup green bell pepper, seeded and cut into ½-inch dice
½ cup celery, cut into ¼-inch dice
2 garlic cloves, minced

Toasted hamburger buns or crusty rolls split in half

Trim excessive fat from brisket. Pat the meat dry with paper towels and season with salt and pepper. Set an electric pressure cooker* on "brown" and add 1 tablespoon of oil to the cooking pot. Add the brisket and brown, 2 to 3 minutes on each side. Lay the onion slices on the brisket.

In a medium bowl, combine the tomato sauce, brown sugar, tomato paste, dry mustard, Worcestershire sauce, red wine vinegar, chili powder, garlic powder, onion powder, salt, and pepper. Pour the mixture over the brisket. Cover and lock the pressure cooker lid into place. Cook on high pressure for 1 hour.

CONTINUED ➡

Let the steam release naturally for 15 minutes, then use the quick pressure release to release the remaining steam. Turn off the pressure cooker, but do not remove the lid. Let the brisket rest in the covered pot for one hour.

While the meat is resting, heat 2 tablespoons of oil over medium heat in a large pot or Dutch oven. Add the chopped onion, green pepper, and celery. Sauté the vegetables until tender and golden, 10 to 12 minutes. Add the garlic and cook for 1 minute more and set aside.

Transfer the rested brisket to a cutting board. Skim the fat from the sauce in the pressure cooker pot, or pour it into a fat separator to remove the fat. Pour the defatted sauce into the pot containing the onion and green pepper mixture and simmer over low heat for 5 minutes, stirring occasionally.

Slice the brisket across the grain, then chop the meat into bite-size pieces. Add the brisket to the sauce and simmer for 5 minutes more. Season the sloppy joe mixture with more salt and pepper, if needed.

To serve, pile the brisket onto toasted buns or rolls.

*If using a stovetop pressure cooker, follow the manufacturer's instructions when preparing this recipe.

Option: This recipe may also be prepared in a slow cooker. Season and brown the brisket in a large skillet. Transfer it to a slow cooker and lay the onion slices on top. Proceed as directed. Set the slow cooker on low heat and cook for 6 to 8 hours, or until tender.

Pachamamas Star Bar Burger

The popular Star Bar Burger was served at Pachamamas Restaurant and Star Bar, the well-known Lawrence establishment owned and operated by Chef Ken Baker for thirteen years. This amazing burger, topped with Chambord-Onion Jam, remained a favorite until the restaurant closed in 2015. The Chambord-Onion Jam can be made ahead and will keep for a week or two in the refrigerator, if it lasts that long.—Chef Ken Baker, Pachamamas Restaurant and Star Bar, Lawrence

MAKES 12 (8-OUNCE) BURGERS

5 pounds ground beef
1 pound bacon, ground
6 garlic cloves, peeled
1 teaspoon salt
4 medium shallots, minced
2 tablespoons Pickapeppa Sauce*
2 tablespoons fresh thyme, chopped
Salt and black pepper, to taste

White cheddar cheese slices (optional)

Premium hamburger buns, lightly grilled or warmed in the oven
Dijon mustard

Chambord-Onion Jam:
4 tablespoons butter
6 cups thinly sliced red onions
1 cup chicken broth
½ cup Chambord liqueur
4 tablespoons dry red wine
¼ cup red wine vinegar
2 teaspoons tomato paste
1 ½ teaspoons fresh thyme, chopped
Salt and black pepper, to taste

Place the ground beef in a large bowl. Grind the bacon in a meat grinder. Add the ground bacon to the beef. Place the garlic cloves in a mortar with pestle. Add 1 teaspoon of salt and, using the pestle, grind the garlic into a paste. Add the garlic paste to the meat along with the minced shallots, Pickapeppa Sauce, and chopped thyme. Mix the meat mixture by hand to make sure all ingredients are evenly combined. Form the ground beef mixture into 8-ounce patties, or desired size. Season the patties liberally with salt and pepper before cooking.

To grill the burgers, prepare a gas or charcoal grill for cooking over high heat. Place the patties on the cooking grate and cover. Cook for 4 to 5 minutes. When the burgers are well browned on the first side, turn them over, cover, and cook for 4 to 5 minutes more, until the meat registers 150 to 155 degrees for medium-well. Move the burgers to a cooler part of the grill, if needed, to prevent burning. During the last 2 minutes of cooking, top each burger with white cheddar cheese slices, if using. Transfer the burgers to a platter, tent with aluminum foil, and let them rest for 5 minutes before serving.

Serve the burgers on warm buns, topped with a spoonful of Chambord-Onion Jam, and Dijon mustard on the side.

CONTINUED ➡

Chambord-Onion Jam: Melt the butter in a large, heavy-bottomed pan over medium heat. Add the sliced onions, cover and sweat them for about 15 to 20 minutes, until soft and translucent. Stir occasionally to prevent burning and lower the heat, if necessary. Do not let the onions brown. Add the chicken broth, liqueur, dry red wine, red wine vinegar, tomato paste, and thyme to the onions. Cook the mixture over medium heat, stirring occasionally, until most of the liquid is reduced and the onions are lightly caramelized, about 30 minutes. As the liquid reduces, lower the heat as needed to prevent burning. Season the jam as it cooks with salt and pepper. Cool to room temperature before using. Cover and refrigerate unused onion jam. Makes about 2 cups.

*Pickapeppa Sauce is a Jamaican pepper sauce and can be found in most supermarkets in the condiment or specialty foods section.

Tip: The jam is a great pairing for almost any meat item or grilled vegetables. It also goes well with baked Camembert cheese.

Old-School Grilled Burgers

Freshly ground beef gives grilled burgers that old-school flavor and texture. We serve them with the works—grilled onion slices, tomato, lettuce, and dill pickles. Grinding the beef is worth the effort for the superior beefy taste. Purchase a chuck roast and grind it at home in a meat grinder or, if you don't own a grinder, ask your butcher to grind the roast for you.—Frank and Jayni

6 SERVINGS

2 pounds chuck roast (arm or
    shoulder)
2 teaspoons salt
½ to 1 teaspoon black pepper, to
    taste

1 large onion, halved and sliced
2 tablespoons olive oil

6 premium hamburger buns

Tomato slices, lettuce leaves,
    dill pickles
Ketchup, mustard, or
    condiments of choice

Cut the chuck roast into 1- to 2-inch chunks, including the fat. Using a meat grinder, grind the meat to a medium texture into a large bowl. For a uniform distribution, grind the pieces of fat interspersed with the meat pieces. Add the salt and pepper and mix gently. Using your hands, form the meat into six patties.

Place the sliced onion in a bowl. Drizzle with olive oil and toss to coat.

Prepare a gas or charcoal grill for cooking over medium-high heat. Place a grill pan on the grate for cooking the onions.

To grill the burgers, place the burgers on the cooking grate and cover. Cook for 4 to 5 minutes, turn them over, and grill for 4 to 5 minutes more, until the meat registers 150 to 155 degrees for medium-well. Move the burgers to a cooler part of the grill if needed to prevent burning. Transfer the burgers to a warm platter and tent with aluminum foil. Let rest for 5 minutes before serving.

To cook the onion slices, place them on the hot grill pan and turn frequently until browned and tender, about 5 minutes.

Toast the buns on the grill, cut side down, until lightly browned, about 30 seconds.

To serve, place the burgers on buns and top each with some of the grilled onion. Serve with a platter of tomato slices, lettuce leaves, and dill pickles. Pass ketchup, mustard, or condiments of choice.

Gourmet Meatloaf with Smoky-Hot Glaze

"My Aunt Rose would open her fridge and make amazing meals just from leftovers. One I loved was her meatloaf using leftover vegetables. Brilliant! I like to add leftover finely chopped broccoli, but you can add just about any cooked vegetable or a combination of several. It's a good way to use up leftovers and adds some extra nutrition to meatloaf."—Kathleen Hodge, Lawrence

4 TO 6 SERVINGS

1 cup bread, torn into small pieces
½ cup heavy cream

2 eggs, lightly beaten
1 tablespoon fresh parsley, chopped
1 heaping teaspoon dried oregano
1 teaspoon dried thyme
1 teaspoon garlic powder
1 teaspoon onion powder
1 teaspoon salt
1 teaspoon black pepper
2 teaspoons Worcestershire sauce
¼ cup Parmesan cheese, grated
¼ cup shallot, finely chopped
1 cup cooked broccoli or other vegetable, finely chopped
1 pound lean ground beef

Smoky-Hot Glaze:
¾ cup ketchup
2 tablespoons hot sauce of choice
1 teaspoon smoked Spanish paprika
1 tablespoon honey
1 tablespoon Worcestershire sauce

Place the bread pieces in a large bowl. Pour the cream over the bread and stir to combine. Let stand until the bread softens and absorbs the cream, about 10 minutes.

Stir the lightly beaten eggs, herbs, garlic powder, onion powder, salt, and pepper into the bread mixture. Add the Worcestershire sauce, grated cheese, shallot, and broccoli. Mix well. Add the ground beef, breaking it up as you gently mix it in to the other ingredients. The mixture will be wet. Form loosely into a round or oval shape and place in a baking dish.

Smoky-Hot Glaze: Combine the ketchup, hot sauce, smoked Spanish paprika, honey, and Worcestershire sauce in a small saucepan. Simmer over medium-low heat for 10 minutes, stirring occasionally. Cool briefly.

Pour the glaze over the top of the meatloaf. Bake in a 350-degree oven for 1 hour. Transfer the loaf from baking dish to a serving platter and tent with aluminum foil. Let rest for at least 15 minutes before slicing.

Variation: Other cooked vegetables can be used, such as green beans, carrots, or corn.

Life on Dale Family Farms

The Dale family has farmed and ranched in Comanche County, Kansas, for more than one hundred years. Kurt and Andi Dale are the fifth generation on the farm and have taken over the reins from Kurt's parents, Bill and Helen Dale. Kurt manages the farm and Andi handles the marketing and distribution of the farm's products. The Dales raise grass-fed, grass-finished beef, pasture-raised pigs, and free-range chickens and turkeys.

Andi says they started the move toward raising grass-fed beef in 2003. The cattle forage on native grasses most of the year, supplemented by grazing on pastures of wheat, rye, triticale, sorghum feed, and turnips. They do not use synthetic growth hormones or antibiotics. The Dales believe that grass-finished beef is healthier than grain-finished beef because it is lower in fat and higher in omega-3 fatty acids and CLAs (conjugated linoleic acids). When prepared properly, grass-finished beef is tender with a rich, full, beef flavor, the Dales have discovered.

The Dales' chickens and turkeys are allowed to range freely during the day, foraging for green grass, seeds, and insects. This "salad bar" approach to their diet improves the flavor and texture of the meat and the eggs they produce. They are housed at night to protect them from predators and moved daily to a fresh forage area.

In recent years, the Dales have added pigs to the mix. They, too, are raised on pasture and are also supplemented with grain rations.

Kurt and Andi Dale are committed to raising healthy animals and being good stewards of the land. As they strive to remain "sustainable," they know they must better utilize natural resources through improved grazing practices and reduce the reliance on fuel and equipment. Andi tells us, "Over the last few years, we have realized that letting our animals remain in their natural environment, doing what they do best—grazing—will be our key to sustainability and another one hundred years for the Dales on the family farm."

Grass-Fed Beef and Bacon Meatloaf

Graze The Prairie is a cattle ranch in the Flint Hills practicing the traditions of the open prairie in a modern way. They raise high-quality, grass-fed beef. The cattle graze year-round on pasture free of chemical fertilizers. They are never given growth hormones or fed grains or concentrates. "Our cattle are moved into paddocks daily in the growing season and at least twice weekly in the dormant season. This mimics the movement of the animals that historically lived on the prairie and is in concert with how the prairie evolved," says Linda Pechin-Long. "This provides our cattle with the best life possible and helps preserve the remaining tallgrass prairie.

"This meatloaf recipe, made with grass-fed beef and topped with bacon, is always a hit with the crew working the cattle. To round out the meal, I serve a fresh garden salad, roasted potatoes, and seasonal vegetables."—Linda Pechin-Long, Graze The Prairie, Beaumont

6 SERVINGS

1 cup fresh breadcrumbs or Panko
    breadcrumbs
1 garlic clove, minced
½ cup lightly packed chopped
    fresh parsley
1¼ teaspoons salt
½ teaspoon black pepper
Pinch of cayenne pepper (optional)
1 cup onion, finely chopped
1 tablespoon honey or molasses
1 egg, beaten
½ cup tomato juice or tomato sauce
1½ pounds grass-fed ground beef

3 bacon slices (optional)

If using fresh breadcrumbs, cut day-old bread slices into large pieces and blend them in a blender or food processor until fine crumbs are produced. Measure 1 cup. In a large mixing bowl, combine the breadcrumbs, garlic, parsley, salt, black pepper, and cayenne pepper, if using. Stir in the chopped onion, honey or molasses, beaten egg, and tomato juice or sauce. Add the ground beef, breaking it up, and blending it into the other ingredients, using a rubber spatula or your hands, until well combined.

Line a baking sheet with parchment paper or aluminum foil. Mound the mixture onto the baking sheet and, with your hands, shape it into a log about 8 inches long and 4 inches wide. Cut the bacon slices in half, if using, and lay them across the top of the loaf with the edges touching to completely cover the top.

Bake the meatloaf in a 375-degree oven for 40 to 45 minutes, until it is well browned and registers 155 degrees. Cool for 10 minutes before slicing.

Weekday Meatloaf

Sometimes a wave of nostalgia rolls over us and we crave our favorite Midwestern comfort food—meatloaf. We've tried many versions of everyone else's favorite, but we always return to the meatloaf recipe we've been making since we first met. We've made a few adjustments over the years, but the big change is using local, naturally raised organic beef.—Frank and Jayni

6 TO 8 SERVINGS

1½ pounds lean ground beef

3 white bread slices
2 eggs
⅔ cup milk
1½ teaspoons salt
½ teaspoon black pepper

2 tablespoons shallot, finely minced
¼ cup celery, finely minced
1 cup onion, finely minced
½ cup carrot, peeled and shredded
¼ cup ketchup

Topping:
¼ cup ketchup
1 teaspoon yellow mustard
¼ cup brown sugar
¼ teaspoon chipotle chile powder

Set the ground beef out of the refrigerator to take the chill off while preparing the other ingredients.

Cut the bread into large dice and place it in a food processor. Blend for a few seconds to make coarse crumbs. Measure 1½ cups of breadcrumbs and set aside. Crack the eggs into a large bowl. Add the milk, salt, and pepper, and whisk to combine. Stir in the breadcrumbs. Let the mixture stand for about 10 minutes to soften the breadcrumbs.

Add the shallot, celery, onion, and carrot to the egg and bread-crumb mixture. Stir in ¼ cup of ketchup. Add the ground beef, breaking it up. Mix until all ingredients are thoroughly combined.

Form the meat mixture into a loaf and transfer to a 9 × 5 × 3-inch loaf pan. Press the meat evenly into the pan.

Topping: Combine the ketchup, mustard, brown sugar, and chipotle chile powder in a small bowl.

Pour the topping mixture evenly over the top of the meatloaf. Bake the meatloaf, uncovered, in a 350-degree oven for 1 hour and 15 minutes, or until the meat registers 155 degrees. Remove the meatloaf from the oven and cool on a wire baking rack for 15 minutes. Using a long metal spatula, carefully remove the meatloaf from the loaf pan and transfer it to a cutting board. Let it cool to warm for easier cutting, about 15 minutes more. Slice the meatloaf to serve.

Ground Beef-Stuffed Yellow Squash with Tomato-Oregano Topping

Linda Pechin-Long stuffs yellow squash halves with cooked ground beef, then tops each one with puréed tomatoes and a sprinkle of oregano. The squash halves make an attractive presentation, and it is a good way to use up an abundance of squash from your backyard garden.

"We raise our cattle in the Flint Hills. We are always looking for recipes where we can use our own grass-fed beef with vegetables that are homegrown or purchased at the farmers' market."
—Linda Pechin-Long, Graze The Prairie, Beaumont

6 TO 8 SERVINGS

3 to 4 medium yellow squash,
    about 8 to 9 ounces each
Salt, to taste

2 tablespoons extra-virgin olive oil
1 medium yellow onion, finely
    chopped
2 garlic cloves, minced
1 pound grass-fed ground beef
1 teaspoon salt
1 teaspoon black pepper
Dash of cayenne pepper

2 fresh tomatoes, or 1 (8-ounce) can
    tomato sauce
Fresh oregano, chopped, or dried
    oregano, to taste

Rinse the yellow squash, trim the ends, and cut each in half lengthwise. Using a large spoon, gently scoop out the seeds leaving a cavity for the filling. If the squash halves do not sit flat, slice a small sliver from the skin side. Sprinkle the cavity with salt and set aside.

Heat the oil in a medium saucepan or skillet over medium-low heat. Add the onion and garlic and cook until the onion is soft and translucent. Raise the heat to medium, add the beef, breaking it up, and cook until browned. Stir in the salt, black pepper, and a dash of cayenne pepper. Cook for 1 minute more. Cool briefly.

Lightly grease a 2- to 3-inch-deep baking dish large enough to hold the squash halves in a single layer (or use two baking dishes, if needed). Fill each squash half with the ground beef mixture and place in the baking dish.

Core the fresh tomatoes and purée in a blender or food processor until smooth. Spoon the puréed tomatoes, or tomato sauce, if using, over the tops of the squash halves. Sprinkle each with fresh or dried oregano.

Cover the baking dish with aluminum foil and bake the stuffed squash in a 350-degree oven for 25 minutes, then remove the foil and bake for 15 to 20 minutes more, or until the squash is tender.

Variation: For smaller servings, use 6 small squash, 4 to 5 ounces each. Cover and bake in a 350-degree oven for 20 minutes. Uncover and bake for 10 to 15 minutes more.

Beef Heart Tacos with Spicy Salsa

"Our forebears began farming in Kansas in 1880, and our farm has been in Janzen hands since 1898," Kristi Bahrenburg Janzen tells us. "In September 2009, the Kansas Farm Bureau conferred Century Farm status on Janzen Family Farms."

This recipe comes from a friend of the Janzen family from Mexico. It calls for beef heart and reflects the Janzens' efforts to branch out and try new things, respectfully utilizing all parts of the animal. Serrano or jalapeño peppers are typically used in this recipe, but if no heat is desired, a bell pepper may be substituted.—Janzen Family Farms, Newton

4 SERVINGS

1 beef heart, 100 percent grass-fed

2 tablespoons olive, vegetable, or canola oil

1 medium onion, chopped

2 to 4 serrano or jalapeño peppers, chopped

3 large tomatoes, seeds removed, and coarsely chopped

1 small bunch fresh cilantro, stemmed and chopped

1 medium-size green cabbage

2 limes

1 garlic clove, chopped or pressed

Salsa:

4 medium-size Roma tomatoes

3 serrano or jalapeño peppers, whole

1 small garlic clove

Salt and black pepper, to taste

Soft corn tortillas, warmed

CONTINUED ➡

Blot the beef heart with paper towels. Cut it into four parts. Boil the quarters in a pot of boiling water for 1½ hours. Drain well and cool briefly. Cut the heart quarters into small chunks or cubes.

Heat the oil in a large skillet over medium-high heat. Add the heart pieces, onion, peppers, chopped tomatoes, and cilantro. Cook, stirring frequently, until the pepper and onion pieces are tender and lightly browned.

Thinly slice the cabbage and place in a large bowl. Season with lime juice and chopped or pressed garlic, to taste. Set aside.

Salsa: Place the Roma tomatoes and serrano or jalapeño peppers into a small pot, cover with water, and bring to a boil. Simmer over low heat for about 15 minutes, until the tomatoes and peppers are soft and cooked. Remove the peppers and tomatoes from the water with a slotted spoon and transfer them to a blender. Add the garlic clove to the blender and season the mixture with salt and black pepper. Blend for a few seconds, until the mixture is uniformly smooth. Pour the salsa into a bowl.

To assemble the tacos, place warm tortillas on a plate. Spoon some of the heart mixture on the tortillas, add some of the seasoned cabbage, and top with the salsa. Fold the tortillas in half to eat.

Slow-Baked Baby Back Ribs with Fennel Seed Spice Rub and Peach Jam Glaze

When it's too cold outside to fire up the grill, slow-bake some baby back ribs in the oven. We like stepping away from the conventional barbecue rub and sauce and, instead, rub the ribs with our own blend of fennel seed, cumin, pure red chile powder, smoked Spanish paprika, and other spices. After the ribs are cooked "low and slow" until fork tender, they are glazed with a blend of peach jam and some of the spice rub.—Jayni

4 TO 6 SERVINGS

2 slabs all-natural pork baby back ribs (about 2 pounds each)

Spice Rub:
4 teaspoons fennel seed, lightly crushed
1 teaspoon cumin seed, lightly crushed
2 teaspoons pure red chile powder, medium or hot
2 teaspoons smoked Spanish paprika
½ teaspoon cayenne pepper
1 teaspoon garlic granules
1 teaspoon onion granules
1 teaspoon black pepper
1 teaspoon salt

½ cup hot water, divided

⅓ cup peach jam

Remove the membrane from the back side of the ribs and place each slab on a large piece of heavy-duty aluminum foil (or a double thickness of regular foil).

Spice Rub: Combine the spices in a small container. Measure 2 teaspoons of the rub and reserve. Sprinkle the remaining rub equally over both sides of each slab of ribs and rub it into the meat. Fold the foil over the ribs to seal tightly. Place the two foil-wrapped slabs of ribs in the refrigerator for at least 3 hours or more. Set out of the refrigerator about 30 minutes before baking.

Place the foil-wrapped ribs on a large sheet pan in a single layer. Open one end of the foil, lift up the end of the slab and pour in ¼ cup of hot water under the ribs. Reseal the foil and repeat with the other slab of ribs. Bake in a 250-degree oven for 2 hours. Check for doneness,

CONTINUED ➡

and if the ribs are not falling-off-the-bone tender, reseal and return to the oven for 15 to 30 minutes more. When done, open one end of the foil and tilt it into a bowl to drain the fat and juices from each slab. Return the ribs to the sheet pan and open the foil.

Heat the peach jam in a small microwavable container in a microwave oven until melted, about 20 seconds. Stir in the 2 teaspoons of the reserved spice rub. Baste the meaty side of each slab of ribs generously, using all of the mixture. Place the ribs about 6 inches under the oven broiler for 1 to 2 minutes, until the tops of the ribs are bubbly and glazed. To serve, cut the ribs into 3- or 4-bone sections.

Slow-Cooked Pork Chops with Madeira and Dried Cherry Sauce

Madeira, a fortified wine, adds a complex earthiness to thick-cut pork chops. Dried tart cherries garnish the sauce with a pleasant touch of sweetness. This is a great dish to serve to company. Since the chops don't require much attention while they cook, you'll have plenty of time to prepare mashed potatoes and perhaps a vegetable side dish. The sauce is made just before serving.—Frank

4 SERVINGS

4 center cut, bone-in pork chops (6 to 8 ounces each), about 1 inch thick
Salt and black pepper

2 tablespoons butter

3 tablespoons shallot, finely chopped
½ cup Madeira wine
1 cup chicken broth

20 dried tart cherries
1 tablespoon potato starch or cornstarch
3 tablespoons water

Trim the pork chops, leaving just a little fat on their outer edge. Pat the chops dry with paper towels. Season the chops with salt and pepper and rub into the meat. Preheat the oven to 300 degrees.

In a 12-inch skillet, melt 2 tablespoons of butter over medium-high heat. Once the butter is hot (foam recedes), add the chops and brown for 2 minutes on each side. Adjust the heat so that the butter does not burn. Transfer the chops from the skillet to a braising pan or baking dish and arrange in a single layer.

Reduce the heat to medium, add the chopped shallot to the skillet drippings, and sauté for about 2 minutes. When the shallot is soft and translucent, but not brown, add the Madeira to deglaze the pan, stirring up the caramelized bits. Allow the Madeira to reduce for about 1 minute and then add the chicken broth. Raise the heat to high and bring to a boil. Pour the broth over the chops in the braising pan, or baking dish, and cover tightly with a lid or aluminum foil. Place in the oven and immediately reduce the oven temperature to 250 degrees. Bake the pork chops for 3 hours and check for doneness. The chops are done when they are fork tender.

Madeira and Dried Cherry Sauce: Transfer the chops to a warm platter and tent with foil. Strain the broth into a small saucepan (or into a fat separator first, if you wish to remove the fat). Add the dried cherries and bring the sauce to a boil over medium-high heat. In a small bowl, make a starch slurry by combining 1 tablespoon of potato starch, or cornstarch, and 3 tablespoons of water. Stir the slurry into the broth a little at a time, letting it return to the boil each time, until the desired thickness is achieved. Taste the sauce and adjust the seasoning with salt and pepper, if needed.

To serve, arrange the pork chops on dinner plates (with mashed potatoes, if desired). Ladle some of the sauce over both, dividing the cherries among the servings. Pass any remaining sauce at the table.

Pork Chops with Whole Grain Mustard Pan Sauce

Weekday pork chops become something special with this simple pan reduction of wine, minced shallot, fresh herbs, and whole grain mustard. Round out the menu with a green vegetable side and creamy mashed potatoes.—Frank and Jayni

4 SERVINGS

4 boneless pork loin or rib chops
   (5 to 6 ounces each)
Salt and black pepper, to taste
1 tablespoon butter
1 tablespoon olive oil

1 tablespoon shallot, minced
½ cup dry white wine
2 teaspoons whole grain or coarse
   ground mustard
1½ teaspoons fresh rosemary,
   chopped
1½ teaspoon fresh thyme, chopped
1 tablespoon butter

Trim excess fat from the pork chops and season with salt and pepper. Heat the butter and olive oil over medium-high heat in a skillet or sauté pan with a cover. Add the pork chops and cook until browned, about 3 minutes. Turn the chops over, cover, and reduce the heat to low. Cook the chops for 3 to 5 minutes more, to an internal temperature of 145 to 150 degrees for medium to medium-well. Transfer the chops to a warm platter, tent with aluminum foil, and let rest for 5 minutes. Reserve the pan drippings.

Add the minced shallot to the pan drippings and cook over low heat for about 1 minute. Add the wine and raise the heat to medium-high. Boil, stirring occasionally, until the wine is reduced by about one-third. Stir in the mustard, rosemary, and thyme. Reduce the heat to low and cook the sauce for 1 minute more. Remove the skillet from the heat and stir in 1 tablespoon of butter.

Grandmother Quillec's Roasted Pork Tenderloin with Prunes
(Rôtis de Porc "Grand Mère Quillec")

Café Provence brings a taste of France to Kansas. The Quillec family has owned and operated this French restaurant in Prairie Village for more than fourteen years. "This adorable, family-owned neighborhood bistro is a hidden monument to flavor and hospitality, providing exquisite French cooking in a terrific atmosphere with a crew that makes you feel at home," says Zagat. Not only has Zagat named Café Provence the best overall restaurant in Kansas City, OpenTable has also named it one of the Top 100 restaurants in the United States. For cooks seeking authentic French ingredients, the family also operates a gourmet store called the French Market, just around the corner from the restaurant.

"I prefer the special French prunes, pruneaux d'Agen, for this recipe. We serve the pork tenderloin with roasted fingerling potatoes and roasted carrots."—Chef Patrick Quillec, Café Provence, Prairie Village

4 TO 6 SERVINGS

2 pork tenderloins (about 1 pound each)
3 teaspoons ground coriander
Salt and black pepper, to taste
1½ tablespoons olive oil

4 whole shallots, thinly sliced (about 1½ cups)
1 cup ruby Port wine
1 cup veal or beef stock
14 pitted prunes, pruneaux d'Agen or other high quality prunes
4 bay leaves, fresh leaves preferred
2 tablespoons butter, cut into pieces

Preheat the oven to 400 degrees. Trim the tenderloins and season them with the ground coriander, then with salt and pepper, to taste.

In a large stainless steel (oven-safe) skillet, heat the olive oil over high heat. Add the tenderloins and brown on all sides, about 3 minutes. Transfer the skillet to the oven and roast the tenderloins until the meat registers 137 to 140 degrees for medium, about 15 minutes. Transfer the tenderloins to a plate, tent with aluminum foil, and let rest while making the sauce.

Slide a handle cover over the skillet handle to prevent burning your hands. Place the skillet over medium heat, add the sliced shallots, and sauté for 1 minute, until tender and

CONTINUED ➡

lightly browned. Add the Port wine and bring to a boil, scraping the bottom of the pan to dislodge any brown bits. Add the veal or beef stock, prunes, and bay leaves. Reduce the liquid slowly to approximately 1 cup. Season with salt, to taste. Remove the skillet from the heat and whisk in the butter.

Slice the tenderloins. Place the tenderloin slices in the sauce to rest for a few minutes before serving.

Fennel-Roasted Pork Loin with Blackberry-Red Wine Sauce

The pleasant aroma of roasting pork with crushed fennel seed will make your mouth water—but not for long. It only takes about thirty minutes in the oven. Today's pork loin is very lean and should not be overcooked. Checking the temperature will prevent a dry roast. Slices of the pork, topped with the blackberry-red wine sauce, tastes great in the fall served with some roasted root vegetables.—Frank and Jayni

6 TO 8 SERVINGS

2-pound center-cut boneless pork
    loin, tied with twine
Salt and black pepper, to taste
1 tablespoon fennel seed

1 tablespoon olive or canola oil

Blackberry-Red Wine Sauce:
1 tablespoon blackberry jam
¾ cup dry red wine

If the pork loin is not tied when purchased, tie with kitchen twine to help hold its shape, or ask the butcher to tie it for you. Place the pork loin on a plastic cutting board and season it with salt and pepper. Coarsely crush the fennel seed with a mortar and pestle or in a spice grinder. Press the crushed fennel seed evenly into the meat.

Heat the oil in a stainless steel oven-safe skillet over medium-high heat. Place the pork loin in the skillet and brown on all sides, 6 to 8 minutes total. Pour off most of the fat and discard. The loin should be positioned fat side up.

Place the skillet with the pork loin in a 400-degree oven. Roast for 30 to 35 minutes, or until the meat registers 145 to 150 degrees for medium-well. Transfer the pork from the skillet to a cutting board, reserving the drippings in the skillet. Tent the pork with aluminum foil. The temperature will continue to rise while the pork loin rests. Before making the blackberry sauce, slide a handle cover over the skillet handle to prevent burning your hands.

Blackberry-Red Wine Sauce: Skim off the accumulated fat in the skillet, retaining the browned bits. Add the blackberry jam and red wine to the skillet and simmer over medium heat, scraping up the brown bits, until the liquid reduces by half and thickens slightly. Meanwhile, slice the pork loin into ½-inch slices. Add the accumulated juices from the pork to the sauce as it reduces. When the sauce is ready, pour it through a fine wire-mesh strainer to remove the blackberry seeds.

To serve, arrange the pork slices on dinner plates and drizzle some of the sauce over each serving.

Pork Butt Braised in Marsala Wine

A Boston butt pork roast is a moderately tough cut of meat. Its high fat content gives it deep flavor but, when cooked slowly over low heat, it becomes fall-apart tender. We braise the roast in Marsala wine and chicken broth, which becomes a rich sauce to spoon over the pork. Serve with roasted vegetables on the side for a satisfying meal. Leftovers make great pulled pork sandwiches.—Frank and Jayni

6 SERVINGS

3-pound boneless Boston butt pork roast
Salt and black pepper

2 tablespoons olive or vegetable oil
1 cup onion, finely chopped
1 medium carrot, peeled and finely chopped
1 celery rib, finely chopped
3 garlic cloves, slivered

1 cup Marsala wine
1 cup chicken broth, or more if needed
1 or 2 sprigs fresh rosemary and thyme, tied together with kitchen twine

CONTINUED ➡

Set the pork butt out of the refrigerator 1 hour before cooking. When ready to cook, pat dry on all sides with paper towels. Tie with kitchen twine, if needed, to hold the roast together. Season with salt and pepper.

Heat the oil in a Dutch oven over medium-high heat. Add the pork roast and brown evenly on all sides. Transfer it to a baking dish or platter. Pour off all but 1 or 2 tablespoons of drippings from the pot. Add the onion, carrot, and celery to the drippings and reduce the heat to medium-low. Cook the vegetables until softened, about 5 minutes. Add the garlic slivers and cook for 1 minute more.

Add the Marsala, raise the heat to medium and bring to a simmer, scraping up the browned bits. Return the pork roast to the Dutch oven. Pour the chicken broth into the pot. The liquid should cover about one third to one half of the roast. If not, add up to one additional cup of chicken broth. Place the tied herbs in the pot. Bring to a simmer, cover the pot with aluminum foil, and then the lid, for a tight seal. Place the roast in a 300-degree oven for 2½ to 3 hours. Check for doneness after 2½ hours. The roast is done when it registers 190 degrees and is fork tender.

Transfer the pork roast to a platter or cutting board and tent with foil. Let rest for 20 minutes. Meanwhile, make the sauce.

Remove the tied herbs from the broth and discard. Pour the broth and vegetables through a wire-mesh strainer into a large fat separator. Reserve the vegetables. Let the broth stand for about 10 minutes to separate the fat. Place the reserved vegetables into a food processor or blender and add ½ cup of the defatted broth. Blend until smooth. Pour the remaining broth into a saucepan and stir in the puréed vegetables. Simmer the sauce over medium heat for 5 to 8 minutes, until it is slightly reduced and thickened. Season with salt and pepper, if needed.

To serve, pull the pork apart into small serving pieces and top each serving with some of the pan sauce.

Garlic Pork Shoulder Roast with Potatoes

"The first year my husband and I were married, this pork shoulder recipe was given to me by my father-in-law, a first-generation Slovene-American. I have been making it for my family ever since. I like to serve the pork roast with steamed carrots and applesauce made from the apples in our orchard."—Wendy Vertacnik, Vertacnik Orchard, Lawrence

6 TO 8 SERVINGS

3½- to 4-pound pork shoulder or butt roast
4 garlic cloves, peeled and sliced into halves or thirds
Salt and black pepper, to taste

½ cup all-purpose flour
2 tablespoons olive oil

6 medium potatoes, peeled and quartered

Set the pork roast out of the refrigerator 1 hour before cooking. Leave the fat on the pork roast. Pat the roast dry with paper towels to remove the moisture. Tie with kitchen twine so that the meat stays in one firm piece. Make several slits in the meat and insert the garlic pieces. Season the pork with salt and pepper.

Place the flour on wax paper. Dust the pork on all sides with the flour, then shake off the excess. Heat the oil over medium-high heat in a large skillet. When the oil is hot, place the pork roast in the skillet and brown on all sides.

Place the browned pork roast fat side up on a rack in a roasting pan. Cook the roast uncovered in a 350-degree oven at 45 minutes per pound, approximately 2½ to 3 hours, or until tender. Add the potatoes to the pan for the last 1½ hours of cooking. Baste the meat and potatoes once or twice during cooking with the drippings in the roasting pan.

Transfer the pork roast and potatoes to a warm platter to serve.

Pork Shoulder Sandwiches

Chef Bryan Williams, along with his wife, Janice (Keller) Williams, own and operate Keller Feed & Wine Company in Cottonwood Falls. "It is a farm-to-table diner that uses fresh produce and herbs grown by us just down the street on our farm. We also have a year-round market inside the diner featuring our locally grown fresh produce and herbs, as well as Hildebrand Dairy items, spices, vinegars, oils, and other kitchen items," says Bryan.

"After many years of smoking the pork shoulder, I began using a slow-roasting method. Believe it or not, our customers (as well as myself) actually prefer the slow-roasted pulled pork to the smoked version. The meat literally falls apart versus being stringy like traditional smoked pulled pork. We serve our pulled pork sandwiches on toasted hard rolls with a fried onion ring, our barbecue sauce, house-made coleslaw, and thick cut spicy pickles."—Chef Bryan Williams, Keller Feed & Wine Company, Cottonwood Falls

MAKES 15 TO 18 SANDWICHES

8-pound pork shoulder (preferably bone-in)
¼ cup yellow mustard

Rub:
¼ cup dark brown sugar
¼ cup smoked Spanish paprika
2 tablespoons granulated garlic
2 tablespoons kosher salt
2 tablespoons coarse ground black pepper
1 tablespoon cayenne pepper

Hard rolls or hamburger buns, toasted or warmed
Barbecue sauce

Set the pork shoulder out of the refrigerator 1 hour before cooking to take the chill off the meat. Pat the pork shoulder dry with paper towels and place it on a large plastic cutting board or a baking sheet. Slather the entire shoulder with the yellow mustard.

Rub: In a small bowl, combine the dark brown sugar, smoked Spanish paprika, granulated garlic, kosher salt, black pepper, and cayenne pepper. Cover the entire pork shoulder with the rub.

Place the shoulder in a roasting pan or a Dutch oven with a lid. Cover and place in a 200-degree oven for 12 hours. When done, the shoulder should be very tender. Remove it from the pan and let rest for 30 minutes on a cutting board. Pull the meat apart, discarding the fat. Pile the pork on hard rolls or buns and serve with barbecue sauce.

Option: For fewer servings, a 4-pound pork shoulder may be substituted. Reduce the amount of mustard and the rub by half. Roast the pork for 12 hours in a 200-degree oven, as directed. Makes about eight sandwiches.

Tip from Bryan: The yellow mustard slathered on the pork shoulder serves a dual purpose. First, it imparts a mustard flavor to the rub. Second, and more importantly, it helps hold the rub to the pork shoulder. This develops a better spice crust—called the bark—on the meat's exterior. A delicious bark on a slow-cooked pork shoulder is arguably the most important part of any pulled pork.

Garlic Pale Ale Sausage

Chef Vaughn Good returned to Lawrence after attending culinary school in New York City. He wanted to embrace the rich culinary traditions of his Midwestern roots and to be near bountiful producers. He opened Hank Charcuterie, a charcuterie, butcher shop, and restaurant rolled into one.

"Our 'Garlic Pale Ale Sausage' is truly a Kansas sausage recipe. We like to use local Duroc pork from Good Family Farms in Olsburg and Copperhead Pale Ale from Free State Brewery in Lawrence to make the sausage."—Chef Vaughn Good, Hank Charcuterie, Lawrence

MAKES 20 SAUSAGE LINKS

5 pounds fatty pork shoulder, diced into 1-inch cubes
3 tablespoons kosher salt
1 tablespoon black pepper
3 tablespoons garlic, minced
1 large yellow onion, cut into small dice

1½ teaspoons yellow mustard seed
1 teaspoon Colman's dry mustard powder
¼ teaspoon cayenne pepper
½ teaspoon dried thyme
1 tablespoon grainy mustard

¼ cup chilled Free State Copperhead Pale Ale, or other pale ale

Hog casings, enough for about 20 links

Olive oil or canola oil, for frying

CONTINUED ➡

Place the diced cubes of pork in a large bowl. Add the kosher salt, pepper, garlic, onion, mustard seed, dry mustard powder, cayenne pepper, thyme, and grainy mustard. Toss until evenly mixed, cover, and refrigerate until completely chilled, at least 8 to 12 hours, to allow the flavors to develop.

Grind the pork mixture through the small die of a meat grinder into a bowl set over a larger bowl filled with ice to keep the sausage cold. Add ¼ cup of beer and mix until the ingredients are well incorporated and the meat looks sticky.

To check the flavor of the sausage, fry a small portion before stuffing and adjust the spices and seasoning, if necessary.

To make sausage links, stuff the sausage mixture into hog casings and twist into 6-inch links. Using a sausage pricker or a sanitized safety pin, prick the casings where air pockets are present. Refrigerate the sausage links overnight to allow the air to release from the casings and develop the flavor of the sausage. If you prefer patties or loose sausage, place the sausage in a sealed container before refrigerating overnight.

To cook the sausage links, heat a small amount of olive or canola oil in a stainless steel or cast iron (oven-safe) skillet over medium heat. Add the sausage links and brown on all sides. Place the skillet in a 350-degree oven and cook the links for about 10 minutes, or until the links reach an internal temperature of 150 degrees.

If making sausage patties, grill them on a gas or charcoal grill, or fry them in a skillet, over medium to medium-high heat. Loose sausage may be used in your favorite sausage recipes.

Hank Charcuterie

Chef Vaughn Good attended the International Culinary Center in New York City, where he learned the art of charcuterie and developed a passion for it. Charcuterie includes a range of methods, such as salting, cooking, smoking, and drying, to preserve foods, especially meats that become sausage, cured meats, and patés. Vaughn's vision was to return to his hometown of Lawrence and open a butcher shop so that he could take advantage of locally grown and raised products to create the best in handcrafted charcuterie.

In 2014, Vaughn opened Hank Charcuterie, where he employs traditional preservation methods mixed with modern techniques to create some of the best sausage, pastrami, and other charcuterie in Kansas. To accompany the charcuterie, he offers creative house-made products such as patés, rillettes, kimchi, pickles, rubs, and more. A selection of local, hand-cut beef, pork, lamb, and duck can also be purchased. Once word got out, Hank Charcuterie's popularity soon resulted in a small restaurant serving lunch, weekend dinners, and Sunday brunch. New customers asking to meet and compliment the owner "Hank" soon learned that the word "hank" refers to a coil or bundle of sausage casings and that their compliments should go to the chef-owner, Vaughn Good.

"At Hank Charcuterie, we appreciate the story behind everything we make," Vaughn tells us. "We strive for our processes to do justice to the work of our local farmers and hope to connect the community back to where their food comes from. In the farm-to-table scenario, *Hank* is the link between the barn and garden, and your plate. We process meat and produce with a respect for the life and heritage of every ingredient we use and our passion is reflected in the foods we create."

Sausage-Stuffed Acorn Squash

It is easy to find a wide variety of fresh, locally made sausages that would work well for this recipe. Many Kansas butcher shops and grocery stores make their own.

"This recipe is very versatile," says Pat Grzenda. "The flavor profile can change with ingredient substitutions. For instance, any type of pork sausage may be used instead of Italian sausage. Adding red or green bell peppers, or jalapeño peppers, to the stuffing mixture will change the dish entirely. You could stuff butternut squash instead of acorn squash, too!"—Pat Grzenda, Lawrence

6 SERVINGS

3 acorn squash, 1 pound each
1 tablespoon olive oil
Salt and black pepper, to taste

Sausage Stuffing:
1 pound mild or medium Italian
    sausage
1 tablespoon olive oil
2 tablespoons butter
1 cup onion, chopped
½ cup celery, chopped
1 tablespoon garlic, chopped
1¼ cups homemade dried bread-
    crumbs or packaged stuffing
    mix
½ to 1 cup homemade or canned
    chicken broth

Cut each squash in half lengthwise (stem to base) and scrape out the seeds. Lay the squash halves flesh side down and cut a thin slice off the skin side to make a stable base. Turn the squash over and brush or rub the flesh side with 1 tablespoon of olive oil and season with salt and pepper.

Place the squash halves flesh side down on a baking sheet and roast in a 375-degree oven for 20 to 25 minutes, or until fairly tender. While the squash is cooking, prepare the stuffing.

Sausage Stuffing: Brown the sausage in a large sauté pan or saucepan over medium heat. Transfer the sausage to a large paper towel-lined plate to drain the fat. Add 1 tablespoon of olive oil and 2 tablespoons of butter to the pan and sauté the onion and celery over medium-low heat until softened, about 5 minutes. Add the garlic and sauté 1 minute more. Return the sausage to the pan and combine it with the onion and celery. Stir in the stuffing, then add the chicken broth, starting with ½ cup. Add more broth as needed, until the desired level of moisture is reached. Season the stuffing with salt and pepper, if needed.

Turn the squash halves cut side up and fill them generously with the sausage stuffing. Place them on a clean baking sheet. Bake in a 375-degree oven for 30 minutes, until the squash is very tender and the stuffing is browned on top. Check the squash after 20 minutes and, if the topping is browning too quickly, tent with aluminum foil during the last few minutes of cooking. Serve warm.

Grilled Lamb Chops

We like to grill lamb chops in the summertime, when fresh herbs are at our fingertips. When rubbed with olive oil, garlic, fresh herbs, and lemon zest, the small chops make a light but satisfying portion of meat for a warm evening. To avoid heating up the kitchen, we grill some fresh tomatoes and asparagus for sides.—Jayni

4 SERVINGS

4 lamb loin chops (4 to 6 ounces each), about 1 inch thick
Olive oil for brushing chops
Salt and black pepper, to taste

3 to 4 garlic cloves, pressed or minced
1 tablespoon fresh rosemary, finely chopped
1 tablespoon fresh thyme, finely chopped
2 teaspoons lemon zest

Trim excess fat from the lamb chops and place them in a shallow baking pan. Brush both sides lightly with olive oil and season with salt and pepper.

In a small bowl, combine the garlic, rosemary, thyme, and lemon zest. Rub about half of the mixture over the tops of the chops, pressing it into the meat. Turn the chops over and repeat. Cover the pan and refrigerate the chops for at least 2 hours. Take the lamb chops out of the refrigerator about 30 minutes before grilling.

Prepare a gas or charcoal grill for cooking over high heat. Place the lamb chops on the cooking grate and cover. Sear for 3 to 5 minutes, turning a quarter turn after the first 2 minutes to mark the meat. When the chops are well browned on the first side,

CONTINUED ➡

turn them over, cover, and cook for 3 to 5 minutes more, until the meat registers 130 to 135 degrees for medium-rare. Transfer the lamb chops to a platter, tent with aluminum foil, and let rest for 5 minutes before serving.

Grill-Roasted Leg of Lamb with Mint Chimichurri Sauce

"Grill-roasting a leg of lamb is quite easy and it really delights dinner guests who may not have seen it prepared this way. Roasting meat on the bone adds more flavor to the end result. As a bonus, you'll have the bone with which to make stock for other dishes.

"You can serve the leg for a summer meal with a green salad and summer vegetables from the garden, or in the winter with mashers and roasted root veggies. Using fresh herbs for the rub and the 'Mint Chimichurri Sauce' makes a big difference! Each time I prepare a leg of lamb, I am amazed at how beautiful it looks on the platter waiting to be carved. Your guests will ooh and aah!"
—Bob Schumm, Lawrence

10 TO 12 SERVINGS

6- to 8-pound whole leg of lamb, bone in
6 to 8 garlic cloves, slivered lengthwise

Wet Rub:
2 tablespoons fresh mint leaves, finely chopped
1 tablespoon fresh rosemary, finely chopped
2 teaspoons flat-leaf parsley, finely chopped
2 teaspoons salt
½ teaspoon freshly ground black pepper
2 tablespoons olive oil

Mint Chimichurri Sauce:
½ cup fresh mint leaves, chopped
¼ cup flat-leaf parsley, chopped
1 garlic clove, minced
½ teaspoon salt
½ teaspoon black pepper
3 tablespoons red wine vinegar
⅓ cup olive oil

Preparing the Leg of Lamb: Pat the leg of lamb dry with paper towels. Using the point of a paring knife, cut ½-inch slits about 2 inches apart over the entire leg. Insert one garlic sliver into each slit. Make sure the garlic slivers are deep enough that they don't pop out during roasting. You should have approximately 35 to 45 insertions.

Wet Rub: In a small bowl, combine the mint, rosemary, parsley, salt, and pepper. Whisk in the olive oil. Apply the rub generously over the entire leg of lamb. Let stand for 30 minutes at room temperature before roasting.

Mint Chimichurri Sauce: Place the mint, parsley, garlic, salt, black pepper, red wine vinegar, and olive oil in a food processor and pulse until the mixture is puréed. Pour the chimichurri sauce into a small bowl and set aside to serve with the lamb.

Grill-Roasting the Leg of Lamb: Prepare a gas or charcoal grill for cooking over medium-high heat. If using a gas grill, place the leg on the cooking grate over indirect heat. If grilling over charcoals, put a drip pan on the charcoal grate and arrange the hot charcoals around either side of the pan. Place the leg on the cooking grate directly over the drip pan. The hot coals should be about 8 inches away from the meat. Cover the grill and maintain a temperature of about 300 degrees for approximately 1 to 1½ hours, depending on the size of the leg. After 30 minutes, check to see if the grill temperature is being maintained, and adjust as needed. After 1 hour of cooking, check the temperature of the meat by inserting a probe thermometer into two or three meaty places on the leg. The meat should register 130 to 135 degrees for medium-rare.

Transfer the leg to a large sheet pan and allow it to rest for 20 minutes before carving. Grasp the narrow end of the leg bone with a folded towel and slice the meat cutting parallel to the leg bone. Serve the sliced lamb with mint chimichurri sauce.

Lamb Hash

Hash is a simple dish of leftover cooked meat, potatoes, and onion with thickened broth to make a light gravy. One of our favorite comfort meals is to make lamb hash with leftover grilled or roasted leg of lamb. Over the years, we've found that this dish is greatly enhanced by adding some fresh herbs and a bit of tomato to brighten up the flavors. We like to serve it with warm garlic bread.
—Frank and Jayni

4 SERVINGS

3 to 4 cups leftover grilled or
    roasted lamb

3 tablespoons olive oil
1 cup onion, chopped
3 cups potatoes, peeled and cubed
2 garlic cloves, minced
Salt and black pepper, to taste

2 tablespoons all-purpose flour
1 cup chicken broth
½ to 1 cup beef broth, divided
½ cup fresh or canned tomatoes,
    diced
1½ teaspoons fresh rosemary,
    chopped
1½ teaspoons fresh thyme,
    chopped

Cut the leftover cooked lamb into ½-inch cubes, removing any excess fat. Measure 3 to 4 cups and set aside.

Heat the olive oil over medium heat in a large nonstick skillet. Add the onion and potatoes and cook, turning often, until tender, 15 to 20 minutes. If browning occurs too quickly, reduce the heat. Add the garlic and cook for 1 minute more. Season with salt and pepper.

Sprinkle the flour over the potatoes and cook for about 2 minutes, stirring often. Slowly stir in 1 cup of chicken broth and ½ cup of beef broth. Add the tomatoes, rosemary, and thyme and simmer over medium-low heat, stirring occasionally, until the mixture is bubbly and slightly thickened. Add the cubed lamb and heat just until warmed. If the sauce needs to be thinned, add ¼ to ½ cup more of beef broth. Taste and add more salt and pepper, if needed.

Variation: Leftover roast beef may be used in place of the lamb.

Farmer Debbie's Shepherd's Pie

Debbie Yarnell's recipe for Shepherd's Pie, made with ground lamb and vegetables and topped with mashed cheddar cheese potatoes, is the perfect comfort food on a wintry Kansas night.

Debbie's farm, Homespun Hill Farm, sits atop rolling hills just outside Baldwin City. A livestock farmer, Debbie raises South Poll cattle and St. Croix sheep. She says the challenge is keeping all of those precious animals comfortable and sheltered from threat of cold weather and blizzards. "Tromping through drifting snow in order to chop ice after a blast from the north has never caused me to question why I raise livestock," says Debbie. "The purity of a newborn lamb and the innocence of a curious calf, with their total dependence on my caretaking ability, motivates me far beyond the inconvenience of an occasional extreme Kansas winter."—Debbie Yarnell, Homespun Hill Farm, Baldwin City

6 TO 8 SERVINGS

Topping:
3 to 4 cups prepared mashed potatoes
½ to ⅔ cup cheddar cheese, shredded

Lamb Filling:
1½ pounds ground lamb
1 cup onion, chopped
1 garlic clove, minced
1 cup peas, cooked or frozen
1 cup sweet corn kernels, fresh or frozen
1 cup beef or chicken broth
½ teaspoon dried thyme
½ teaspoon salt
¼ teaspoon black pepper
2 cups diced tomatoes, fresh or canned
2 tablespoons red wine vinegar

Topping: Prepare mashed potatoes with butter, milk, salt, and pepper. Measure 3 to 4 cups and stir in the cheddar cheese. Set aside.

Lamb Filling: In a large skillet over medium-high heat, brown the ground lamb, breaking it up as it cooks. Remove the lamb from skillet with a slotted spoon and transfer it to a bowl, reserving the drippings in the skillet. Sauté the onion and garlic in the drippings over medium heat until tender. Return the lamb to the skillet and add the peas, corn, broth, thyme, salt, and pepper. Increase heat to medium-high and stir for about 1 minute. Stir in the diced tomatoes and red wine vinegar. Reduce the heat to medium and cook for about 5 to 8 minutes more, stirring occasionally, until the juices are slightly reduced and thickened.

Transfer the lamb filling to a lightly greased 3-quart baking dish. Spoon the mashed potatoes over the filling and smooth the top with a rubber spatula or the back of a large spoon. Bake the shepherd's pie in a 400-degree oven for 15 to 20 minutes, or until the top is lightly browned and the pie is hot and bubbly. Let stand for 5 to 10 minutes before serving.

Grilled Tequila-Lime Goat Chops

Pete Rowland hails from Alice, Texas, but has lived in Lawrence for more than thirty years. He is well known for introducing Kansans to the Texas custom of roasting goat—and to their first taste of goat meat.

These days, Pete prefers to grill goat chops, rather than the whole goat, because the chops are easy to find locally and they are quick to cook. He says marinating the chops in an herb and spice mixture containing lime and tequila promotes tenderness and tempers the finish. "I like to serve the goat chops with roasted parsnips and carrots, or with guacamole to start and pinto beans on the side. A Petite Syrah is my wine of choice to serve with this recipe."—Pete Rowland, Lawrence

4 SERVINGS

8 goat chops, 1 to 1½ inches thick
Salt and black pepper, to taste

Tequila-Lime Marinade:
½ cup fresh-squeezed lime juice
¼ cup tequila
⅓ cup low-sodium soy sauce
6 to 8 garlic cloves, crushed
1 tablespoon fresh ginger, peeled and shredded
½ cup fresh cilantro leaves, chopped
2 teaspoons cumin, fresh ground preferred
2 teaspoons pure red chile powder
½ cup olive oil

½ cup thick tomato salsa

Rub the chops with salt and black pepper. Place them in a baking dish large enough to hold them in a single layer.

Tequila-Lime Marinade: In a bowl, combine the fresh lime juice, tequila, soy sauce, garlic, ginger, cilantro, cumin, and chile powder. Whisk in the olive oil.

Pour the marinade over the goat chops and turn to coat. Cover and marinate in the refrigerator for at least 4 hours.

Remove the chops from the marinade, reserving the marinade, and let them stand at room temperature for 30 minutes to 1 hour before grilling.

Tequila-Lime Salsa: Pour the reserved marinade into a saucepan and bring to a boil over medium-high heat for 2 minutes. Add ½ cup of tomato salsa and simmer the sauce over low heat for 3 minutes. Set aside.

Prepare a gas or charcoal grill for cooking over medium heat. Place the goat chops on the cooking grate and cover. Grill for 3 to 5 minutes each side, or until the meat registers 130 to 135 degrees for medium-rare.

Transfer the goat chops to a platter, tent with aluminum foil, and let rest for 5 minutes before serving.

Serve the grilled goat chops with the tequila-lime salsa.

Goat Roast

Pete Rowland, originally from Alice, Texas, brought his family's tradition of roasting "cabrito" to Kansas when he moved to Lawrence more than thirty years ago to join the faculty at the University of Kansas as a professor of political science. "If you live in Texas, it's not a goat roast, it's a barbecue. Anyone invited to a barbecue assumes it will be goat, or cabrito, as it is called there. If you're cooking another meat, you'd better say so," says Pete.

When Pete was growing up in South Texas, his dad used an outdoor brick oven with a grill grid for roasting the goat, and he always slathered it with some kind of sauce. Pete says he tried roasting a goat in a pit years ago but found it was too much trouble. "Now I quarter the goat and either spit roast it or cook it 'low and slow' over indirect heat on the grill over hot charcoals and mesquite chips. Cooking the meat in quarters allows the cook to control the cooking time and temperature of each piece."

The most important thing is to choose the right goat. "It must be young, twenty pounds or less, and have some fat on it," Pete says. He tells us that goat meat benefits from a marinade and that he likes a mixture of beer, garlic, lemon or lime juice, and olive oil. After rubbing the meat with salt and pepper, it is marinated for several hours or overnight. How long does it take to roast the goat? "About twelve beers," Pete says with a chuckle, "or pretty much all day. If you put it on the grill in the morning, it will be done by dinnertime."

Grilled Rack of Goat

Goat meat is growing in popularity in Kansas as well as nationwide. Approximately 63 percent of red meat consumed worldwide is goat meat. Various cuts of organic goat meat can be purchased directly from some small farmers around the state, farmers' markets, or natural food stores.

Rack of goat is lean and tender and benefits from slow cooking. When grilling, apply a wet rub to the meat and marinate for several hours for added flavor.—Frank and Jayni

4 TO 6 SERVINGS

2 racks of goat (12 to 16 ounces each), frenched

Wet Rub:
3 garlic cloves, peeled
1 teaspoon salt
¼ teaspoon black pepper
½ teaspoon dried oregano
½ teaspoon dried marjoram or 1 teaspoon fresh marjoram, chopped
½ teaspoon dried thyme or 1 teaspoon fresh thyme, chopped
2 tablespoons lemon juice
2 tablespoons olive oil

Wipe or pat the goat racks dry with paper towels, if needed. Place the two racks in a baking dish large enough to hold them in a single layer.

Wet Rub: Place the peeled garlic cloves and salt in a mortar with pestle. Using the pestle, grind the mixture to a paste, or press the garlic into a small bowl and add the salt. Add the black pepper, oregano, marjoram, and thyme. Stir in the lemon juice and olive oil until well combined.

Brush or spoon the wet rub onto both sides of the goat racks. Cover the baking dish and refrigerate the racks for at least 3 hours. Take them out of the refrigerator 30 minutes before grilling.

Prepare a gas or charcoal grill for cooking over high heat. Place the goat racks meaty side down on the cooking grate and cover. Sear for 3 to 5 minutes, until browned. Turn the racks over and place them over indirect heat, or move them to a cooler part of the grill. Cover and cook for 10 to 12 minutes, until the meat registers 135 to 140 degrees for medium-rare to medium, or until cooked to desired doneness.

Transfer the goat racks to a platter, tent with aluminum foil, and let rest for 5 minutes before serving. Cut the racks into single or double chops to serve.

Jamaican-Style Goat

Jessica Pierson and Jen Humphrey own The Red Tractor Farm, located in rural Douglas County. They have been farming since 2008 on land that has been in Jessica's family for four generations. They raise Boer meat goats, laying hens, and a diverse selection of vegetables that are certified organic.

"Goat meat is very lean, so to achieve tenderness, it must be cooked low and slow. This recipe calls for goat stew meat, but we tried the recipe recently with goat chops. It's delicious with any cut of goat, including shanks. Don't let the long list of ingredients intimidate you—it's an easy dish."
—Jen Humphrey, The Red Tractor Farm, Lawrence

4 TO 6 SERVINGS

3 tablespoons vegetable oil
2 pounds goat stew meat (from a
    roast cut, such as a shoulder
    roast), trimmed and cut into
    bite-size pieces

1 large onion, chopped
1 teaspoon garlic, minced
3 tablespoons curry powder
1 teaspoon allspice
½ teaspoon dried thyme
1 teaspoon salt
1 teaspoon black pepper

2 cups vegetable or beef broth
2 tablespoons brown sugar
1 tablespoon wine vinegar
3 dashes of hot sauce
1 tablespoon lime juice
1 cup unsweetened coconut milk

Cooked white rice
2 green onions, thinly sliced, for
    garnish

Heat the vegetable oil over high heat in a Dutch oven or other heavy pot. Add the goat meat and brown quickly in batches. Remove the meat from the pot and set aside.

Add the onion to the pot and add another tablespoon of oil, if needed. Sauté the onion over medium heat until softened, about 5 minutes. Add the garlic and sauté for 2 minutes more. Add the curry powder, allspice, thyme, salt, and pepper to the onions and cook, stirring for about 1 minute more.

Return the browned goat meat to the pot. Stir in the broth, brown sugar, vinegar, hot sauce, lime juice, and coconut milk. Cover and simmer over low heat for 2 hours, or until the meat is tender.

Serve the goat meat over rice and garnish with sliced green onion.

Option: Prepare the goat meat as directed and cook in a slow cooker set on low heat for 4 to 6 hours, or until tender.

Chapter 7
Poultry

Not so long ago, commercially processed poultry from the grocery store was all that was available unless you raised and butchered your own. These days in Kansas, if you search a little further, you may find fresh, organic, pasture-raised chickens, turkeys, or ducks at a natural foods store, the farmers' market, or perhaps you can purchase them directly from the farmer. Large supermarkets have gotten in the game in recent years and often carry these birds as well.

Perhaps it's no surprise that Americans consume a large quantity of chicken. Chicken costs less than other meats and has less fat, a real advantage for today's food trends. Another advantage is that chicken lends itself to a variety of preparations. A succulent whole roasted bird still stands as a gourmet classic but, if spatchcocked and grilled, as in "Hot Rosemary Grilled Chicken," an equally delicious crispy brown chicken will be ready for the table about fifteen minutes sooner with less fuss, and supercharged with the flavors of cayenne, brown sugar, and rosemary.

The dilemma of choosing between white or dark meat was put to rest years ago when supermarkets began packaging chicken by its parts, including skinless and boneless pieces. Purchasing parts has generated a new genre of chicken recipes that allow cooks to focus on cooking times suitable for the piece and expand the range of flavor options these separated parts can provide.

Consider the nutritional benefits of skinless, boneless chicken breasts, coated with almond meal, quickly sautéed in coconut oil and drizzled with honey as in "Almond Meal-Encrusted Chicken Breasts with Honey," or the convenience of chicken breasts topped with a cheese and crumb topping and baked in wine, broth, and cream as in "Cheddar Chicken Bake."

With a little more time to spend in the kitchen, try the slow-cooked "Braised Chicken Thighs with Tomatillo and Green Chile Gravy" or "Chicken Braised in White Wine," which both feature bone-in chicken pieces that yield a pan sauce with complex flavor.

Turkey still commands center stage for the holidays. Whole turkeys appear in the grocery stores as Thanksgiving comes up on the calendar, and these days you can opt for an organic turkey available from one of Kansas's own farms. When tradition calls for a whole stuffed bird, carved at the table, try "Maple and Brandy Brined Turkey with Red-Eye Gravy." A turkey breast recipe such as "Turkey Breast Roll with Corn-bread and Date Stuffing" offers an enticing option for a smaller gathering. Or prepare "Turkey Pie with Broccoli and Cheddar Cheese Sauce" for a new twist on an old family favorite.

If you do value tradition and wish to go deeper, seek out a heritage turkey with a genealogy reaching back to the Pilgrims. The Good Shepherd Poultry Ranch in Lindsborg raises heritage turkeys, chickens, ducks, and geese conforming to standards intent on keeping the breed's lineage tasting the way grandmother's poultry used to.

Why not go wild and recreate the first Thanksgiving by hunting your own bird? Wild turkeys, reintroduced into Kansas in the 1960s, have been a great success. Huntable populations of turkeys now exist in every county in the state.

For those who enjoy duck but do not hunt, whole ducks or duck breasts can usually be purchased anywhere you can find chicken and turkey. For an easy way to enjoy duck, try "Grilled Duck Breasts with Port Wine Sauce." "Duck Street Tacos," made with duck confit, offers something for the adventurous.

Almond Meal-Encrusted Chicken Breasts with Honey

In this gluten-free recipe, the chicken breasts are dipped in an egg and milk mixture, coated with almond meal, and quickly fried in coconut oil.

"I like to experiment with different ways to cook chicken breasts, and all the ingredients in this recipe really complement each other. For a touch of sweetness, I serve the chicken with a drizzle of honey."—Isaac Combs, Lawrence

4 SERVINGS

4 skinless, boneless chicken breasts
   (about 6 ounces each)
Sea salt, to taste

1 egg
⅓ cup milk
1 cup almond meal*

½ cup coconut oil

Honey

Place the chicken breasts on a plate and season them with sea salt.

In a wide, shallow bowl, whisk together the egg and milk. Pour the almond meal into a plastic storage bag. Dip a chicken breast in the egg and milk mixture, place it in the bag, and shake to coat with the almond meal. Place the chicken breast on a baking sheet and repeat the process with the remaining chicken breasts.

Heat a nonstick skillet over medium heat. Add the coconut oil, and when hot, carefully place the chicken breasts in the skillet. Fry the chicken for 4 to 5 minutes, until browned, turn and fry for 4 to 5 minutes more, or until the chicken is cooked through.

CONTINUED ➡

Lower the heat, if necessary, to prevent burning the coating.

Transfer the chicken breasts to a paper towel-lined plate to drain briefly, and then place them on dinner plates. Top each chicken breast with a drizzle of honey.

*Almond meal, also called almond flour, is blanched almonds that have been ground.

Cheddar Chicken Bake

We are always looking for new and easy ways to prepare the versatile chicken breast. In this recipe, chicken breasts are topped with chopped shallot cooked in butter; covered with a cheese and bread-crumb mixture; then baked in chicken broth, wine, and cream. We like to serve the chicken with a rice pilaf, or on buttered noodles with some of the broth spooned on top.—Frank and Jayni

4 SERVINGS

4 boneless chicken breasts (about 6 ounces each)
Salt and black pepper, to taste

3 tablespoons butter
2 ounces shallot, chopped

½ cup Panko breadcrumbs
2 ounces sharp cheddar cheese, shredded
1 teaspoon Hungarian paprika

¼ cup dry white wine
¼ cup chicken broth
¼ cup heavy cream

Season the chicken breasts with salt and pepper and place them in a 9-inch baking dish in a single layer. Set aside.

Heat the butter in a small skillet over medium-low heat. Add the chopped shallot and cook until softened, about 5 minutes. Set aside.

In a medium bowl, combine the Panko breadcrumbs, shredded cheese, and paprika and set aside.

Combine the white wine, chicken broth, and cream in a 1-cup glass measuring cup. Pour the mixture over the chicken breasts. Top each with some of the cooked shallot and butter mixture. Cover the chicken with the breadcrumb and cheese mixture.

Bake the chicken, uncovered, in a 350-degree oven for 35 minutes, or until the topping is browned, the liquids are bubbly, and the chicken is cooked through. Let stand for 10 minutes before serving.

Spiced Chicken with Carrots, Artichoke Hearts, and Rice

A trip around the world is as close as your spice drawer. Mix together a blend of aromatic spices to season chicken pieces and rice, and suddenly, you're not in Kansas anymore! Add carrots and artichoke hearts to complete this unique one-pan meal. This recipe is definitely not your mother's chicken and rice!—Frank and Jayni

6 SERVINGS

4 chicken thighs
2 skinless, boneless chicken breasts

Spice Blend:
1 teaspoon smoked Spanish paprika
¾ teaspoon salt
¼ teaspoon black pepper
½ teaspoon cinnamon
½ teaspoon turmeric
½ teaspoon ground cumin
½ teaspoon ground cloves
⅛ teaspoon ground saffron

⅓ cup all-purpose flour

2 tablespoons olive oil
1 cup onion, chopped
1 cup basmati rice

3 medium carrots, peeled and
    sliced into ¼-inch rounds
1 (14-ounce) can artichoke hearts,
    drained and quartered
2¼ cups chicken broth

Remove the bones from the chicken thighs, leaving the skins intact. Cut each thigh in half. Cut the chicken breasts in half.

Spice Blend: Combine the spices in a small container.

Place the flour in a wide, shallow bowl. Add 2 teaspoons of the spice blend and stir to combine. Dust the chicken pieces with the flour mixture.

Heat the olive oil in a large braising pan over medium-high heat. Add the chicken pieces in batches and brown on both sides. Reduce the heat if necessary to prevent burning. Transfer the chicken to a tray or baking dish. Add the onion to the pan, along with another tablespoon of olive oil, if needed, and cook over medium heat for about 3 minutes, stirring often. Stir in the remaining spice blend and cook for 1 minute. Add the rice and cook for 1 to 2 minutes more, stirring frequently.

Scatter the carrots and artichoke hearts over the rice. Add the chicken broth. Arrange the

CONTINUED ➡

chicken pieces on top. Bring the mixture to a boil, cover, and reduce the heat to low. Simmer for 25 to 30 minutes, until all the liquid is absorbed and the chicken pieces are cooked through.

Place some of the rice, carrots, and artichoke hearts on six dinner plates and top with chicken pieces.

Variation: Use any combination of chicken thighs and breasts, so long as you have six pieces of chicken.

Braised Chicken Thighs with Tomatillo and Green Chile Gravy

Kansans love Southwestern flavors, and tomatillos play a key role in this recipe. Fortunately, we have the climate to grow tomatillos in a backyard garden. Tomatillos are part of the nightshade family and distantly related to tomatoes, though these green beauties are mostly used to make sauces and salsas. The plants are quite attractive in the garden and fun to watch grow. Amid its green foliage, the plant sets bright yellow flowers, which turn into papery husks that resemble tiny Chinese lanterns. Each tomatillo grows into one of these husks as it ripens. Tomatillo plants are prolific, and you will need only two or three plants to produce an abundant crop. For this recipe, we like to serve some buttery mashed potatoes alongside the braised chicken, both generously topped with the tomatillo and green chile gravy.—Frank and Jayni

4 SERVINGS

1 pound tomatillos
2 tablespoons vegetable oil

2 Hatch or Anaheim green chile
    peppers

4 chicken thighs
Salt and black pepper, to taste
2 tablespoons olive or vegetable oil
1 garlic clove, finely chopped
1 teaspoon cumin seed, coarsely
    ground
½ teaspoon dried oregano
½ cup chicken broth

To prepare the tomatillos: Remove the papery husks from the tomatillos. Rinse off the sticky substance and dry them with paper towels. Cut the tomatillos into quarters. Heat 2 tablespoons of oil in a skillet over medium-high heat. When hot, add the tomatillos and cook them, shaking the skillet occasionally, until they are lightly browned and begin to break down. Cool the tomatillos briefly, then place them in a blender, and blend until smooth. Measure 1 cup of the sauce and set aside. (Freeze any remaining tomatillo sauce for another use.)

To roast the green chile peppers: Arrange the chiles on a baking sheet and place them about 6 inches under the oven broiler, or on a hot grill grate, until charred and blistered on all sides. Immediately enclose the charred chile peppers in a plastic or paper bag and let them "sweat" for about 20 minutes for easier peeling. Peel the chiles and remove the stems and seeds. Chop the chiles into ½-inch pieces and set aside.

Pat the chicken thighs dry with paper towels. Season with salt and pepper. Heat 2 tablespoons of olive or vegetable oil over medium-high heat in a braising or sauté pan. Place the chicken thighs in the pan, skin side down, and brown the skins, 3 to 4 minutes. Turn the thighs over and spoon off excess fat. Add the tomatillo sauce, chopped green chiles, garlic, cumin, oregano, and chicken broth. When the mixture begins to simmer, cover the pan and reduce the heat to low. Simmer for 35 to 40 minutes, or until the thighs are tender. Baste the chicken with the pan juices once or twice during cooking. When done, transfer the thighs to a warm platter. Raise the heat to medium-high and simmer the gravy for 2 to 3 minutes to reduce slightly, stirring frequently. Season with salt and pepper, to taste.

Serve the chicken thighs topped with the tomatillo and green chile gravy.

Baked Chicken Thighs with Apricot-Brandy Glaze

We like to serve these beautifully glazed chicken thighs tucked alongside some creamy mashed potatoes and whatever green vegetable is in season. The sweet, savory, and sticky apricot-brandy glaze is so irresistible you may want to double the recipe.—Frank and Jayni

4 SERVINGS

4 chicken thighs
Salt and black pepper, to taste

Apricot-Brandy Glaze:
½ cup apricot jam
2 tablespoons butter, melted
2 tablespoons brandy
1 tablespoon fresh tarragon, finely
    chopped

2 tablespoons olive oil

Wine Sauce (optional):
⅓ cup dry white wine

Pat the chicken thighs dry with paper towels. Season with salt and pepper and set aside.

Apricot-Brandy Glaze: Combine the apricot jam, melted butter, brandy, and tarragon in a small bowl. Set aside.

Heat 2 tablespoons of olive oil in a stainless steel (oven-safe) skillet over medium heat. Place the thighs in the skillet, skin side down, and cook until skins are golden, 3 to 4 minutes. Turn the thighs over and remove the skillet from the heat. Pour or spoon off the accumulated fat in the skillet. Brush the apricot-brandy glaze generously over the tops of the thighs.

Place the skillet in a 350-degree oven and bake for 20 minutes, then baste the thighs with some of the remaining glaze. Continue baking for 25 to 30 minutes more. Baste two more times with either the remaining glaze or the skillet drippings, about every 10 minutes. The thighs are done when they are tender and cooked through. Serve the glazed chicken as is, or make the following sauce from the pan drippings.

Wine Sauce (optional): When the chicken is done, remove the skillet from the oven and cover the handle to prevent burning hands while making the sauce. Transfer the chicken thighs to a warm platter. Pour the pan drippings into a fat separator. Let stand for 3 to 5 minutes, then pour the defatted juices back into the skillet. Add ⅓ cup dry white wine and bring to a simmer over medium heat. Cook for about 3 minutes to reduce the sauce slightly, stirring frequently. Drizzle the sauce over the chicken thighs to serve.

Unforgettable Chicken Pot Pie

"Chicken pot pie is comfort food at its best, and a family favorite," Betty Stambaugh tells us. "One time, my daughter didn't have time to make a from-scratch chicken pot pie for her family so she bought a frozen one instead. Oh boy, did she ever hear about it! The family thought it was the worst pot pie they had ever eaten! This recipe has been entered in many pie contests and has won numerous times."—Betty Stambaugh, Topeka

6 TO 8 SERVINGS

Pie Filling:
2 to 3 cups cooked, deboned chicken
¼ cup butter
⅓ cup all-purpose flour
½ teaspoon salt
Black pepper, to taste
1½ cups chicken broth
1 cup milk
10 ounces peas and diced cooked carrots, or cooked mixed vegetables of choice

Pie Crust:
2¼ cups all-purpose flour
1 teaspoon salt
1 to 2 teaspoons celery seeds
1 teaspoon paprika
⅔ cup canola or vegetable oil
5 tablespoons ice cold water

Pie Filling: Cut the chicken into small pieces and set aside. Melt the butter in a large skillet over medium heat. Stir in the flour, salt, and pepper and cook for 1 minute. Stir in the chicken broth and milk and cook until thickened. Add the chicken and vegetables. Set aside while preparing the crust.

Pie Crust: Combine the flour, salt, celery seeds, and paprika in a large bowl. Stir in the oil, then the cold water, a little at a time, until the mixture can be formed into a ball. Divide the dough into two portions. Roll out one portion of dough between two sheets of waxed paper. Transfer it to a large pie plate. Press the dough gently into the plate. Pour in the filling. Roll out the remaining dough, place over the filling, trim off the excess dough, and crimp the edges of the two crusts together. Cut slits in the top to allow the steam to escape.

Bake the pot pie in a 425-degree oven for 20 minutes. Reduce the heat to 350 degrees and bake 30 to 40 minutes more, until the pastry is golden brown. Let the pie rest for at least 10 minutes before cutting to allow time for the filling to set up.

Heritage Poultry

"Prior to World War II, there was really only one source for chicken—the farm-raised chicken," Frank Reese recalls. "My family established a farm near Lindsborg after coming to Kansas following the Civil War. We've always raised Barred Rock chickens."

Though many farmers keep a small flock of chickens and even folks in the city have caught on to the trend of keeping a few laying hens in the backyard, Frank Reese's vision of raising poultry goes far beyond the quaint and sentimental. He is likely not the first farmer to feel his grip on his life's work slipping, and that his alerts have fallen upon deaf ears. He speaks with passion about his devotion to the well-being of his birds and condemns the commercial trends that undermine the

established traditions of raising healthy animals. The heritage chickens, turkeys, ducks, and geese, raised on Frank's Good Shepherd Poultry Ranch in Lindsborg, are born through natural mating, live outdoors, and are free to forage. Because they are allowed to grow more slowly, it takes them twice as long to reach market weight compared to the intensively managed modern hybrids. These traditional accommodations develop a greater depth of flavor, though at a higher cost to the consumer. There is a problem, as Frank observes ironically: "The best way to save the old-time poultry is to return them to our dining tables."

Frank is a poultry rancher who is renowned for his expertise and, as a guardian of heritage poultry, he has caught the attention of celebrity chefs, food writers, and organizations devoted to preserving heritage breeds. As told by Heritage USA, help arrived in 2001 when a young man from Brooklyn, NY, visited the Good Shepherd Poultry Ranch. Patrick Martins, who was the president of Slow Foods USA at the time, was passionate about saving heritage foods. Slow Foods USA is a nonprofit organization with the goal to protect foods that are part of America's heritage by creating a market for heritage breeds. It was a unique opportunity for Patrick to do more than simply acknowledge the plight of Frank's heritage birds. Patrick promised Frank that if he would increase his production, he would sell them. Soon afterward, *New York Times* food writer Marian Burros wrote an article about her search for the country's best-tasting turkey. She chose a

Bourbon Red as her favorite and mentioned the Slow Foods project, creating a lot of chatter in the food world. More tasting contests and high-profile comparisons followed. "My birds have won every time," Frank boasts, and, as a result, the ranch's production has grown tenfold over the years.

Even with his success, Frank fears that the heritage genetic strains will be lost as well as the knowledge and experience he has acquired over the years. "I can hardly keep up," he says, "and there is no one to take over the farm." But again, Frank has found a partner to help with his cause. Kansas Wesleyan University in Salina will soon create the Good Shepherd Poultry Center, an accredited program for college students that combines coursework in environmental science, social science, economics, and the sustainability of heritage breeds. "The institute will be a place to preserve the heritage genetics," Frank says, "and keep the poultry farmer's knowledge for future generations."

Roasted Spatchcocked Chicken

Spatchcocking, or butterflying a chicken, makes it easier to marinate the bird since it will fit neatly into a large plastic storage bag along with the marinade. To spatchcock the chicken, split it open by removing the backbone to allow it to lie flat. The bird will brown more evenly and cook more quickly.—Frank and Jayni

4 SERVINGS

3½- to 4-pound whole chicken

Marinade:
¼ cup lemon juice
3 garlic cloves, smashed
1 teaspoon Hungarian paprika
1 teaspoon salt
1 teaspoon black pepper
1 tablespoon fresh rosemary, chopped
1 tablespoon fresh thyme, chopped
2 tablespoons olive oil

To spatchcock the chicken, place it on a cutting board, breast side down. Using kitchen or poultry shears, start at the thigh and cut along one side of the backbone. Cut along the other side and remove the backbone. Alternatively, the backbone can be removed in the same fashion using a sharp knife. Remove any excess fat from inside the carcass. Turn the chicken over, breast side up, and press firmly on the breast to crack the breastbone. Wipe the chicken with paper towels, if needed. Place the chicken in a large plastic storage bag while preparing the marinade.

Marinade: In a small bowl, combine the lemon juice, garlic, paprika, salt, pepper, rosemary, and thyme. Whisk in the olive

CONTINUED ➡

oil. Pour the mixture over the chicken and seal the storage bag. Turn the bag over several times until the chicken is well coated with the marinade. Refrigerate for at least 8 hours, or overnight.

Place a baking rack in a large baking dish. Remove the chicken from the marinade and place it on the baking rack, breast side up. Pour about half of the marinade over the chicken. Discard the remaining marinade.

Roast the chicken in a 400-degree oven for 30 minutes. Baste with the pan drippings and continue roasting for 30 to 45 minutes more, until cooked through, or an instant-read thermometer inserted into the thickest part of the thigh reaches 165 degrees.

Remove the chicken from the rack to a cutting board and let rest for 10 minutes. Cut the chicken into quarters to serve.

Roast Chicken with Quinoa-Vegetable Pilaf

We like to prepare a classic roast chicken for Sunday dinner. We skip the mashed potatoes and serve it with a quinoa-vegetable pilaf plus a green salad for a complete meal. —Frank and Jayni

4 SERVINGS

3½-pound whole chicken

2 teaspoons kosher salt
Fresh-ground black pepper, to taste

Quinoa-Vegetable Pilaf:
2 tablespoons olive oil
1 cup carrot, peeled and cut into small dice
½ cup onion, finely chopped
1 cup red quinoa, rinsed and drained
1¼ cups low-sodium chicken or vegetable broth
1 cup fresh tomato, chopped
½ teaspoon salt
1 cup frozen peas, slightly thawed
4 ounces feta cheese, crumbled or cut into ¼-inch dice

Pat the chicken completely dry, inside and out, with paper towels. Using kitchen twine, truss the chicken to hold the wings and thighs firmly against the body. Tie the drumsticks together. Let the chicken stand at room temperature for about 30 minutes before roasting.

Preheat the oven to 425 degrees. Sprinkle the kosher salt and black pepper over the chicken. Transfer the chicken, breast side up, to a baking dish or roasting pan.

Place the chicken in the center of the oven and roast for 15 minutes, reduce the heat to 375 degrees, and continue roasting for 45 minutes to 1 hour, until an instant-read thermometer inserted into the thickest part of the thigh reaches 165 degrees. When the chicken is done, remove it from the oven and baste with the pan drippings. Let rest for 10 minutes before carving.

After the chicken has been in the oven for about 30 minutes, prepare the Quinoa-Vegetable Pilaf.

Quinoa-Vegetable Pilaf: Heat the olive oil in a saucepan over medium-low heat. Add the carrot and onion and cook until tender-crisp, about 5 minutes. Stir in the rinsed quinoa, chicken or vegetable broth, tomato, and salt. Bring the mixture to a boil over high heat, cover, and reduce the heat to low. Simmer for 20 to 25 minutes, or until the liquid is absorbed. Remove the pan from the heat and immediately stir in the peas and feta cheese. Cover and let stand for 5 to 10 minutes.

CONTINUED ➡

When ready to serve, remove the trussing string from the chicken and cut it into quarters (breast-wing and leg-thigh combinations). Spoon some of the pilaf on each plate and arrange the chicken quarters on top.

Chicken Braised in White Wine

Chicken gently braised in white wine with shallot, garlic, and herbs is simple enough to prepare for the family, or makes a main course special enough to serve to guests. The herbs and wine make a lovely pan sauce that can be served over the chicken with mashed potatoes or rice.

Many wineries in Kansas offer a suitable dry or off-dry white wine for making this recipe. Choose a dry Seyval Blanc from Wheat State Wine Co. in Winfield, Holy-Field Winery in Basehor, or Davenport Orchards & Winery in Eudora. Another white wine, Vidal Blanc, is produced by Smoky Hill Vineyards & Winery in Salina, Shiloh Vineyard & Winery in WaKeeney, or Prairie Fire in Paxico, to name a few.—Frank and Jayni

4 TO 6 SERVINGS

3½- to 4-pound whole chicken, cut into 8 serving pieces
Salt and black pepper, to taste

2 tablespoons unsalted butter
2 tablespoons olive oil

2 tablespoons shallot, finely minced
1 garlic clove, minced
2 teaspoons fresh thyme, chopped, or 1 teaspoon dried thyme
2 teaspoons fresh tarragon, chopped, or 1 teaspoon dried tarragon
1¼ cups dry or off-dry white wine

Pat the chicken dry with paper towels and season with salt and pepper.

In a large braising pan, or skillet with a lid, heat the unsalted butter and olive oil over medium-high heat. When hot enough to sizzle, place the chicken pieces in the pan. Do not crowd. Brown the chicken on all sides (in two batches, if necessary), turning occasionally. Reduce the heat if necessary to prevent burning. Transfer the chicken pieces to a platter.

Pour off all but 2 tablespoons of the pan drippings from the pan. Add the minced shallot and cook over low heat until softened, about 3 minutes. Add the garlic and cook for 1 minute more. Return the chicken pieces to the pan and sprinkle with the thyme and tarragon. Pour in the white wine and bring to a simmer over medium-high heat. Cover the pan, reduce the heat to medium-low, and maintain a slow, steady simmer, adjusting the heat as needed. After 30 minutes, baste the chicken with the pan juices, cover and continue cooking for 20 to 25 minutes more, until tender.

Transfer the chicken pieces to a warm platter or individual plates. Skim the fat from the pan juices, if desired. To serve, spoon the pan juices over the chicken.

Hunter-Style Chicken
(Pollo alla Cacciatora)

The Kansas-Nebraska Act of 1854 opened Kansas land for settlement and, in 1862, the Homestead Act allowed settlers to claim land. Many immigrants came to Kansas, bringing with them recipes from their home countries. The tradition continues. John Bellome, whose grandfather came to New York from Italy, grew up in Brooklyn and eventually landed in Kansas. Cooks enjoy preparing recipes that reflect their family heritage, and John stirs up memories each time he prepares this dish. "I still remember the sweet aroma of this meal permeating the entire house," he recalls.—John Bellome, Lawrence

4 TO 6 SERVINGS

4-pound chicken, cut into 8 to 10 pieces
Salt and black pepper, to taste
⅓ cup olive oil

1 large garlic clove, crushed
1 large onion, sliced
1 large green bell pepper, seeded and chopped
1 celery rib, chopped

1 carrot, peeled and sliced
3 large fresh tomatoes, peeled and chopped, or 1 (14.5-ounce) can diced, undrained tomatoes (preferably San Marzano)
½ cup Marsala wine
1 teaspoon salt
½ teaspoon black pepper
½ teaspoon dried oregano
8 ounces button mushrooms, cleaned and sliced

1 loaf crusty Italian bread

CONTINUED ➡

Pat the chicken pieces dry with paper towels. Season them lightly with salt and pepper. Heat the oil over medium heat in a large skillet or braising pan. Add half of the chicken pieces (do not crowd) and brown on all sides. Transfer the browned pieces to a platter while browning the remaining pieces. Transfer the second batch to the platter.

Drain off all but 1 tablespoon of the fat from the skillet. Add the garlic and cook for about 1 minute. Add the onion, green pepper, celery, and carrot to the skillet. Stir in the tomatoes, Marsala wine, salt, pepper, and oregano. Do not add the mushrooms at this time. Return the chicken pieces to the skillet. Cover and simmer over medium-low to low heat for 40 minutes. Adjust the heat as needed to maintain a gentle simmer. Stir occasionally and spoon the pan juices over the chicken. After 40 minutes, add the sliced mushrooms, cover and continue cooking for 15 minutes more, or until the chicken is tender.

Serve the chicken with crusty Italian bread to dip in the sauce.

Hot Rosemary Grilled Chicken

A brown sugar and cayenne pepper rub heats up this grilled chicken with just a touch of sweetness. Rosemary adds an herbal flavor and an enticing aroma. Spatchcock the chicken by cutting out the backbone and flattening the bird for easy grilling and crisp, spicy skin.—Frank and Jayni

4 SERVINGS

3½- to 4-pound whole chicken

Hot Rub:
2 tablespoons brown sugar
2 tablespoons fresh rosemary, minced
½ teaspoon cayenne pepper
1 teaspoon salt
¼ teaspoon black pepper

1 tablespoon olive oil

To spatchcock the chicken, place it on a cutting board, breast side down. Using kitchen or poultry shears, start at the thigh and cut along one side of the backbone. Cut along the other side and remove the backbone. Alternatively, the backbone can be removed in the same fashion using a sharp knife. Remove any excess fat from inside the carcass. Turn the chicken over, breast side up, and press firmly on the breast to crack the breastbone. Wipe the chicken with paper towels, if needed.

Hot Rub: In a small bowl, combine the brown sugar, rosemary, cayenne pepper, salt, and pepper.

Place the butterflied chicken in a shallow baking pan, breast side down. Measure 1 tablespoon of the rub and sprinkle it over the chicken and press it into the meat using your fingers. Turn the chicken over, breast side up, and brush with 1 tablespoon of olive oil. Sprinkle the remaining rub over the breast side of the chicken and press it into the skin. Cover and refrigerate for at least 3 hours or more before grilling.

Prepare a gas or charcoal grill for cooking over medium indirect heat. Place the chicken breast side up on the cooking grate over indirect heat. Cover the grill and cook the chicken for 1 hour to 1 hour 15 minutes, until an instant-read thermometer inserted into the thickest part of the thigh reaches 165 degrees.

Remove the chicken from the grill to a cutting board and let rest for 10 minutes. Cut the chicken into quarters to serve.

Time to Grill!

When Kansas was granted statehood in 1861, an open fire was about the only option for cooking a hot meal. Let's skip over that dismal period when pioneers had to use buffalo chips for fuel. Eventually, modern indoor stoves, first fueled by wood and later by gas and electricity, became the norm in Kansas. Still, the desire for cooking outdoors and the romance of smoke and flame calls to us. There is just no substitute for that smoky taste and the primal caveman desire for cooking over hot coals.

Grilling, as we now call it, began after World War II and continued to grow in popularity along with the invasion of the Hawaiian shirt and tiki torches. Come warm weather, dads across Kansas opened the garage door, rolled out the barbecue grill, and took charge of the fire. The more zealous grillers of the era went as far as to build a permanent brick barbecue, complete with a concrete patio, in their backyard—a virtual outpost dedicated to cooking with fire.

The popularity of grilling continues to be boundless and, as women have joined the ranks of serious grillers, our desire for fire seems to have pulled the barbecue grill closer to the house. In fact, it's just outside the back door. Melding the convenience of the kitchen with the call of the wild, we now enjoy an entertaining evening outdoors, salivating happily, as we listen to the fire crackle, watch dinner roast before our eyes, and let the aroma of smoke and caramelizing juices waft under our noses.

No longer confined to the kitchen, the griller appears center stage, with tongs aloft amid the flame and smoke, orchestrating the evening's meal. Hungry helpers are eager to attend to the maestro's every whim, whether it's for a longer set of tongs, the digital thermometer, or a spray bottle to tame the unruly flames. There is drama and danger when cooking with fire and, as the helpers know, allowing the cook to become distracted could result in disaster— worse, of course, would be dinner overdone.

And so, the challenge becomes a question: what to put on the grill for our family and guests? Let's face it; for the griller standing at the helm with all that firepower, hot dogs alone won't cut it. Fortunately, across the chapters in this book is a wide array of recipes for grilling nearly everything: chicken, red meat, fish, vegetables, and even peaches for a dessert!

Grilled Lemon-Tarragon Chicken

We love the taste of tarragon with chicken. This marinade and spatchcocking the chicken makes this recipe one of our favorite ways to prepare a whole chicken for a summer meal. There are three reasons to spatchcock the chicken: it will fit neatly into a storage bag for marinating, it cooks evenly on the grill in about an hour or so with zero fuss, and you can easily separate the grilled bird into breast-wing and leg-thigh servings.—Frank and Jayni

4 SERVINGS

3½- to 4-pound whole chicken

Lemon-Tarragon Marinade:
¼ cup lemon juice
2 tablespoons fresh tarragon, finely chopped
1 teaspoon salt
1 teaspoon coarsely crushed black pepper
2 tablespoons olive oil

To spatchcock the chicken, place it on a cutting board, breast side down. Using kitchen or poultry shears, start at the thigh and cut along one side of the backbone. Cut along the other side and remove the backbone. Alternatively, the backbone can be removed in the same fashion using a sharp knife. Remove any excess fat from inside the carcass. Turn the chicken over, breast side up, and press firmly on the breast to crack the breastbone. Wipe the chicken with paper towels, if needed. Place the chicken in a large plastic storage bag and set aside while preparing the marinade.

Lemon-Tarragon Marinade: In a small bowl, combine the lemon juice, tarragon, salt, and pepper. Whisk in the olive oil. Pour the marinade over the chicken and seal the storage bag. Turn the bag over several times until the chicken is well coated with the marinade. Marinate the chicken in the refrigerator for at least 8 hours, or overnight.

Prepare a gas or charcoal grill for cooking over medium indirect heat. Remove the chicken from the marinade and discard the marinade. Place the chicken, breast side up, on the cooking grate over indirect heat. Cover the grill and cook the chicken for 30 minutes. After 30 minutes, check the chicken for even browning. Cover and continue cooking

CONTINUED

30 to 45 minutes more, until an instant-read thermometer inserted into the thickest part of the thigh reaches 165 degrees.

Transfer the chicken from the grill to a cutting board and let rest for 10 minutes. Cut the chicken into quarters to serve.

Maple and Brandy Brined Turkey with Red-Eye Gravy

Chef Vaughn Good, chef and owner of Hank Charcuterie, suggests you choose a locally raised organic turkey for this recipe. Brining the turkey adds a couple of days to the preparation but the results should guarantee a moist, well-seasoned turkey. To guarantee the best outcome of this recipe, the chef prefers to use weight measurements for some of the ingredients.

"I like to serve this turkey with garlic mashed potatoes or cornbread dressing, along with some blistered greens or Brussels sprouts."—Chef Vaughn Good, Hank Charcuterie, Lawrence

8 TO 12 SERVINGS

Maple and Brandy Brine:
2 gallons water (1 gallon water plus
    1 gallon ice water)
3 cups maple syrup
3 cups brandy
3.5 ounces sugar
12.3 ounces kosher salt
4 bunches fresh thyme
8 bay leaves

10- to 15-pound fresh organic
    turkey*

Garlic and Herb Compound Butter:
½ cup (1 stick) butter, softened
1½ teaspoons fresh sage leaves,
    finely chopped
1½ teaspoons fresh thyme, finely
    chopped
2 garlic cloves, minced

Stuffing:
1 small bunch fresh thyme
1 small bunch fresh sage
1 large shallot, peeled
5 garlic cloves, crushed with the flat
    side of a knife

Red-Eye Gravy:
2.5 ounces rendered bacon fat
1 medium shallot, minced
2.5 ounces all-purpose flour
4 cups duck or chicken stock
3 sprigs fresh thyme
1 bay leaf
3 ounces black coffee
Kosher salt and freshly ground
    black pepper, to taste

Maple and Brandy Brine: In a large pot, combine 1 gallon of water with the maple syrup, brandy, sugar, kosher salt, thyme, and bay leaves. Bring the mixture to a simmer over medium-high heat, stirring to dissolve the sugar and salt. Remove the pot from the heat and add the gallon of ice water. Cool the brine to room temperature, then refrigerate until completely chilled.

Place the turkey in a large nonreactive container and add the brine. Make sure the turkey is fully submerged in the brine. Refrigerate for 12 to 16 hours.

Remove the turkey from the brine and place it on a sheet pan fitted with a wire rack. With a clean towel, pat the surface dry. Refrigerate the turkey uncovered for 24 hours before cooking. This allows the skin to dry so it will become brown and crisp while roasting.

Garlic and Herb Compound Butter: In a mixing bowl of a stand mixer fitted with a paddle, or by hand, mix together the butter, sage, thyme, and garlic. Set aside.

Allow the turkey to come to room temperature so it will cook more evenly and the skin will become crispy. Preheat the oven to 425 degrees. While the oven is heating, prepare the bird for roasting.

Stuffing: Stuff the cavity of the turkey with bunches of thyme and sage, one large peeled shallot, and five crushed garlic cloves. Using kitchen twine, tie the legs together and tuck the wings under the bird. Stuff 6 tablespoons of the compound butter between the skin and the breast. Rub the remaining 2 tablespoons of butter on the outside of the bird.

Roast the turkey in a 425-degree oven for 30 to 45 minutes, until the skin begins to brown, then lower the oven temperature to 325 degrees. Continue roasting the turkey until the internal temperature, when measured at the meatiest part of the thigh, registers 165 degrees. The temperature of the turkey will rise 5 to 10 degrees while it is resting. Tent the turkey with aluminum foil and let it rest for 30 to 40 minutes before carving.

Red-Eye Gravy: In a 2-quart saucepan, heat the bacon fat over medium heat. Add the minced shallot and sauté until tender and translucent. Whisk the flour into the bacon fat and cook over medium heat for 2 to 3 minutes, stirring occasionally. Stir in the stock and add the thyme sprigs and bay leaf. Bring the mixture to a boil and cook until it begins to thicken. Reduce the heat to a low simmer, add the coffee, and simmer for 3 to 5 minutes. Season the gravy with kosher salt and fresh ground black pepper. Remove the thyme sprigs and bay leaf before serving.

To serve, slice the turkey and top with some of the red-eye gravy.

*For best results, choose a fresh organic turkey for this recipe. Commercial turkeys labeled "enhanced" or "self-basting" have been injected with a salt solution, and brining could make the turkey too salty.

Kansas Governor's One Shot Turkey Hunt

How do you call a turkey? According to Mike Hayden, the forty-first governor of Kansas, one could use a "yelper," a call made from the wing bones of a wild turkey. Mike, who also served as secretary of the Kansas Department of Wildlife, Parks, and Tourism under Gov. Kathleen Sebelius, is an avid turkey hunter and has always enjoyed the natural resources of Kansas.

In 1987, Gov. Mike Hayden founded the Kansas Governor's One Shot Turkey Hunt. Every year, famous people from around the country come to participate in the hunt. Well-known Kansans such as former astronauts Joe Engle and Ron Evans, as well as many Kansas City sports figures and celebrities have participated. The mission is to provide an opportunity to hunt and to raise money for youth programs and education scholarships. The event serves to pass on the heritage of hunting and showcases the natural resources of Kansas to promote tourism.

Kathleen Sebelius, the forty-fourth governor of Kansas and the twenty-first secretary of the US Department of Health and Human Services, tells us, "The turkey hunt is a widely loved event. It is a unique hunting experience and is truly a celebration of Kansas. I didn't grow up around guns or hunting, but thanks to Mike Hayden and the Kansas Highway Patrol, I learned to handle a shotgun. When Mike Hayden was governor, he instituted a number of outdoor activities to keep the tradition of hunting, fishing, and other outdoor pursuits alive and well in Kansas. There is no better experi-ence than being outdoors with Mike. His breadth of knowledge and love of the outdoors fascinated me. As governor, I wanted to continue the tradi-tion." While filming a turkey hunt, Kathleen bagged a "boss gobbler"—a Tom turkey so large it was preserved and mounted for display at the National Wild Turkey Federation in Edgefield, South Carolina.

"The first year," Kathleen recalls, "the one shot turkey hunt coincided with the annual Easter egg roll held at the governor's mansion. My husband, Gary, also known as the First Dude, had to preside over the event and greet the children along with the Easter bunny, while I was out in Butler County dressed in camouflage, hunting for turkey. Quite a role reversal!" Mike Hayden proudly says, "Kathleen proved to be a very determined and steadfast turkey hunter."

Kansas is now a popular destination for turkey hunting. Beginning in the 1860s, Kansas settlers killed and consumed nearly all the turkeys in the state. By the 1890s, and for the next seventy years, wild turkeys were nearly impossible to find. In the early 1960s, the Kansas Department of Wildlife, Parks, and Tourism reintroduced turkeys into Western Kansas through the trap-and-transplant program. Thanks to this program, growing the turkey population is one of the great conservation success stories in Kansas. Over the years, the turkeys have adapted, their numbers have grown, and now there are turkeys in every county in the state.

Mike, who has guided many people through their first turkey hunt, says, "If you want to eat the bird, you should hunt for a hen turkey, also known as a Jenny, or young male turkey, called a Jake, because they are the most tender and best for eating. A mature male turkey, known as a Tom, is tough and is usually only hunted for a trophy." When it comes to eating wild turkey, Mike says, "Wild turkeys can be roasted or deep-fried just like commercial turkeys. I like to cut the breast meat into strips and fry it for fajitas, and the legs and thighs make great turkey and noodles."

Turkey Breast Roll with Cornbread and Date Stuffing

When you're in the mood for a turkey dinner but don't want to prepare an entire feast, a turkey breast roll is the answer. First, you must butterfly a split turkey breast so that it can be stuffed and rolled before roasting. To serve, the breast is cut into rounds to display the beautiful cornbread and date stuffing center.—Frank and Jayni

4 TO 6 SERVINGS

Cornbread and Date Stuffing:
6 tablespoons butter
1 cup onion, chopped
⅓ cup celery, chopped
⅓ cup walnuts, coarsely chopped
⅓ cup pitted dates, chopped
1½ cups packaged cornbread
    stuffing

1 tablespoon fresh sage leaves,
    finely chopped
2 tablespoons fresh parsley, finely
    chopped
4 to 6 tablespoons chicken broth
Salt and black pepper, to taste

2- to 2½-pound split (half) turkey
    breast
Salt and black pepper, to taste

Baste:
2 tablespoons butter, melted
2 tablespoons dry white wine

CONTINUED ➡

Cornbread and Date Stuffing: Melt the butter in a large saucepan over medium-low heat. Add the onion and celery and cook until softened. Add the chopped walnuts and dates and cook for about 2 minutes more. Remove the pan from the heat and stir in the cornbread stuffing, sage, and parsley. Add enough of the chicken broth to moisten the stuffing and season it with salt and pepper. Let the stuffing cool slightly while preparing the turkey breast.

Place the turkey breast on a work surface, skin side down. Remove the rib bones. Cut a long, shallow slit along the length of the breast and gently press it open. Make another slit on either side of the first slit and press the meat to flatten. Do not cut completely through the meat, and keep the skin intact. Place the breast between two sheets of plastic wrap or waxed paper. Pound the meat gently with the flat side of a meat mallet to a thickness of about ½ inch. Season the cut side of the turkey with salt and pepper.

Evenly spread as much of the stuffing as needed on the cut side of the breast, leaving a 1-inch border around the edges. Roll one long side of the breast around the stuffing to form a cylinder, keeping the stuffing inside and the skin in place. An extra pair of hands will make this process easier. Tie the rolled turkey breast with four to six pieces of kitchen twine. Season the roll with salt and pepper. Place the turkey roll, seam side down, in a baking dish just large enough to hold it.

Baste: Combine the melted butter and wine in a small container.

Baste the turkey roll with the butter and wine mixture. Roast it in a 400-degree oven for 40 minutes, basting twice, at 15-minute intervals. The turkey is done when the internal temperature reaches 165 degrees and the skin is lightly browned. When done, transfer the turkey roll to a warm platter, tent with aluminum foil, and let rest for 10 minutes before slicing.

To serve, slice the turkey roll into ½- to ¾-inch slices.

Turkey Pie with Broccoli and Cheddar Cheese Sauce

If you're between holidays but craving the taste of turkey, here's a new twist on an old favorite. Turkey pie is often made with leftovers, but a small split turkey breast cooks easily with much less fuss. The twist: a broccoli and cheddar cheese sauce. It may just become the new family favorite.—Frank and Jayni

6 TO 8 SERVINGS

2-pound split (half) turkey breast
Salt and black pepper

Pie Crust:
2 cups unbleached all-purpose
**   flour**
½ teaspoon salt
⅓ cup chilled butter, diced
⅓ cup chilled vegetable shortening
5 to 7 tablespoons cold water

2 broccoli tops, 7 to 8 ounces each

Cheddar Cheese Sauce:
¼ cup butter
¼ cup all-purpose flour
½ teaspoon salt
1 cup milk
1 cup chicken broth
4 ounces room-temperature sharp
**   cheddar cheese, shredded**

Salt and white pepper, to taste

Sprinkle the turkey breast with salt and pepper and place it on a rack in a shallow baking pan. Bake in a 350-degree oven for about 1 hour to 1 hour and 20 minutes, or until it reaches an internal temperature of 165 degrees. Remove the turkey breast from the oven and tent with aluminum foil. Let rest for 15 minutes, or until cool enough to handle. Remove the skin and bones and cut the breast meat into bite-size pieces. Measure about 3 cups for the recipe. While the turkey bakes, prepare the pie crust.

Pie Crust: In a large bowl, combine the 2 cups of flour and salt. Using a pastry blender, blend in the butter and shortening until the mixture is crumbly. Add the cold water 1 tablespoon at a time, stirring with a fork, until the dough can be formed into a ball. Divide the ball in half and press each half into a flat disk. Wrap each disk in plastic wrap and chill in the refrigerator for 30 to 60 minutes.

To prepare the broccoli, cut off the stalks of each broccoli top just below where the florets begin. Break or cut the florets into tiny, bite-size pieces. Measure 3 to 4 cups. Drop the florets into a pot of boiling water and cook for 2 to 3 minutes, until tender-crisp. Drain the florets and drop into a bowl of ice water to stop the cooking and preserve the color. Drain well.

Cheddar Cheese Sauce: Melt the butter in a large saucepan over

CONTINUED ➡

medium heat. Stir in the ¼ cup of flour and the salt and cook for 1 minute. Pour in the milk and chicken broth and stir until thickened. Cook the sauce for about 1 minute, stirring constantly. Remove the pan from the heat and immediately add the cheddar cheese and stir until melted.

Fold the cooked turkey and broccoli into the cheese sauce and season with salt and white pepper, to taste. Set aside.

To make the pie shell, roll out half the chilled dough on a lightly floured surface to a thickness of about ⅛ inch. Fold the dough loosely in half and place it in a 9½-inch pie plate. Unfold the dough and press it gently into the plate. Pour the turkey and broccoli filling into the pie shell. For the top crust, roll out the remaining dough to a thickness of about ⅛ inch. Dampen the edges of the bottom pie crust with a little cold water. Fold the dough in half and place over the filling. Unfold and trim off the excess dough. Crimp the edges of the two crusts together. Prick the top with a knife or fork to allow the steam to escape.

Place the turkey pie in a 425-degree oven and bake for 20 minutes. Reduce the heat to 350 degrees and bake 30 to 35 minutes more, until the crust is lightly browned. Remove the pie from the oven and place on a wire rack. Let cool for 15 minutes before cutting.

Variation: Cooked chicken breasts may be substituted for the turkey.

Grilled Duck Breasts with Port Wine Sauce

Kansas duck hunters will enjoy this recipe, and for those who don't hunt, you may find farmers in your area who raise ducks, or you can purchase frozen duck breasts at natural foods stores and large supermarkets.

Grilling duck breasts is one of the easiest ways to prepare the cut. A Port wine sauce to serve over the duck is quickly simmered on the range top just before serving.—Frank and Jayni

4 SERVINGS

2 whole boneless duck breasts
(about 2 pounds total)
Salt and black pepper, to taste

Port Wine Sauce:
¾ cup chicken broth
¾ cup ruby Port wine
2 tablespoons shallot, finely
chopped
1 teaspoon black currant jam
1 teaspoon cornstarch combined
with 1 tablespoon chicken broth
1 tablespoon cold butter, cut into
small pieces

Pat the whole duck breasts dry with paper towels. Place them skin side down on a cutting board. Cut each breast in half between the two lobes and trim any fat that may extend past the exposed meat. Using a sharp knife, score the skin of each breast half, taking care not to cut through to the meat. Season the breasts with salt and pepper.

Prepare a gas or charcoal grill for cooking over medium-high heat. Place the duck breasts, skin side down, on the cooking grate and cover the grill to prevent flare-ups. Sear for 3 to 4 minutes, turning a quarter turn after 2 minutes to mark the skins. Turn the breasts over and place them over indirect heat, or move them to a cooler spot on the grill for 4 to 6 minutes more, until the breasts register 135 to 140 for medium-rare to medium, 155 to 160 for medium-well, or longer to reach desired doneness. Place the duck breasts on a platter and tent with aluminum foil. Let rest for 5 to 10 minutes.

CONTINUED ➡

Port Wine Sauce: In a small saucepan, bring the chicken broth, port wine, and chopped shallot to a boil over medium heat and reduce to ¾ cup. Strain out the shallot, return the sauce to the pan, and bring to a simmer over medium heat. Stir in the black currant jam until dissolved. Slowly stir in the cornstarch slurry, adding just enough to slightly thicken the sauce. Let the sauce boil gently for a few seconds. Off heat, whisk in the butter until melted.

To serve, slice each duck breast into thin slices and fan out on four dinner plates. Top each with some of the Port wine sauce.

Duck Street Tacos

Though duck confit requires advance preparation, the steps of this age-old method of preservation are actually quite easy. In a few days, the result is moist, tender, and deeply flavorful meat that is more often found on high-end restaurant menus than at home.

Depal Patel shreds the preserved duck meat, fries it until crispy, then tucks it, along with some toppings, into corn tortillas for "street tacos," but they are hardly pedestrian.—Depal Patel, Lawrence

8 TO 12 SINGLE SERVINGS

Duck Confit:
8 to 12 duck leg and thigh quarters
2 tablespoons coarse salt
30 to 40 garlic cloves, smashed (don't peel), divided
25 to 30 sprigs fresh thyme, divided
8 to 10 bay leaves, crushed
5 whole cloves
20 to 30 black peppercorns

6 to 8 cups rendered duck fat, lard, olive oil, or vegetable oil (enough to completely cover the duck quarters)

Taco Toppings:
1 cup radishes, thinly sliced
1 cup red onion, finely chopped
4 to 6 serrano peppers, seeded and finely chopped

1 cup Mexican crema or sour cream
1 cup tomatillo salsa or salsa of choice
½ cup fresh cilantro leaves, finely chopped

8 to 12 soft corn tortillas

Duck Confit: Rub the duck leg and thigh quarters with the coarse salt. Place them in a plastic storage bag or container. Add half of the garlic and half of the thyme sprigs, reserving the remaining garlic and thyme sprigs for later. Add all of the bay leaves, whole cloves, and black peppercorns. Seal the bag and refrigerate for 12 to 48 hours. Drain the accumulated liquid every 12 hours or so.

After the duck has been refrigerated for 12 to 48 hours, heat the rendered duck fat or lard, if using, in a saucepan over low heat to liquefy it. Cool to warm or room temperature before using.

Using paper towels, brush the salt and seasonings off the duck quarters. Place the duck in a baking dish. Add enough of the duck fat, lard, or other oil to cover the duck completely. Sprinkle the reserved garlic and thyme over the top. Loosely cover the baking dish with aluminum foil and place the duck in a 200- to 225-degree oven for 12 to 14 hours. Remove the baking dish from the oven and cool the duck to room temperature. The preserved duck may be used immediately. If using later, refrigerate in an airtight container with the fat covering the duck.

Set the container out of the refrigerator and bring the duck to room temperature before making the tacos.

To make the tacos, scrape the fat off the duck quarters and remove the meat from the bones. Shred the duck meat and place it in a skillet over medium-high heat. Fry the duck, turning occasionally, until the meat is warm and slightly crispy. If the meat does not yield enough fat when frying, add 1 or 2 tablespoons of duck fat or other oil to the skillet. Transfer the shredded duck meat to a warm platter.

Toppings: Prepare the toppings as directed and place in bowls for self-serving.

Just before serving, warm the tortillas in a microwave oven or a skillet.

To serve, place the platter of warm duck meat, the warm tortillas, and toppings in the center of the table or on a buffet table, and let guests prepare their own tacos.

Tip: Rendered duck fat can be purchased at some specialty stores or butcher shops.

Chapter 8
Freshwater Fish and Seafood

By the early 1870s, fresh, salted, and smoked fish, as well as shellfish, rode the rails to Kansas and was offered on the menu at the famous Harvey House restaurants. Fred Harvey, the famed restaurateur, contracted with the Atchison, Topeka, and Santa Fe Railroad to build his restaurants along the train routes, which allowed passengers, as well as locals, to dine first class. In 1876, Harvey opened the Topeka Harvey House in the state capital's Santa Fe train depot, and it remained open until 1940. These days, most large grocery stores in urban areas have a seafood counter to sell fresh, or freshly frozen, fish and shellfish flown in to the state on a regular schedule. Kansas's borders may not touch the sea, but its residents crave seafood all the same.

There is plenty of freshwater fishing within the state as well, and the craving for food with fins has a lot of people angling for its taste.

For Kansas fishermen, wild-caught walleye, crappie, bass, and trout are favorites that make an exciting catch as well as an exciting meal. There are numerous fishing tournaments for walleye, bass, and catfish enthusiasts that take place in the large reservoirs, lakes, and rivers around the state. Thanks to stocking the reservoirs with small fry, the variety and abundance of game fish continues to make fishing a great family sport for Kansans. Other fishermen like to go deep in order to catch a channel catfish lurking on the bottom of a river or pond.

In this chapter, the recipes span from the simple to the sublime. What could be easier than baking "Crispy Baked Walleye Fillet," or "Striped Bass Fillets with Capers and Lemon?" If you prefer to grill-smoke your fish, try "Planked Ruby Trout with Orange Butter, Citrus, and Rosemary." Then again, we often hear that "nothing is better than battered," and so you'll find the recipe "Deep-Fried Catfish Nuggets," which is sure to please the kids.

When fishing for something different at the seafood counter, consider tempting your Midwestern taste buds with more exotic saltwater catches. Shrimp, crab, and salmon are among the selection available, and they often appear on our menus for special occasions. In this chapter, you'll find a way to prepare "Crispy Grilled Garlic Shrimp," or if you're a fan of salmon, try "Grilled Salmon with Rosemary-Rhubarb Sauce." And what could be more elegant than easy-to-make "Perfect Crab Cakes"?

Deep-Fried Catfish Nuggets

If you're hooked on catfish, perhaps you can catch your own for this recipe. Nonanglers can go fishing for catfish nuggets at the fish and seafood counter in the supermarket. Adding beer to the batter makes a light, crisp coating on deep-fried catfish nuggets. Of course, tartar sauce is the classic accompaniment. Serve French fries on the side.—Frank and Jayni

4 SERVINGS

1 pound catfish nuggets

Beer Batter:
1 cup all-purpose flour
1 tablespoon paprika
½ teaspoon salt
⅛ teaspoon garlic granules
⅛ teaspoon onion granules
12 ounces beer, room temperature

Tartar Sauce:
1 cup mayonnaise
⅓ cup onion, minced
1 teaspoon yellow mustard
⅓ cup sweet pickle relish
1 tablespoon lemon juice, or to taste
¼ teaspoon garlic granules
¼ teaspoon onion granules
1 tablespoon parsley, finely chopped

Vegetable or canola oil, for deep-frying

1 cup all-purpose flour
Salt, to taste

If the catfish nuggets are larger than desired, cut them into bite-size pieces. Place the nuggets in a covered container and refrigerate until ready to use. Pat the nuggets dry with paper towels just before using.

Beer Batter: In a shallow bowl, combine the flour, paprika, salt, garlic granules, and onion granules. Whisk in the beer. Let the batter stand at room temperature for 1 hour.

Tartar Sauce: In a small bowl, combine the mayonnaise, onion, yellow mustard, pickle relish, lemon juice, garlic granules, onion granules, and parsley. Cover and refrigerate until ready to use. Let stand at room temperature for 15 minutes before serving.

CONTINUED ➡

In a Dutch oven or large pot, pour vegetable or canola oil no farther than one-third of the way up to avoid hot oil bubbling over when frying the nuggets. Heat the oil over high heat until it is hot enough to sizzle.

Place 1 cup of flour on a plate or baking sheet. Dredge the catfish nuggets in the flour, four to six at a time, and shake off the excess. Dip the nuggets into the beer batter to coat them. Carefully lower the nuggets into the hot oil and fry until the coating is golden brown and the nuggets are cooked through, 2 to 3 minutes. To ensure even browning, turn the nuggets over with metal tongs or a slotted spoon after about 1 minute of frying. Remove the nuggets with a slotted spoon, drain them on paper towels, and sprinkle with salt. Repeat the process with the remaining catfish nuggets. If the coating cooks too quickly, lower the heat to medium-high.

Serve the catfish nuggets immediately with the tartar sauce.

Variation: Tilapia fillets, cut into strips or cubes, can be substituted for catfish nuggets.

Option: Use the fried nuggets as a filling for fish tacos. For the tartar sauce, substitute chipotle hot sauce (or hot sauce of choice), to taste, for the sweet pickle relish. Top the tacos with shredded lettuce.

Pan-Fried Crappie with Brandy-Lemon Sauce

Crappie, one of the most popular sport fish in the state, is abundant in Kansas's lakes and reservoirs. It is a lean fish with mild white flesh, which makes it great for pan-frying. An easy pan sauce of butter, brown sugar, brandy, and lemon juice adds sparkle to the pan-fried crappie.—Frank and Jayni

4 SERVINGS

½ cup butter, divided
1 cup fine, dried breadcrumbs, or
    more as needed
4 to 8 crappie fillets (depending on
    size), about 1 pound
Salt and black pepper, to taste

Brandy-Lemon Sauce:
2 tablespoons butter
2 tablespoons brown sugar
¼ cup brandy
¼ cup lemon juice

2 tablespoons fresh parsley,
    chopped

Melt ¼ cup of the butter in the microwave or in a small saucepan over low heat. Place the breadcrumbs on a plate. Generously brush the crappie fillets on both sides with the melted butter and season them with salt and pepper. Dip the fillets into the breadcrumbs to coat and shake off the excess.

Heat the remaining ¼ cup of butter in a large, nonstick skillet over medium heat. When hot, add the fillets and fry until lightly browned, about 2 to 3 minutes each side. Lower the heat, if necessary, to prevent burning the crumb coating on the fish. Remove the fillets from the skillet and keep warm. Reserve the pan drippings.

Brandy-Lemon Sauce: Add 2 tablespoons of butter to the pan drippings and melt over medium heat. Add the brown sugar, brandy, and lemon juice. Stir constantly until the brown sugar dissolves and the mixture begins to caramelize and thicken slightly, 2 to 3 minutes. Do not overcook the sauce or it will separate.

To serve, drizzle the sauce over the fish fillets and garnish with the chopped parsley.

Variation: Tilapia, or other white-flesh fish fillets can be substituted for crappie fillets.

Crispy Baked Walleye Fillet

Walleye is a popular game fish with Kansas anglers, and has been stocked in many reservoirs and some larger state and community lakes. The walleye's thick white flesh and mild flavor make it suitable for baking, grilling, or deep-frying. We prefer it baked with Panko Japanese breadcrumbs and butter for a crispy topping.—Frank and Jayni

4 SERVINGS

2 tablespoons butter, cut into
    pieces

1 walleye fillet, 1 to 1¼ pounds
1 tablespoon lemon juice
Salt and black pepper, to taste

½ cup Panko breadcrumbs*
1 teaspoon paprika
1 tablespoon butter, melted

4 lemon wedges

Preheat the oven to 400 degrees. While the oven is heating, place 2 tablespoons of butter in an oval or rectangular baking dish just large enough to hold the fillet and let it melt in the oven for 2 to 3 minutes.

Remove the baking dish from the oven, place the walleye fillet, flesh side down, in the melted butter to coat, then turn the fillet over, flesh side up. Pour 1 tablespoon of lemon juice over the fillet, and season it with salt and pepper.

In a small bowl, combine the Panko breadcrumbs and paprika. Stir in 1 tablespoon of melted butter and sprinkle the crumbs evenly over the fillets to cover.

Bake the walleye fillet for about 15 minutes, or until the topping is lightly browned and the fish flakes easily when pierced with a knife. Cut the fillet into four servings. Serve with lemon wedges.

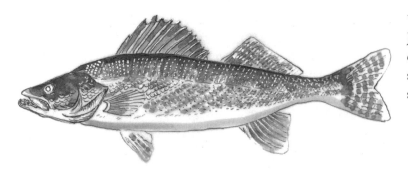

* Panko breadcrumbs are Japanese-style dried breadcrumbs and are available in specialty stores and most large supermarkets.

Gone Fishin'

Kansans love to fish, and the more serious anglers have the opportunity to participate in fishing tournaments across the state. There are at least seven to ten regional or nationally affiliated organizations that hold sanctioned tournaments in Kansas, along with small local tournaments in cities, counties, and townships, usually sponsored by local fishing clubs.

David Breth of Pratt, fisheries program specialist for the Kansas Department of Wildlife, Parks, and Tourism, tells us, "Tournament anglers are also known as weekend warriors, since most of their fishing happens on the weekend. And it's not just a boys' club. Many women fish and compete right along with the guys. The interest in fishing extends to Kansas high school and college students. K-State competes in fishing tournaments on the collegiate level, along with other colleges across the nation."

Eric Craft, a schoolteacher in Erie, likes to compete in bass tournaments. In 2014, Eric competed at the local level in the American Bass Anglers of America Fishing Tour (AFT). He won a divisional title and went on to compete in the AFT national championship on Old Hickory Lake, near Nashville, Tennessee. Eric took second place in that competition, but won the prestigious National Angler of the Year title. His prize was a fully rigged Triton bass boat,

which he now enjoys using when he fishes. Eric says, "I enjoy competitive fishing because the rules are straightforward, so it's just about you and the fish. You put them on the scales to be weighed and you know where you're at." He says he is proud that all bass tournaments are catch and release. "Bass anglers like to preserve and prolong the resource," Eric says, which gives him incentive to get back out on the lake in his new bass boat and fish for the big one.

How does one compete in a fishing tournament? First, buy your fishing license and agree to abide by state fishing regulations and the rules of the tournament, and pay an entry fee. Next, choose your fish— bass, walleye, or catfish—and third, pick your tournament. Most walleye and bass tournaments are daylong events on a given lake, while a catfish tournament may take place for up to forty-eight hours in multiple lakes so that night fishing can be included.

"Your choice of bait will depend on the kind of fish you're angling for. For bass, it's strictly artificial lures, so contestants are always on the lookout for the newest lure on the market that promises to hook the biggest bass. When it comes to walleye or catfish, live or cut bait is used, and the choice is up to the angler," David Breth says.

In spite of the fact that those who compete appreciate a day out on the lake—enjoying the surrounding beauty from sunrise to sunset—the goal is to win the tournament. Catching the biggest fish is what it's all about. The fish are usually judged by weight or length, and the winner generally goes home with a cash prize. The others can only talk about the one that got away.

Striped Bass Fillets with Capers and Lemon

Striped bass is a mild white-flesh fish that tastes best when prepared with the least amount of fuss. In this recipe, the fillets are dusted with flour, quickly pan-seared, and finished in a hot oven. A garnish of capers and lemon wedges is all that is needed to reel the family in to the table.

The striped bass is a saltwater native fish that has adapted to freshwater, and many Kansas lakes are stocked with them. Smallmouth, largemouth, or white bass can be found nearly everywhere in the Sunflower State's lakes and can be used in this recipe.—Frank and Jayni

4 SERVINGS

4 striped bass fillets (about 6 ounces each), or other firm, white-flesh fish fillets, ½ inch thick
Salt and black pepper, to taste
¼ cup all-purpose flour

3 tablespoons peanut or vegetable oil

¼ cup capers, rinsed and drained
Lemon wedges

Sprinkle the bass fillets with salt and pepper. Dust each lightly with flour.

Heat the oil over medium-high heat in a stainless steel (oven-safe) skillet, large enough to comfortably hold the fish fillets without touching each other. When the oil is hot, place the fillets in the skillet, flesh side down, and cook for about 1½ minutes, until light gold. Turn the fillets over, reduce the heat to medium, and cook for 30 seconds more. Spoon off all but about 1 tablespoon of fat from the skillet.

Place the skillet in a 400-degree oven and cook the fillets for 4 to 5 minutes, until they reach 130 to 135 degrees, or the flesh is opaque and flakes easily with a fork.

Serve the bass fillets sprinkled with capers. Serve lemon wedges on the side.

Harry's Rainbow Trout

Located in the Historic Wareham Hotel in Manhattan, Harry's is known as the city's premier fine dining establishment. The restaurant is best known for its classic-contemporary cuisine and gracious service.

"This main course was a favorite among Harry's regulars for more than a decade and pairs very well with fresh green beans, or even some fried potatoes."—Executive Chef Cadell Bynum, Harry's, Manhattan

4 SERVINGS

4 boneless rainbow trout fillets (about 8 ounces each), butter-flied, boneless, skin on

Red Pepper Aioli:
¾ cup mayonnaise
¾ teaspoon garlic, chopped
1 tablespoon Sriracha hot sauce
½ teaspoon kosher salt
1½ to 2 teaspoons fresh-squeezed lemon juice, or more to taste

Pecan-Focaccia Breading:
1 cup pecans, coarsely chopped
2½ cups fresh focaccia, ground into breadcrumbs
Pinch of kosher salt

6 tablespoons butter, divided

Prepare the rainbow trout as directed, cover, and refrigerate until ready to use.

Red Pepper Aioli: In a medium bowl, combine the mayonnaise, garlic, Sriracha hot sauce, and kosher salt. Add lemon juice, to taste. Set aside if using soon, or cover and refrigerate for later use.

Pecan-Focaccia Breading: In a medium bowl, combine the coarsely chopped pecans, focaccia breadcrumbs, and a pinch of kosher salt.

Preheat the oven to 375 degrees. Have two large stainless steel (oven-safe) sauté pans or skillets ready to cook the trout fillets.

CONTINUED ➡

Spread about half of the red pepper aioli on a plate. On a second plate, evenly spread out half of the breading. Dredge one trout fillet through the aioli, coating both sides. Use a rubber spatula to spread the aioli evenly on the fillet, if needed. Dredge the fillet through the breading to coat both sides. Repeat with the remaining trout fillets, adding more aioli and breadcrumbs to the plates as needed.

Melt 3 tablespoons of butter over medium heat in one of the sauté pans or skillets. Place two breaded trout fillets in the sauté pan, flesh side down, and pan-fry for 1 to 2 minutes to brown. Carefully turn the trout fillets over and place the sauté pan in the oven for 6 to 8 minutes, or until desired doneness is achieved. While the trout cooks, bread the remaining two fillets and cook in the second pan as directed.

Transfer the trout to dinner plates and pass Sriracha at the table, if desired.

Option: As an alternative to cooking the fish in two sauté pans, preheat a baking dish large enough to hold four fillets. Brown the breaded trout fillets as directed in two batches and transfer them, along with the pan drippings, to the preheated baking dish. Bake as directed.

Grilled Trout Fillets

Rainbow trout is stocked in many lakes across Kansas, so anglers looking for a tasty way to cook them on the grill will appreciate this recipe. Ruby or golden trout, which can be purchased at most seafood counters, works well for this recipe, too. Simply top the trout fillets with the ingredients below, marinate them in the refrigerator for thirty minutes, and grill over gas or charcoal.—Frank and Jayni

4 SERVINGS

4 trout fillets (6 to 8 ounces each),
    rainbow, ruby, or golden
Olive or vegetable oil
Salt and black pepper, to taste
¼ cup butter, melted
¼ cup lemon juice
2 tablespoons fresh tarragon,
    chopped
2 tablespoons brown sugar

Lemon wedges

Brush the skin of each trout fillet generously with olive or vegetable oil and place them in a large baking dish, flesh side up. Season each fillet with salt and pepper. Drizzle or brush 1 tablespoon of melted butter over each. Sprinkle the top of each fillet with some of the lemon juice and the chopped tarragon. Sprinkle an equal amount of the brown sugar over each of the fillets. Cover and refrigerate for 30 minutes before grilling.

Prepare a gas or charcoal grill for cooking over high heat. Place the trout fillets on the cooking grate, skin side down. Cover and cook for 2 to 3 minutes to cook the skins. Turn the fillets over using a large metal spatula and remove the loosened skins, if desired. Cover and cook for 2 to 3 minutes more. Carefully turn the fillets over again and check for doneness. Cook 1 to 2 minutes more, if needed. The fillets should be cooked to medium, and still moist in the center.

Transfer the trout fillets from the grill to a warm plate and tent with aluminum foil for about 5 minutes before serving. Serve the trout fillets with lemon wedges.

Planked Ruby Trout with Orange Butter, Citrus, and Rosemary

We grill year-round at our house, and we like to make this planked trout recipe in the winter months, when oranges and grapefruits taste best. The aroma and smoky flavor from the wood planks plus the toppings of winter citrus and orange butter make the trout a cozy treat on a winter night.—Frank and Jayni

4 SERVINGS

4 (4 × 9-inch) or 2 (6 × 15-inch) untreated alder wood or cedar grilling planks

1 large orange, peeled and segmented

1 pink grapefruit, peeled and segmented

Orange Butter:
3 tablespoons fresh-squeezed orange juice

¼ cup butter, diced into small pieces

4 ruby trout fillets (6 ounces each)
Vegetable oil
Salt and black pepper
Fresh rosemary branches cut into 12 (1-inch) sprigs

Soak 4 individual planks (or 2 large planks) in water for 1 hour or more.

To segment the orange and grapefruit, slice the peel off the top and bottom to expose the fruit, using a sharp knife. Cut away the peel and pith following the curve of the fruit. Cut between the membrane walls and remove the segments. Set aside.

Orange Butter: Heat the orange juice over medium heat in a small saucepan. Simmer for 2 to 3 minutes, until the juice is reduced to 1 tablespoon. Off heat, whisk in the butter until melted. Pour the mixture into a small container and let partially solidify before using.

To prepare the fish for grilling: Pat the trout fillets dry with paper towels. Lightly oil the fish skins to prevent sticking to the grilling planks. Place the fillets flesh side up on a baking sheet or plastic cutting board and season with salt and pepper. Spoon about 1 tablespoon of the orange butter over the flesh of each fillet. Top each fillet with two orange sections and two grapefruit sections, alternating them. Arrange three rosemary sprigs on each fillet.

Prepare a gas or charcoal grill for cooking over high heat. Drain the soaked planks. To "season" the planks, place them on the grill, cover and heat for 3 to 5 minutes, until they begin to smoke. Turn the planks over and place them over medium heat, or move them to a slightly cooler part of the grill. Using a large metal spatula, transfer the trout fillets to the planks. Cover and grill the fish for 10 to 12 minutes. Use the tip of a knife to check the interior for desired doneness.

Remove the fillets from the planks and serve immediately.

Grilled Salmon with Rosemary-Rhubarb Sauce

Rhubarb, though botanically a vegetable, is generally eaten as a fruit. Many Kansans even call it the "pie plant." It has a tart flavor but, when tempered with sugar, rhubarb makes delicious sweet-tart pies and jams. In this recipe, rhubarb lends itself nicely to a sauce for grilled salmon. Adding Dijon mustard and fresh rosemary creates a sauce with a savory quality.—Frank and Jayni

4 TO 6 SERVINGS

Rhubarb Sauce:
8 ounces red rhubarb, cut into ¼-inch dice
¼ cup sugar
¼ cup water
1 teaspoon Dijon mustard
1 teaspoon fresh rosemary, minced

4 to 6 salmon fillets (about 6 ounces each)
Olive or canola oil
Salt and black pepper, to taste

4 to 6 rosemary sprigs

Rosemary-Rhubarb Sauce: In a small saucepan, combine the diced rhubarb, sugar, and water. Cook over medium-low heat, stirring occasionally, until the rhubarb breaks down, 5 to 7 minutes. Remove the pan from the heat and cool to warm. Transfer the rhubarb mixture to a blender and blend until smooth, or blend with a stick blender. Return the blended rhubarb to a clean saucepan, add the mustard and rosemary, and set aside. Just before serving, simmer the sauce over low heat for about 1 minute. The sauce should be somewhat thick, but if it's too thick, thin it with a tablespoon or two of water while heating.

Brush both sides of the salmon fillets with olive or canola oil and season them with salt and pepper.

Prepare a gas or charcoal grill for cooking over high heat. Place the salmon fillets on the cooking grate, skin side down. Cover the grill and cook for 2 to 4 minutes to brown the skins. Turn the

CONTINUED ➡

fillets over and, using a large metal spatula or tongs, remove the skins. Cover and cook for 2 to 3 minutes more. Carefully turn the fillets over again and check for doneness. The salmon should be cooked to medium and still moist in the center. If needed, continue cooking the salmon fillets for 1 to 2 minutes over indirect heat, or move the fillets to a cooler part of the grill. When done, transfer the salmon fillets to a warm plate, tent with aluminum foil, and let rest for 5 minutes.

To serve, top each salmon fillet with some of the warm rosemary-rhubarb sauce. Garnish with rosemary sprigs.

Perfect Crab Cakes

Crab cakes are easy to make at home, so why wait to go to a restaurant to enjoy them? Use fresh lump crabmeat, if you can find it super fresh, or keep a few cans of premium lump crabmeat on hand for an impromptu meal during the week. Serve the crab cakes with a vegetable side and a salad, or a cup of your favorite soup.—Frank and Jayni

4 SERVINGS

12 ounces fresh lump crabmeat, or 2 (6½-ounce) cans premium lump crabmeat

1 egg, beaten
3 tablespoons mayonnaise
2 green onions, finely chopped
1 teaspoon fresh dill, finely chopped, or ¼ teaspoon dried dill
⅛ teaspoon sea salt
⅛ teaspoon white pepper
⅛ teaspoon garlic granules
⅛ teaspoon onion granules
¼ cup Panko or other dried breadcrumbs, plus more, if needed

Sauce:
¼ cup mayonnaise
2 tablespoons ketchup
1 tablespoon lemon juice
½ teaspoon Worcestershire sauce
⅛ teaspoon garlic granules
⅛ teaspoon cayenne pepper
⅛ teaspoon white pepper
2 tablespoons heavy cream

½ cup Panko or other dried breadcrumbs, for coating

¼ cup peanut or vegetable oil

Fresh dill sprigs, or dried dill

If using fresh crabmeat, pick it over for bits of shell. If using canned, drain the crabmeat in a wire-mesh strainer. Chill a small bowl in the refrigerator for whipping the cream later.

In a medium bowl, whisk together the egg and mayonnaise. Stir in the green onion, dill, sea salt, white pepper, garlic granules, and onion granules. Gently fold in the crabmeat. Fold in ¼ cup of breadcrumbs. If the mixture is too wet to form the crab mixture into small cakes, fold in 2 to 3 more tablespoons of breadcrumbs, adding only enough breadcrumbs to hold the mixture together. Cover the crab mixture and chill for 30 minutes or more. This will make the mixture easier to handle.

Shape the crab mixture into eight small cakes about 2½ inches in diameter and 1 inch thick (the mixture will still be moist). Place the crab cakes on a platter, cover, and chill for at least 30 minutes before cooking. Make the sauce for the crab cakes just before cooking them.

CONTINUED ➡

Sauce: In a small bowl, combine the mayonnaise, ketchup, lemon juice, Worcestershire sauce, garlic granules, cayenne pepper, and white pepper. Pour the heavy cream into the chilled bowl and whisk with a wire whisk until soft peaks form. Fold the whipped cream into the mayonnaise mixture.

To fry the crab cakes, place ½ cup of breadcrumbs on a plate. Coat the crab cakes on both sides with the breadcrumbs. Handle carefully; they will be very fragile.

Heat the peanut or vegetable oil in a large nonstick skillet over medium heat. Carefully transfer the crab cakes to the skillet and fry for 2 to 3 minutes on each side, until golden brown.

To serve, arrange two crab cakes on each dinner plate. Spoon a dollop of the sauce on the crab cakes, or serve the sauce on the side. Garnish the crab cakes with fresh dill sprigs or sprinkle dried dill on the sauce.

Crispy Grilled Garlic Shrimp

Although Kansas is a landlocked state, we can get a "glimpse of the sea" at larger grocery stores where the ocean's offerings are shipped in, both fresh and frozen, two to three times a week. Grilling shrimp is quick and easy, so in the summertime we prefer this method to avoid heating up the kitchen. We like to coat the shrimp with Panko Japanese-style breadcrumbs for a light and crunchy exterior.—Frank and Jayni

4 SERVINGS

1 pound large shrimp (21 to 25 count)	2 tablespoons butter	Lemon wedges
Salt, to taste	½ teaspoon garlic granules	
	½ cup Panko breadcrumbs	

Peel and devein the shrimp, leaving the last segment of shell and the tails intact. Place them in a large bowl and sprinkle with salt.

Place the butter in a small microwave-safe container and melt in a microwave oven. Stir in the garlic granules and let cool briefly. When cool, pour the melted garlic butter over the shrimp and toss to coat. Sprinkle half of the breadcrumbs over the shrimp and toss. Add the remaining breadcrumbs and toss again to make sure all the shrimp are lightly coated.

Prepare a gas or charcoal grill for cooking over medium to medium-high heat. Preheat a large grill pan on the cooking grate. When hot, place the shrimp in a single layer on the grill pan using grilling tongs. Cover the grill and cook for 2 to 3 minutes, until the shrimp are lightly browned on the undersides. Turn the shrimp over and grill for 2 to 3 minutes more, until cooked through. Do not overcook the shrimp.

Transfer the shrimp to a platter. Serve immediately with lemon wedges.

Spicy Lime Shrimp with Coconut Rice

The number of Asian immigrants to Kansas increased as Vietnamese, Laotians, and Cambodians came to work in the meatpacking plants in Dodge City and Garden City after the end of the Vietnam War in 1975. Since then, these immigrants have opened restaurants in the surrounding areas and across the state and are serving delicious dishes from their homelands. This shrimp and coconut rice recipe borrows from the wonderful flavors of Southeast Asia—lemongrass, coconut milk, and lime juice.—Frank and Jayni

4 SERVINGS

Coconut Rice:
2 tablespoons peanut oil or vegetable oil
½ cup onion, finely chopped
1 cup basmati rice
1 lemongrass stalk (about 4 to 5 inches)
1 cup unsweetened coconut milk
1 cup chicken broth
½ teaspoon sea salt

2 pounds extra large shrimp (16 to 20 count)
Sea salt, to taste

6 tablespoons butter
3 large garlic cloves, finely minced
½ teaspoon crushed red pepper
1 tablespoon lime zest
¼ cup fresh-squeezed lime juice

Lime slices, for garnish

Coconut Rice: Heat the oil in a medium saucepan over medium-low heat. Add the onion and cook until tender. Add the rice and cook for about 2 minutes, stirring frequently. Remove the tough outer layer of the lemongrass stalk and discard. Using a sharp knife, cut the lemongrass into three pieces and add to the rice. Stir in the coconut milk, chicken broth, and sea salt. Raise the heat to high and bring to a boil. Stir, cover, and reduce the heat to low. Cook the rice for 14 minutes, or until the liquid is absorbed and the rice is tender. Let the rice stand, covered, for 5 to 10 minutes. Remove the lemongrass before serving.

Shell and devein the shrimp. Wipe the shrimp or pat dry with paper towels. Sprinkle with sea salt.

Heat the butter over medium-low heat in a large skillet or sauté pan. Add the garlic and crushed red pepper and cook for 1 minute. Add the shrimp and lime zest and cook until the shrimp are cooked through, about 3 minutes. Stir in the lime juice and briefly return to a simmer.

Immediately, divide the shrimp among four dinner plates and spoon the butter and lime pan sauce over top. Serve the coconut rice on the side. Garnish each plate with lime slices.

Chapter 9
Bread and Pizza

Beneath a flawless blue sky, a gentle breeze buffets fields of golden wheat stretching endlessly to the horizon. In early summer, the image is a souvenir for travelers crossing the plains of Kansas. Katharine Lee Bates, traveling from Massachusetts to Colorado, inspired by this vision, wrote the line "amber waves of grain" into her poem "Pike's Peak," which became the patriotic song "America the Beautiful."

Early settlers in Kansas began growing wheat, and, eventually, the state would become known as the "breadbasket of the world," but it wasn't an easy path. The story of wheat in Kansas is an epic tale wrought through struggle. Prior to 1874, harvesting spring wheat was as unpredictable as Kansas's weather. Turkey Red wheat, brought to Kansas by German Mennonites arriving from Russia, was a heartier variety and became the ideal crop for Kansas. Following decades of successful harvests, tragedy struck in the form of drought, and so began the Dust Bowl of the 1930s. The wheat farmers persevered, however, and as agricultural science advanced with new wheat varieties and technological methods, wheat production again flourished. Kansas became known as the "Wheat State" and it is always among the top-ranked producers of wheat and milled flour in the United States.

When it comes to flour for baking breads and rolls, traditional whole wheat is often used for hearty yeast breads, while a newer variety, white whole wheat, is gaining in popularity because it lightens up the texture and flavor of breads and other dough recipes. This chapter offers bakers a variety of yeast bread and pizza recipes.

"Accidental Bread" combines traditional whole wheat flour with spelt flour to make a bread that is superb for making toast or sandwiches. "Whole Grain Wheat 'n' Oats Bread" makes use of leftover oatmeal combined with white whole wheat flour or traditional whole wheat flour to make what one family calls their "favorite" daily bread. If you have a bread machine, "Healthy and Hearty Three-Seed Bread" makes nourishing bread for the family while eliminating the work of kneading and baking.

For a large group, make a big batch of "Brown-and-Serve Wheat Rolls." And, even if your group is not so big, for convenience, they can be made ahead, parbaked, and frozen for later use. On the sweeter side, "Ann's Caramel-Walnut Cinnamon Rolls" are bound to be a crowd pleaser—so deliciously fragrant, they make a warm breakfast surprise.

Pizza has long been a part of the American diet, thanks to the Italian immigrants, many of whom came to the United States in the early 1900s and eventually settled in Kansas. Pizza lovers say there is no substitute for the taste of homemade, and it is as much about the crust as it is about the toppings.

For a party pleaser in the summer when basil and tomatoes are prolific, try "Pepperoni and Pineapple Pizza with Pesto-Cheese Topping." In the fall when fresh apples are available for the picking, make "Pizza with Apple, Marinated Red Onion, and Bacon." It can be served as a party starter, brunch, or for dinner with a side salad.

In the story "Homestead Pizza," children at a field-to-table day camp learn about where their food comes from by milling wheat for the flour to make the dough, harvesting herbs and tomatoes from the garden for the sauce, and milking a cow for the milk to make fresh cheese for the topping. On their last day at camp, they put together a pizza from the ingredients made on the homestead. Now that's a happy ending to the story of wheat.

Whole Grain Wheat 'n' Oats Bread

"This bread, our family's daily bread, is made from leftover oatmeal—sometimes intentionally leftover—and the power of Kansas hard wheat flour."—Sharon Davis, family and consumer sciences educator, Home Baking Association, Manhattan

MAKES 2 PAN LOAVES, OR 2 OR 3 ROUND LOAVES

2 cups warm water (95 to 100 degrees)
½ to 1 cup leftover oatmeal (any kind), cooked and cooled*
0 to ¼ cup brown sugar, honey, molasses, or sorghum, to taste
¼ cup butter or vegetable oil
1 large egg
2 packages (¼ ounce each) active dry yeast
3 cups white whole wheat flour or regular whole wheat flour

1¾ teaspoons salt
2¾ to 3 cups unbleached bread flour

In a large mixing bowl, combine the warm water; leftover oatmeal; choice of sweetener, if using; butter or vegetable oil; egg; dry yeast; and 3 cups of white or regular whole wheat flour. Using a mixer, mix on low speed until blended, then on medium speed for 3 to 4 minutes. Cover the bowl lightly with plastic wrap or a clean, damp tea towel and let rest for 15 to 45 minutes.

To the mixture, add the salt, then the bread flour, mixing until a rough, shaggy dough forms. If the dough is too sticky, add ¼ cup more flour. If it is too dry, add 1 or 2 tablespoons of water, until pliable. Knead by hand using as little flour as possible or with a stand mixer fitted with a dough hook. Knead until the dough cleans the counter or mixing bowl, about 10 to 12 minutes. Place the dough in an oiled bowl, cover lightly again, and let rise in a draft-free, warm place.

CONTINUED ➡

After the dough doubles in size, about 35 to 45 minutes, deflate the dough and shape it into a smooth ball. Cover with a bowl, or a tea towel, and let rest for about 5 minutes. Meanwhile, grease two 8½ × 4½-inch loaf pans, or a large cookie sheet.

If using loaf pans, divide the dough in half, shape into loaves, and place them into the pans, seam side down. Or, if using a large cookie sheet, divide and shape the dough into two large round loaves, or three smaller round loaves. Place them on the cookie sheet, allowing 3 inches or more between loaves. Cover the loaves lightly and allow to double in size in a warm place.

When the loaves are doubled in size, preheat the oven to 360 degrees. If making two pan loaves, bake for 30 to 35 minutes. If making round loaves, make a ¼-inch-deep "X" in the top of the loaves before baking. Bake two large round loaves for 30 to 35 minutes, or three small round loaves for 20 to 25 minutes. All loaves should register 190 to 210 degrees at the center when done.

Cool the bread on wire cooling racks. Wrap the bread when completely cool.

*Oatmeal prepared with milk is preferred. If oats are prepared with water, scald 1½ cups milk, cool, and substitute for an equal amount of the warm water.

Variation: Before baking, sprinkle raw oatmeal on the pan or cookie sheet under the loaves, or brush the tops with an egg wash and sprinkle with oats to garnish the loaf.

White Whole Wheat Bread

Hard white wheat is the newest class of wheat marketed in the United States, and it is now grown in the western and central parts of Kansas. Breads and other products made with white wheat flour have become increasingly popular in recent years, not only for home bakers, but for food manufacturers as well. White whole wheat flour yields bread that is lighter in color, softer in texture, and milder in flavor than bread made with traditional whole wheat flour. Both flours are nutritionally equal, so the choice comes down to a matter of taste.—Jayni

MAKES 2 LOAVES

2 packages (¼ ounce each)
    fast-rising instant yeast
6 to 6½ cups white whole wheat
    flour, divided
2½ cups lukewarm water (110 to
    115 degrees)

2½ teaspoons salt
⅓ cup honey
⅓ cup vegetable oil

Combine the yeast and 3 cups of the white whole wheat flour in the bowl of a stand mixer, or in a large bowl, if mixing by hand. Stir in the warm water using the dough hook, or a wooden spoon. Cover with a tea towel and let stand for 10 minutes.

Add the salt, honey, and vegetable oil to the flour mixture and mix with the dough hook on low to medium speed, or stir to combine. Gradually add 3 cups more of the flour. Knead with the dough hook, or by hand, for 10 to 15 minutes, until smooth and elastic. If the dough is too sticky while kneading, add additional flour, up to ½ cup. Shape the dough into a smooth ball, place in a greased bowl, and turn to grease the top. Cover with a tea towel and let rise in a warm place until doubled in size, about 45 minutes.

After the dough has risen, punch it down and divide in half. Shape the dough into two smooth loaves. Place them into two greased 9 × 5 × 3-inch loaf pans. Cover lightly with a tea towel and let rise for 30 to 40 minutes.

Bake the loaves in a 350-degree oven for 45 minutes, or until they are golden brown and reach an internal temperature of 195 to 200 degrees.

CONTINUED ➡

Allow the loaves to cool in the loaf pans for about 5 minutes. Remove the loaves and place them on a wire rack to cool.

Variation: For half wheat, half white loaves, substitute 3 to 3½ cups of unbleached all-purpose flour for the portion of white whole wheat flour added before kneading.

The Wheat Harvest at Mead Farms

Mead Farms Inc. in Lewis boasts of six generations since it was taken over by the Mead family from the original homesteaders in 1902. Since 1980, Lynn and Julie Mead have run the family farm along with Lynn's parents, Jeff and Zelma Mead. Their son, Dustin, has recently returned and has become a partner. Nicole, their daughter, teaches at an elementary school in nearby Lewis, and lives a couple of miles away with her husband, Blake, and their two children. Nicole helps out with the meals at harvest time, when the whole family is needed. The Meads' major crop is hard red winter wheat, though they also grow food-grade milo, corn, and soybeans.

The Mead family exemplifies how harvest time has changed over the years. "Until the mid-nineties, we were still making the big harvest meals at noontime for the crew," Julie Mead explains. "Planning was essential for timing the cooking and carrying the meal to the field, usually in the back of a pickup truck. If it was windy, it was hard to serve the food.

And if it wasn't, we had heat, gnats, and flies to deal with. The gnats would fly into the food so we just called them 'pepper!' In those days, we made fried chicken, potatoes and gravy, and garden vegetables for the crew and, of course, pies. The evening meal, or supper, as it's called, was simpler. It usually consisted of burgers, hot dogs, or sloppy joes, and simple sweets like cookies and banana bread. The big meals were nice back then because the children were young, and it gave Lynn some time with them during the busy season."

A change in farming equipment has brought changes to the harvest meals. These days, the huge, modern combines with air-conditioned cabs are guided by computer programs so the harvest is more efficient and less taxing on the body. With the lightened workload, the crew no longer requires the big noon meal. "Now they prefer a sack lunch so they can eat on the go, " says Julie. "Sack lunches include sandwiches or wraps; chips; apple or banana; iced tea or lemonade; homemade cookies;

and raw vegetables such as carrots, cucumbers, peppers, and celery. This way, they can eat inside the cab of the combine, tractor, or truck without stopping. When the evening meal rolls around, it is a time for the harvesters to take a break, and we will take something much more interesting to the field to eat. The crew has their favorites and expect certain meals every year such as Zelma's barbecue meatballs and my lasagne in a bun. Nicole has brought some new dishes to the harvest table that are also becoming quite popular with the crew. The evening meal provides a time to rest, visit with family, and enjoy some good food together, then it's time to crank up the machines and finish up the rest of the day's harvesting."

What hasn't changed is the anxiety that comes with each wheat harvest—another reason to keep meals simpler. Timing is everything because the crop must be harvested at the optimal time, and there is no room for error. "The crew must be ready to go at a moment's notice," Lynn Mead says. Weather is always a factor, as the wheat must be dry enough to cut. An equipment breakdown or a computer going out can cause a major delay. "It's a stressful time," says Lynn. "Everything has to come together for a successful harvest."

For many wheat farmers, the big noontime meals are disappearing. The women don't miss cooking the massive feasts in hot kitchens and the crews prefer a lighter sack lunch so they can continue to cut the wheat. Still, the camaraderie remains, along with some of the crew's favorite dishes and, when served at the end of a long hard day, this food is reason enough for celebration.

Accidental Bread

"This bread, first created by accident out of necessity, has been through several permutations involving different combinations of flour—unbleached, whole wheat, and spelt. This final version makes superior toast. The bread also has structural integrity, so it does not crumble when used for a sandwich. I make this bread once a week, keeping the second loaf in the freezer until the first loaf is gone."—Shirley Domer, Lawrence

MAKES 2 LOAVES

For the Sponge:
2 cups lukewarm water
2 teaspoons active dry yeast
1 cup unbleached flour
2 cups whole wheat bread flour
2 teaspoons salt

1 cup lukewarm water
2 tablespoons vegetable oil
2 tablespoons honey
1 cup whole wheat flour
2 to 3 cups spelt flour, plus extra for kneading

To make the sponge, pour 2 cups of lukewarm water into a mixer bowl and sprinkle in the yeast. Do not stir. Let sit until the yeast expands and rises to the top. This will take several minutes. In a separate bowl, combine the unbleached flour, whole wheat bread flour, and salt. Beat the flour mixture into the yeast mixture 1 cup at a time. Continue beating until the mixture forms ribbons as it is stirred. Cover the bowl with plastic wrap or a tea towel. After 1 hour, check the sponge for activity; it should be bubbling and doubled in size.

To make the dough, stir down the sponge and mix in the water, oil, and honey. Add 1 cup of whole wheat flour and mix well. Add the spelt flour a cup at a time, mixing only until the flour is incorporated, as the gluten in spelt flour breaks down quickly. Once the flour is incorporated (it will be sticky), turn the dough out onto a kneading cloth or surface sprinkled with flour. Knead, adding more spelt flour as needed to keep the dough from sticking. Bread made with spelt flour requires less kneading than bread made with whole wheat. The dough will be soft, but knead only until it is no longer sticky on the outside.

Place the dough in an oiled bowl and turn it over so there is a coating of oil on the top. Cover and let rise until doubled, 45 minutes to 1 hour.

Divide the dough into two portions. Shape into loaves and place them in buttered 9-inch bread pans. Cover with a tea towel and let rise until the dough mounds up above the pans, 30 to 45 minutes.

Bake the loaves in a 350-degree oven for 45 minutes. Let the loaves cool in the pans for about 5 minutes. Turn the loaves out onto a rack to cool.

Healthy and Hearty Three-Seed Bread

"I am a spokesperson for the Kansas Wheat Commission, and I have used my bread machine for years. It makes bread-making simple. This bread is filled with healthy, wholesome ingredients. It takes a bit longer to measure out all the ingredients, but the outcome is well worth your time!"
—Kathy Walsten, spokesperson, Speak for Wheat, Kansas Wheat Commission, Manhattan

MAKES 1 LOAF
(BREAD MACHINE RECIPE)

2 cups bread flour
1 cup whole wheat flour
1½ teaspoons salt
1 tablespoon vital wheat gluten
2 tablespoons dry milk powder
4 tablespoons whole flaxseeds
3 tablespoons raw, hulled sunflower
seeds
2 tablespoons chia seeds or poppy
seeds
2 tablespoons olive oil
2 tablespoons honey or agave
nectar
1½ cups water (80 degrees)
2 teaspoons active dry yeast

Add the ingredients to the bread machine in the order suggested by your bread machine manufacturer. Select the basic cycle, medium crust setting. The time-bake feature can be used.

Check the dough after 5 minutes. The dough should form a soft ball around the kneading blade. If the dough is too wet, add 1 tablespoon of flour at a time. If the dough is too dry, add 1 tablespoon of water at a time until the dough forms a soft ball around the kneading blade.

When the cycle is done, remove the bread from the machine and let it cool on a wire rack.

Brown-and-Serve Wheat Rolls

"This roll recipe is unusual because the rolls can be made ahead of time, parbaked, and frozen. Whenever you want to serve fresh, hot rolls, they can be baked for about ten minutes and served. I included about half white whole wheat flour for flavor and nutrition. These rolls are amazingly light.— Cindy Falk, nutrition educator, Kansas Wheat, Onaga

MAKES 4 DOZEN ROLLS

3 cups white whole wheat flour
2 (¼-ounce) packages fast-rising
    instant yeast
½ cup sugar
2½ teaspoons salt

1½ cups 2 percent low-fat milk
1½ cups water
½ cup (1 stick) butter

2 large eggs, beaten
5½ to 6 cups bread flour, divided

In a mixer bowl, combine the white whole wheat flour, undissolved yeast, sugar, and salt.

Heat the milk, water, and butter in a saucepan over medium heat until very warm (120 to 130 degrees). For best results, check the temperature with a thermometer. The butter does not need to melt completely. Add the milk mixture to the dry ingredients and beat with a mixer for 2 minutes at medium speed, scraping the sides of the bowl.

Add the eggs and 2 cups of the bread flour and beat for 2 minutes, scraping the bowl. Gradually mix in enough additional bread flour to make a soft dough.

Knead the dough by hand on a lightly floured surface, or with a stand mixer fitted with a dough hook, for 10 to 12 minutes. Cover the dough and let rest for 10 minutes.

Divide the dough into three equal portions. Divide one portion of the dough into fifteen (1.5-ounce) pieces. Shape into 1-inch balls. Place them smooth side up in a greased 13 × 9-inch baking pan, about ½ inch apart. As you work, cover the dough that is not being shaped so it does not dry out. Cover the rolls and let rise in a warm place (80 to 90 degrees) until doubled in size, 45 to 60 minutes. Continue shaping the remaining dough, filling two more 13 × 9-inch baking pans, or extra pans if needed.

Parbake the rolls in a 300-degree oven for 20 to 25 minutes, or until they are set and just starting to change color. Cool them in the pans for 10 minutes. Transfer the rolls to a wire baking rack and cool completely.

Place the rolls in plastic storage or freezer bags, label, and date. Store in refrigerator up to 1 to 2 days, or in the freezer up to 1 month.

To finish baking the rolls, defrost frozen rolls at room temperature for about 1 hour. Refrigerated rolls can go directly into the preheated oven. Place the rolls on a baking sheet and bake in a 400-degree oven until golden brown, about 10 minutes.

Ann's Caramel-Walnut Cinnamon Rolls

My mother, Ann Amos, loves to bake these heavenly cinnamon rolls and generously gives them to our family and friends. The glistening caramel and nut topping is showy and irresistible. We enjoy her rolls for breakfast or as a dessert with a cup of coffee or tea. They are a favorite to serve guests during the holiday season. If you are lucky enough to taste my mom's cinnamon rolls and let her know you liked them, you may be added to her list when she prepares the next batch. Can't wait? Neither could we! I coaxed her into sharing her recipe. —Jayni

MAKES 18 TO 20 ROLLS

Yeast Dough:
2 (¼-ounce) packages fast-rising instant yeast
½ teaspoon sugar
⅓ cup lukewarm water

1 cup milk
½ cup sugar
1 teaspoon salt
½ cup vegetable oil
2 eggs, beaten
2 cups unbleached all-purpose flour, plus additional flour (up to 2½ cups more)
½ teaspoon baking powder

Filling:
1 cup firmly packed brown sugar
½ cup granulated sugar
2 tablespoons cinnamon
½ cup butter, melted

Topping:
6 tablespoons butter, melted
½ cup firmly packed brown sugar
2 cups walnuts, broken or coarsely chopped

CONTINUED ➡

Yeast Dough: In a measuring cup, dissolve the yeast and ½ teaspoon sugar in the warm water. Set aside.

Pour the milk into a measuring cup and heat in a microwave oven on full power for 1½ to 2 minutes, until hot and steamy, but not boiling. Or, heat the milk in a small saucepan over medium-high heat. Pour the hot milk into a large bowl and stir the sugar and salt until dissolved and the milk has cooled to warm. Stir in the oil. Blend in the beaten eggs. Add the dissolved yeast. In a separate bowl, combine 2 cups of flour and the baking powder. Add the flour mixture to the wet ingredients, beating with a wooden spoon until smooth. Gradually add additional flour (1½ to 2½ cups more) to form a soft dough that can be easily handled.

Place the dough in an oiled bowl and turn to grease the top. Cover with a warm, wet tea towel and let rise until doubled in size, 45 minutes to 1 hour. Punch down the dough and

divide it in half. Cover with a dry tea towel and let rest for 10 minutes. Meanwhile, make the filling and prepare the topping.

Filling: Combine the brown sugar, granulated sugar, and cinnamon. Stir in the melted butter and set aside.

Topping: Pour 3 tablespoons of the melted butter into the bottom of each of the two 9½-inch round baking dishes, about 1½ inches deep. Sprinkle half of the brown sugar over the butter in each baking dish, and top each with half of the nuts. Set aside.

Roll out half of the rested dough on a lightly floured surface into a rectangle, approximately 15 × 11 inches. Spread half of the filling on the dough, 1 inch from the edges. Start with a long side and roll up the dough evenly and tightly. Slice the roll into 1½-inch-thick slices (nine or ten rolls) and arrange them in one of the prepared baking dishes with a little space between them. Repeat with the remaining dough and filling. Cover each batch of rolls with a dry tea towel and let rise until doubled in size, 30 to 45 minutes.

Bake the rolls in a 350-degree oven for 25 to 30 minutes, until golden brown. Remove the rolls from the oven and let rest for 2 minutes before removing them from the baking dishes. To remove the rolls, place a plate on top of one batch of rolls and carefully invert the baking dish to release them. Gently slide the rolls off the plate and onto a baking rack to cool. Repeat with the second batch of rolls.

Serve warm, or heat for a few seconds in a microwave oven before serving.

Variation: Whole pecans can be used in place of the walnuts. Arrange the pecans with their top sides down in the baking dish for the best presentation.

Tip: To freeze baked rolls, place them in freezer-proof storage bags or containers. The rolls freeze well for 1 month. Thaw in the refrigerator. To serve, reheat them in a microwave oven for a few seconds.

Pepperoni and Pineapple Pizza with Pesto-Cheese Topping

Even with all the grab-and-go pizza choices available, we still prefer to make our own crust and pizza sauce. We love pepperoni for the main topping, but adding a few bits of fresh pineapple and mixing some pesto into the cheese really makes the flavors pop.—Frank and Jayni

MAKES 2 (16-INCH) PIZZAS

Pizza Dough:
2 (¼-ounce) packages fast-rising instant yeast
⅛ teaspoon sugar
½ cup warm water
3½ cups all-purpose flour
1 teaspoon salt
¼ cup olive oil
½ to 1 cup ice water

Pizza Sauce:
4 cups fresh tomatoes, peeled, seeded, and chopped (juices included), or 1 (28-ounce) can diced tomatoes
2 tablespoons olive oil
2 or 3 garlic cloves, finely chopped
1 tablespoon fresh chopped basil, or 1 teaspoon dried basil
1 teaspoon dried oregano
¼ teaspoon sugar
⅛ teaspoon salt
⅛ teaspoon crushed red pepper

Cornmeal, for dusting pizza pan
6 ounces pepperoni slices
⅔ cup fresh or canned pineapple, chopped into small pieces
12 ounces mozzarella or Monterey jack cheese, shredded
3 tablespoons pesto sauce, homemade or purchased

CONTINUED ➡

To make pizza dough in a food processor: In a measuring cup, dissolve the yeast and sugar in ½ cup of warm water. Place the dough blade in a food processor bowl. Add the flour and salt to the bowl and pulse a few times to mix. Add the dissolved yeast mixture and the olive oil. Close the lid and turn on the food processor. Very slowly add ½ to 1 cup of ice water through the feed tube, just until the dough forms a ball. Do not let the dough become too wet. Let the processor knead the dough for about 15 seconds. Stop the processor, turn the dough over, and process for 15 seconds more. If the dough should become excessively warm during this process, stop and allow it to cool down before continuing. The dough should be smooth and elastic. Place the dough in a lightly greased bowl and turn once to grease the top. Cover and let rise in a warm place until doubled in size, 45 minutes to 1 hour. While the dough is rising, prepare the pizza sauce and toppings.

Pizza Sauce: Place the fresh or canned tomatoes in a blender and blend for a few seconds until the tomatoes are mostly smooth. Set aside. Heat the olive oil over medium-low heat in a saucepan. Add the garlic and cook for 1 minute, or until softened, but not browned.

Add the blended tomatoes, basil, oregano, sugar, salt, and crushed red pepper. Simmer the sauce, uncovered, over low heat for about 10 minutes, or until slightly thickened. Cool to warm or room temperature before using. Makes 2½ to 3 cups of pizza sauce.

When the dough has risen, punch it down, divide it in half, and form it into two balls. Cover the dough balls with a towel and let rest for 10 minutes. Place an oven rack on the lowest rung in the oven. Preheat the oven to 500 degrees.

To make the pizza, lightly oil a 16-inch pizza pan and sprinkle with cornmeal. Shape one ball of pizza dough into a disk by hand, then roll it out on a lightly floured surface to fit the pan. Ladle some of the sauce over the dough and smooth it evenly to cover. Arrange half of the pepperoni slices on the sauce. Scatter half of the chopped pineapple over the pizza. Combine the shredded cheese and pesto in a large bowl. Sprinkle half of the cheese and pesto mixture evenly over the top.

Place the pizza on the lowest rack in the oven and bake for 10 to 12 minutes, or until the crust is lightly browned and the cheese is bubbly. Transfer the pizza to a baking rack to cool while making the second pizza.

Homestead Pizza

You can learn a lot by making a pizza—and the kids will love it. It's one of their favorite meals, so they'll have the patience to wait while it's being prepared. Okay kids, roll up your sleeves; it'll be ready in about four days.

Four days! Why so long? Is it being delivered by stagecoach? Can't we just go to the store, buy a prepared crust and a jar of sauce? Sorry, no delivery. No store-bought ingredients. This pizza is beyond homemade; it's *homestead* made. It's a lesson not only about the ingredients, but also about where the ingredients come from.

Each day at Amy Saunders' Field-to-Table Day Camp in rural Jefferson County, the focus is on one of the pizza's ingredients. The children learn hands-on how to thresh wheat and grind it for the flour, milk a cow in order to make the cheese, pick tomatoes from the vine, dig up the onions, and snip fresh herbs for the sauce.

"All the while, the children are learning about the farm and being a caregiver to the animals and the land," Amy says. "The reward for their effort is one of kids' most favorite meals—pizza!" The lessons learned are equally nourishing.

"When I first started Amy's Meats in 2002, my husband and I quickly realized that education was a large part of what we did when selling at our farmers' market booth. At the time, we only sold naturally raised Angus beef, which contains no added hormones. Since then, we've added two kids, bought our own place, and I ventured into the world of homesteading. I am now able to farm with a diverse cross section of animals and veggies, offering our own version of a CSA and educational classes on site. I love to share the experience of farm life with people of all ages, allowing children to hold their first kitten, create foods they have only seen purchased, and taste the amazing simplicity of fresh, warm bread and butter."

Amy continues, "My goal is to show how easy it is to create foods we all love from foods we can all grow, harvest, and preserve."

On the last day of the camp, it's time to make Homestead Pizza. The kids gather around while Amy measures out the ingredients:

1¼ cups warm water
2 teaspoons active dry yeast
1 tablespoon honey
2 teaspoons sea salt
3 tablespoons olive oil
2 cups all-purpose flour
2 cups whole wheat flour

Amy makes the dough in her well-seasoned, hand-carved wooden bread bowl purchased at the farmers' market. "If you've never had the pleasure of using a bread bowl, you must try it!" she says, dissolving the yeast in warm water and the freshly harvested Bees In The Meadow Honey. She lets the liquid rest in a warm place for 10 minutes, until it is bubbly and smells yeasty.

Amy adds the sea salt and olive oil and slowly stirs in the all-purpose flour and the whole wheat flour. The whole wheat was raised and freshly ground at the Homestead. She continues stirring the mixture with her favorite wooden spoon and, holding it up with admiration, says, "My son carved it from wood from our land." The dough comes together into a soft blob, but is still slightly sticky to the touch.

"A great part of this recipe is that by passing the bowl around, the children can all have a turn with adding and mixing," Amy explains, sprinkling the flour over the dough and around the bowl. She then kneads the dough in the bread bowl for about 10 minutes. When all dough is collected, she re-oils the bowl, making sure to swipe the dough ball through the bowl, covering it with oil.

She covers the bowl with a damp tea towel and lets the dough rise until double in volume, about 1½ to 2 hours.

Amy cuts the dough into quarters and sprinkles a flour and cornmeal mixture over paper plates to allow the children to shape their own pizzas. One could also roll out all the dough to make a single large pizza.

To assemble the pizza, the children start by spreading on the tomato sauce made from fresh tomatoes, onions, and herbs collected from the garden. Next, they layer the pizza with fresh cheeses made from the Jersey cow everyone learned to milk the day before. They finish by garnishing with additional freshly picked veggies from the Homestead's heirloom garden. Amy lets the pizzas rise for 15 minutes before baking them in a preheated 400-degree oven for 20 minutes, or until the cheese is bubbly and golden.

"Sometimes the children's creations may take longer to bake if the dough is thicker. Whole and personal pizzas are fantastic grilled, too!" she says. "Slice the pizza and let it cool before eating. A burned mouth ruins the rest of the experience!"

Pizza with Apple, Marinated Red Onion, and Bacon

Hungry for a new twist on pizza? Try this one! Thin slices of sweet-tart apple and thinly sliced and marinated red onion sit on a bed of rich and creamy cheese. A final garnish of crumbled bacon adds just the right touch of smoke and salt. Serve this pizza anytime, including breakfast.—Frank and Jayni

MAKES 1 (16-INCH) PIZZA

Pizza Dough:
1 (¼-ounce) package fast-rising instant yeast
Pinch of sugar
⅓ cup warm water
1¾ cups all-purpose flour
½ teaspoon salt
2 tablespoons olive oil
¼ to ½ cup ice water

Marinated Red Onion:
½ small red onion, about 4 ounces
1 tablespoon red wine vinegar
Pinch of salt
2 tablespoons olive oil

4 bacon strips

2 medium tart apples (Jonathan apples preferred), cored and thinly sliced
2 tablespoons olive oil

6 ounces Gruyère cheese, shredded

To make pizza dough in a food processor, dissolve the yeast and sugar in a measuring cup with ⅓ cup of warm water. Place the dough blade in the food processor bowl. Add the flour and salt to the bowl and pulse a few times to mix. Add the dissolved yeast mixture and the olive oil. Close the lid and turn on the food processor. Very slowly add ¼ to ½ cup of ice water through the feed tube, just until the dough forms a ball. Do not let the dough become too wet. Let the processor knead the dough for about 15 seconds. Stop the processor, turn the dough over, and process for 15 seconds more. If the dough should become excessively warm during this process, stop and allow it to cool down before continuing. The dough should be smooth and elastic. Place the dough in a lightly greased bowl and turn once to grease the top. Cover and let rise in a warm place until doubled in size, 45 minutes to 1 hour. While the dough is rising, prepare the toppings.

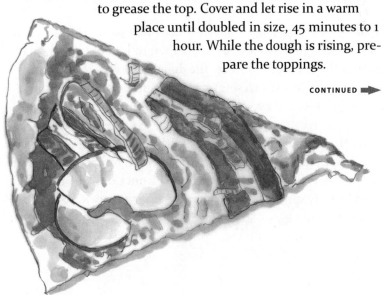

CONTINUED ➡

Marinated Red Onion: Thinly slice the onion. Put the slices in a wire-mesh strainer and rinse under cold running water. Drain well. Place the sliced onion in a bowl. In a separate bowl, whisk together the vinegar, salt, and olive oil. Pour over the sliced onion and toss to coat. Let stand at room temperature 30 minutes or more before using.

Fry the bacon in a large skillet over medium heat until crispy. Drain on paper towels and chop or crumble into small pieces.

Just before rolling out the pizza dough, place the apple slices in a microwave-safe bowl and toss with 2 tablespoons of olive oil. Microwave the slices on full power for 1 minute, turn them over, and microwave for 30 seconds to 1 minute more, just until the apples slices soften slightly. Cool briefly.

When the dough has risen, punch it down and form it into a ball. Cover the dough ball with a towel and let rest for 10 minutes. Place an oven rack on the lowest rung in the oven. Preheat the oven to 500 degrees.

To make the pizza, lightly oil a 16-inch pizza pan. Shape the ball of pizza dough into a disk by hand, then roll it out to fit the pan. Scatter the cheese evenly over the dough. Arrange the apple slices on the cheese in a single layer. Drain the marinade from the onion slices and scatter them over the apple slices.

Place the pizza on the lowest rack in the oven and bake for 10 to 12 minutes, until the crust is lightly browned on the bottom and the cheese is bubbly. Remove the pizza from the oven and immediately sprinkle the chopped bacon over top. Slice and serve immediately.

Chapter 10
Breakfast and Brunch

The morning meal deserves some recognition for its lavishness. Ignore the cold cereal and the gas station doughnut. We're talking about the meal where you're coaxed from bed by the smell of sizzling sausage, buttery baked biscuits, and freshly brewed coffee. The ingredients may be common and fundamental, but the luxury lies in the pace and comfort. Is there a better way to be awakened?

Kansans love the tradition of the classic farm breakfast with its generous portions of potatoes, ham, and eggs. In this chapter, you'll find recipes for breakfasts that stick to your ribs and wake up your senses. Our recipe for "Ham, Potato, and Egg Stacks" will satisfy the desire for a traditional farm breakfast. For a spicy wake-me-up, try the one-pan meal, "Chorizo Skillet Breakfast." After the rooster crows, why not start your day with our twist on a breakfast classic, "Frank's Biscuits and Jayni's Italian Sausage Gravy"?

Brunch, on the other hand, is the manufactured word for melding two meals, breakfast and lunch, into one. Though the origin of this mash-up is uncertain, speculation suggests the collision of early-rising churchgoers preferring Sunday dinner with late-rising revelers desiring eggs for their noon meal. To address these intermingling demands, cooks began to cross-pollinate recipes in order to satisfy the appetites of both the wide-eyed and the drowsy.

The brunch menu usually offers dishes both savory and sweet. If eggs are a must on the menu, try "Sausage, Red Pepper, and Sweet Corn Frittata." For something sweet, serve your guests "Signature Scones," "Banana Muffins with Brown Sugar-Walnut Topping," or "Chocolate Waffles." For those who prefer the lunch side of brunch, try "Stovetop Smoked Trout with Cucumber-Dill Sauce" and, for the adventurous, a baking dish full of "Cheddar Apples with Buttery Beer Drizzle." If you think political unrest might break out at your gathering, "Bipartisan Chicken Salad" is the recipe for you.

Ham, Potato, and Egg Stacks

The family will rise and shine for this hearty farm-style meal-in-one breakfast! A slice of seared ham, stacked with fried potatoes and topped with a poached egg, then drizzled with a mustard vinaigrette, is worth waking up for.—Frank and Jayni

4 SERVINGS

2 tablespoons olive oil
12 ounces potatoes, peeled and cut
    into ½-inch dice
½ cup onion, finely chopped
Salt and black pepper, to taste
1 garlic clove, finely chopped

Mustard Vinaigrette:
2 tablespoons red wine vinegar
½ teaspoon Dijon mustard
⅛ teaspoon salt
Black pepper, to taste
3 tablespoons extra-virgin olive oil

4 eggs

2 teaspoons olive oil
4 ham slices, about ¼-inch thick

1 medium tomato chopped, or ½
    cup cherry tomatoes, halved

Heat the olive oil in a nonstick skillet over medium-low heat. Add the diced potatoes and onion, and season with salt and pepper. Fry the mixture, turning often, until the potatoes are tender and golden. Add the garlic during the last 2 minutes of cooking. While the potatoes are cooking, make the mustard vinaigrette.

Mustard Vinaigrette: In a small bowl, combine the red wine vinegar, Dijon mustard, salt, and pepper. Whisk in the olive oil. Set aside.

Fill a deep pot with water and bring to a boil over high heat. Add the eggs to the boiling water, two at a time, and poach them for about 2½ minutes. Remove the eggs from the pot with a slotted spoon and place on a warm plate.

Heat 2 teaspoons of olive oil in a skillet over medium heat. Add the ham slices and sear for about 1 minute on each side.

To serve, place a seared ham slice in the center of each plate. Stack some of the fried potatoes on top of the ham. Place a poached egg on top of the potatoes. Garnish each with the chopped tomato. Drizzle each stack with some of the mustard vinaigrette.

Variations: Substitute your favorite salsa for the mustard vinaigrette. Or, to serve as a brunch item, place each stack on a bed of chopped romaine lettuce leaves or arugula dressed with the mustard vinaigrette.

Egg Slips

The Bauman family purchased their farm near Garnett in 2001. To date, the farm supports and employs three generations, with the next generation on the way. They raise grass-fed beef and poultry, including chickens, ducks, and turkeys. The farm grows non-GMO grains such as corn, soybeans, oats, barley, and wheat to feed their poultry a healthy diet.

The Baumans also have laying hens, and the eggs are sold in surrounding areas from Garnett to Lawrence. When you purchase a dozen eggs from Bauman's Cedar Valley Farms you get a little something extra. No, it's not an extra egg; it's more like the message you find in a fortune cookie. Rosanna Bauman calls them "egg slips." The egg slips aren't intended to give you a glimpse into the future, but you do get something that is likely to bring you pleasure—a peek into Kansas farm life. "We wanted to find a way to let people know they are

purchasing eggs from a small family farm," Rosanna explains. "Another farmer suggested the idea, and now our customers look forward to the egg slips, so the tradition continues."

Over the years, we have saved a few favorite egg slips as if they are dispatches from the farm. We often post them on our refrigerator to share with others. One egg slip welcomes Roper, the new Lab puppy, into the Bauman family. It describes how he has adjusted to his new life as a farm dog, including the thrill of riding in the truck bed.

Our favorite egg slip, entitled "Goodbye Grandpa," is insightful and joyful, yet bittersweet. It reads, "For the past year, our family has been privileged to experience life in a three-generation household. Our maternal grandma moved in so that we could help her care for [Grandpa] after his strokes. A lifelong farmer, he enjoyed spending his days on a busy farm and watching his grandchildren's

farming endeavors. To his delight, the boys repaired and restored his old Ford tractor. It was a comfort to him to see his descendants utilizing the skills and knowledge that he had cultivated. We enjoyed hearing more of his life's story around the supper table, because grandparents' stories are important. Sadly, a massive stroke took his life this week. Thankfully, all of his children were in attendance at his death and we all got to say goodbye. There's an empty spot in our home, and a bigger one in our hearts. —The Baumans, less one."

Chorizo Skillet Breakfast

¡Buenos días! This tasty Mexican breakfast in a skillet will feed a family of four and keep preparation time for breakfast to a minimum. Though simple to make, it can also serve as an eye-catching good-morning breakfast for overnight guests. Chances are, you can find locally made fresh chorizo at your local butcher shop or supermarket.—Frank and Jayni

4 SERVINGS

3 tablespoons olive or canola oil
1 pound potatoes, peeled and diced
1 cup onion, diced
1 Anaheim green chile, seeded and finely chopped
Salt and black pepper, to taste

1 pound fresh Mexican chorizo

4 eggs
½ cup pepper jack cheese, shredded

Salsa
Corn or flour tortillas, warmed

Heat the oil in a large nonstick skillet over medium heat. Add the diced potatoes, onion, and green chile, and season with salt and pepper. Fry, turning often, until the potatoes are lightly browned and tender. Reduce the heat if needed to prevent burning. Set aside.

In a large (oven-safe) cast iron or stainless steel skillet, fry the chorizo over medium heat, breaking it up as it cooks. Spoon off most of the excess fat, leaving the chorizo in the skillet.

Spoon the potato mixture over the chorizo and stir gently to combine. Using the back of a large spoon, make four holes in the potato and chorizo mixture to accommodate the eggs. Crack the eggs, one at a time, into a custard cup, then pour each egg into one of the holes. Season the eggs with salt and pepper. Sprinkle the shredded cheese on and around the eggs.

Place the skillet in a 375-degree oven 5 to 6 minutes, or until the eggs are set. Cut into four portions and serve with salsa and warm tortillas.

Frank's Biscuits and Jayni's Italian Sausage Gravy

When it comes to making biscuits and gravy, we're a team. Jayni makes the sausage gravy, while I bake a batch of biscuits. She prefers hot Italian sausage for a spicy gravy and, to make it more tender, simmers the browned sausage in a little chicken broth before adding the milk. The broth enhances the flavor and turns the gravy an appetizing golden-brown color. To keep up with Jayni's upgrade, I've added some sour cream to my recipe for basic biscuits to give them a rich and moist interior.—Frank

8 SERVINGS

Italian Sausage Gravy:
2 tablespoons butter
½ cup onion, finely chopped
1 pound Italian sausage, hot or mild
½ cup chicken broth
3 tablespoons unbleached
    all-purpose flour
3 cups milk
Salt and black pepper, to taste

Biscuits:
1½ cups unbleached all-purpose
    flour
2 teaspoons baking powder
¼ teaspoon salt
2 teaspoons sugar
2 tablespoons cold butter, cubed
¼ cup vegetable shortening, chilled
1 tablespoon sour cream
½ cup milk

Italian Sausage Gravy: Melt the butter in a large skillet or braising pan over medium-low heat. Add the onion and cook until tender, stirring frequently. Raise the heat to medium and add the sausage, breaking it up into small pieces with a spatula or a large wooden spoon. Cook the sausage until browned. Add the chicken broth and simmer over medium-low heat, stirring occasionally, until the liquid is completely absorbed, 8 to 10 minutes. Sprinkle the flour over the sausage and stir for 2 to 3 minutes to cook the flour. Raise the heat to medium, stir in the milk and scrape up the brown bits on the bottom of the skillet. When the gravy begins to simmer, reduce the heat to low and cook slowly, stirring occasionally, for 10 minutes. Season the gravy with salt and pepper. Prepare the biscuits while the sausage gravy is simmering.

Biscuits: Sift the flour, baking powder, salt, and sugar together in a medium bowl. Cut in the butter and shortening using a pastry blender until the mixture is crumbly. Add the sour cream and the milk, and stir just until the mixture is moist. Do not over-mix. Place the dough on a lightly floured surface. Knead lightly, until the dough can be formed into a ball. Add more flour, if necessary, to keep the dough from becoming too sticky to handle. Pat the dough into a circle about ½ inch thick. Cut into biscuits with a 2-inch biscuit or cookie cutter. Re-form the dough in order to cut more biscuits. There should be eight biscuits.

Place the biscuits on an ungreased baking sheet and bake in a 450-degree oven for 12 to 14 minutes. To serve, split the biscuits in half and top with sausage gravy.

Option: For larger biscuits, pat the dough into a circle about ¾ inch thick and cut into five biscuits.

Variation: Serve fried or poached eggs on top of each serving of biscuits and gravy.

Sausage, Red Pepper, and Sweet Corn Frittata

The frittata, also known as an Italian omelet, is the tastiest way to provide an egg dish for a brunch. A frittata is fun to make because it gives the cook creative license to choose the ingredients for the egg base. Our favorite frittata includes locally made sausage and peppers and sweet corn from the farmers in our community.—Frank and Jayni

8 SERVINGS

12 eggs
¼ teaspoon salt
¼ teaspoon black pepper

1 ear sweet corn

1 tablespoon butter
1 tablespoon olive oil
1 small onion, cut in half, thinly
    sliced
1 cup red bell pepper, seeded and
    diced
8 ounces pork sausage
1 cup shredded sharp cheddar
    cheese, divided

1 to 2 tablespoons fresh chives,
    chopped

CONTINUED ➡

Break the eggs into a large bowl. Add the salt and pepper and whisk to blend. Set aside.

Trim the dried tassel off the ear of corn, but do not shuck it. Place the ear in a microwave oven and cook on full power for 1 minute. Turn the ear over and cook for 1 minute more. Let the ear rest for 3 to 5 minutes in the microwave, or on the countertop. Hold the warm ear with a tea towel or paper towels to shuck. Grasping the leaves and silks together with your fingers as you shuck them will help to get all the silks off easily. Cut the kernels off the cob using a sharp knife. Measure ½ cup of kernels.

Preheat the oven to 350 degrees. Heat the butter and olive oil over medium-low heat in a 12-inch (oven-safe) cast iron skillet, stainless steel skillet, or sauté pan. Add the onion and red pepper and cook until tender, 10 to 12 minutes, stirring frequently. Transfer the mixture to a bowl. Raise the heat to medium and add the sausage to the skillet, breaking it up as it cooks. Remove the skillet from the heat and drain the excess fat. Spread the sausage evenly in the skillet. Return the onion and pepper mixture to the skillet. Scatter the corn kernels over the mixture, then top with half of the shredded cheese.

Place the skillet over medium-high heat and pour in the beaten eggs. Top with the remaining cheese. Do not stir. Cook for about 3 minutes until the eggs are set on the bottom and around the edges of the skillet. Place the skillet in the oven and cook for 8 to 10 minutes. The frittata is set when the center jiggles slightly as the skillet is shaken gently.

Remove the skillet from the oven, garnish the frittata with chopped chives, and let stand for 5 to 10 minutes before serving. Slice into eight wedges to serve.

Option: Though the frittata is often served warm from the oven, it is also delicious served cold or room temperature for lunch paired with a soup or salad.

Stovetop Smoked Trout with Cucumber-Dill Sauce

The trout in Kansas's waters like it cold, and if you're angling for them, you'd better dress warm. Trout are stocked between November 1 and April 15 in about thirty sites around the state. For an easy catch—but perhaps not as much fun—hike over to your local supermarket for some farm-raised trout fillets. In this recipe, we add a campfire flavor to this mild fish by using a stovetop smoker; you can also fashion your own from an old Dutch oven. Serve the smoked trout as part of a brunch buffet, or with eggs and hash browns for breakfast.—Frank

8 TO 10 SERVINGS

Cucumber-Dill Sauce:
1 small cucumber
1 cup sour cream
½ cup mayonnaise
2 teaspoons lemon juice, or more
    to taste
2 teaspoons fresh dill, chopped, or
    1 teaspoon dried dill
¼ teaspoon sugar, or more to taste
¼ teaspoon salt, or more to taste

2 trout fillets, about 6 ounces each
Vegetable oil
Salt and black pepper
6 fresh tarragon sprigs, plus extra
    for garnish

Heavy-duty aluminum foil
¼ cup apple wood smoking chips,
    small pieces

Cucumber-Dill Sauce: Peel the cucumber and cut it in half, lengthwise. Using a spoon, scoop out most of the seeds. Cut the cucumber into small dice and measure ½ cup. Reserve any remaining cucumber for another use. Place the diced cucumber in a blender, add the sour cream and mayonnaise, and blend until smooth. Pour the mixture into a bowl and add the lemon juice, dill, sugar, and salt. Cover and refrigerate the sauce for at least 2 hours to allow the flavors to develop.

Pat the trout fillets dry with paper towels. Brush a large piece of aluminum foil with vegetable oil and lay the fillets, skin side down, on the foil. Season the flesh side with salt and pepper and lay three tarragon sprigs on each fillet. Set aside while you prepare the stovetop smoker.

CONTINUED ➡

Follow the manufacturer's directions for your stovetop smoker or fashion your own by placing a piece of aluminum foil in the bottom of a cast iron or stainless steel Dutch oven, or other large heavy-bottomed pot with a lid. The pot should be large enough to lay the fillets flat in a single layer. Place the apple wood smoking chips (small pieces work best) on the foil. Cover the pot and heat over high heat until the wood smolders, about 5 to 10 minutes.

Place the foil sheet with the fillets directly on top of the smoldering wood chips. Cover the pot and reduce the heat to low. Cook the fillets for 8 to 10 minutes until the flesh is opaque and can be flaked with a fork, or the internal temperature reaches 125 degrees. Note: To avoid smoke in the kitchen, turn on a kitchen exhaust fan while smoking the fish fillets, or smoke them outdoors on the side burner of a gas grill.

Lift out the foil holding the fillets from the pot and place it on a cutting board or the countertop. To serve the fillets without the skin, carefully insert a large, metal spatula between the flesh and the skin of each fillet to remove the skin. Transfer the fillets to a serving dish and replace the wilted tarragon sprigs with fresh tarragon sprigs for garnish. Pour the cucumber-dill sauce into a small decorative bowl and place alongside the smoked trout.

Bipartisan Chicken Salad

This simple chicken salad, filled with fruit and nuts and served on lettuce leaves, is a welcome addition to any brunch menu, regardless of your political affiliation.

"I call this recipe 'bipartisan' because I am a Democrat and have adapted this recipe shared by a dear Republican friend and neighbor, now deceased."—Barbara Watkins, Lawrence

4 TO 6 SERVINGS

2 cups cooked chicken, chopped
1 cup seedless red or green grapes (or mixed)
1 large orange
3 small or 2 large celery ribs, cut in half lengthwise and thinly sliced
2 green onions (including some green tops), thinly sliced
½ cup black or English walnut pieces

3 to 4 tablespoons of bottled honey mustard dressing, or more to taste
Salt and black pepper, to taste

Lettuce leaves

Place the chopped chicken in a large bowl. Cut the grapes in half and add them to the bowl. Peel the orange, cut into sections, and cut each section into thirds. Add the orange pieces to the bowl along with the sliced celery, green onions, and the walnut pieces.

To dress the salad, gently fold in 3 or 4 tablespoons of honey mustard dressing, taste and add more, if needed. Season lightly with salt and pepper. Cover and refrigerate for at least 2 hours before serving.

To serve, place a few lettuce leaves on the plates and top with some of the chicken salad.

Variation: In place of the honey mustard dressing, combine ⅓ cup of mayonnaise and 2 tablespoons of sour cream, and stir into the salad.

Cheddar Apples with Buttery Beer Drizzle

"We're so lucky here in Kansas to have local sources for everything in this dish, from the apples and beer to the butter and cheese—even the honey and nuts! Of course, the flavors here scream fall and winter, but the recipe also works well in summer with lighter beer, like a pilsner or wheat. Besides for brunch, the apples make a nice appetizer or side dish, especially on a holiday table, or top a big tossed salad with two halves and call it a light meal."—Kerri Conan, freelance food writer and editor, Lawrence

12 SERVINGS

1 tablespoon butter, softened
6 crisp medium apples, red or green

1 (12-ounce bottle) flavorful beer
    (stout or pale ale)
¼ cup honey
2 tablespoons butter

6 ounces sharp white or yellow
    cheddar cheese, shredded
½ cup chopped raw pecans (op-
    tional)

Coarse sea salt, to taste
Freshly ground black pepper, to
    taste

Grease a 13 × 9-inch baking dish with the softened butter and set aside. Cut the apples in half from top to bottom. Remove the seeds and core the apple halves with a sharp spoon or melon baller, leaving a small crater in the center. Put the apples cut side down in a single layer in the prepared baking dish. Bake the apples in a 400-degree oven, undisturbed, until they are just tender enough to pierce with a knife tip, 10 to 15 minutes. Remove them from the oven.

Meanwhile, pour the beer and honey in a small saucepan and heat over medium-high heat, watching and stirring until the mixture comes to a boil, but does not overflow. Lower the heat to medium or medium-low so the mixture bubbles steadily. Cook, stirring occasionally, until the liquid reduces by half, 8 to 12 minutes. (It will lightly coat the back of a spoon when it's ready.) Remove the pan from the heat, add 2 tablespoons of butter, and stir until it melts.

Turn the apples over and pour the beer glaze over them all, filling all the craters as well as

possible. Top the apples with the cheese and the pecans, if using, then return them to the oven. Bake until the cheese is bubbly and browned in places and the liquid thickens a bit, 8 to 12 minutes. The apples should be soft but not falling apart.

Sprinkle the apples with coarse sea salt and pepper and drizzle them with some of the baking juices. Serve warm.

Signature Scones

Nutrition educator Cindy Falk says scones are a favorite because they are so quick to make. Cindy skips the traditional way of making scones with butter and cream; instead, she bakes a tasty low-fat version using Greek yogurt. She also combines white whole wheat flour with all-purpose flour for added nutrition.

"This recipe allows bakers to customize their scones by choosing a flavored Greek yogurt and their favorite fresh or dried fruit. Today, everyone—even the younger generation, who are not frequent bakers—has yogurt in the refrigerator."—Cindy Falk, nutrition educator, Kansas Wheat, Onaga

MAKES 12 SCONES

1 cup white whole wheat flour
1 cup all-purpose flour
2 teaspoons baking powder
¼ teaspoon baking soda
½ cup dried fruit or fresh fruit, chopped
2 tablespoons sugar or agave nectar
½ cup (5.3-ounce carton) nonfat Greek yogurt, flavor of choice
¼ cup vegetable oil or olive oil
¼ cup low-fat milk
1 large egg, slightly beaten

Topping:
1 tablespoon low-fat milk or whipping cream
2 teaspoons sparkling white decorating sugar or granulated sugar (optional)

In a large bowl, combine the flours, baking powder, and baking soda. Add the dried or fresh fruit, sugar or nectar, yogurt, oil, milk, and slightly beaten egg. Stir just until ingredients are combined and the dough clings together. (The mixture will be sticky. If using fresh fruit, several more tablespoons of flour may be needed.)

CONTINUED ➡

Turn the dough onto a lightly floured surface and knead lightly for a few turns. Divide the dough in half and pat into two 6-inch circles. Cut each circle into six equal wedges. Place the wedges 2 inches apart on a parchment-lined or lightly greased baking sheet.

Topping: Brush the tops of the scones with 1 tablespoon of milk or whipping cream. Sprinkle with sparkling white decorating sugar or granulated sugar, if using.

Bake the scones in a 350-degree oven for 20 to 25 minutes, or until lightly golden. Transfer the scones to a wire rack to cool. Serve warm or at room temperature.

Flavor Variations:

Double Pineapple: pineapple yogurt with ½ cup chopped dried tropical pineapple.

Lemon Ginger: lemon yogurt, 1 tablespoon grated lemon zest plus ¼ to ½ cup finely minced crystallized ginger.

Lemon Blueberry: lemon yogurt, 1 tablespoon grated lemon zest and ½ cup fresh blueberries.

Three Tractors, Three Generations

Walking with Jeff and Zelma Mead on their wheat farm near Lewis, we came upon a handsome little Caterpillar tractor resting under a shade tree near the old barn. Having tracks instead of wheels, it sat there square and solid, and though there was more rust than paint, it gave us the impression that it wouldn't take much of a spark to bring it to life.

Jeff Mead began to speak: "In 1927, my grandfather, Lawrence Jefferis, purchased his first Caterpillar tractor. This is it."

As we gathered around it, Jeff continued, "The tractor was delivered to the dealership in Kinsley, about twenty miles from here. The roads were dirt back then, so it was okay to drive on them with tracks instead of wheels." Then, with a chuckle he added, "It would only go 3¾ miles per hour in high gear. It took my grandfather all day to get home!"

Tractors were scarce during the World War II years, and in 1944 Lawrence Jefferis purchased his next tractor—a new, D 1944 John Deere. This new tractor could do six miles per hour and it had rubber tires so it could travel between the fields using the paved roads. Jeff was fourteen years old then, and his grandfather allowed him to drive the new tractor home from Kinsley. The route included an important detour. "I drove it by my school in Centerview to show all the kids," Jeff said proudly, the memory still fresh.

In 1953, Jeff and Zelma married. In 1961, Jeff made the decision to stop working at the Ford garage and begin farming his grandfather's land. Jeff's grandfather had just purchased a used 1950 Case LA tractor and gave it to Jeff. It was Jeff's first tractor and the first big tractor on the farm. "We worked the farm together," Zelma Mead says. "I could drive that tractor, but more often, I drove a truck while Jeff drove the combine." They farmed with the Case tractor for ten years before selling it to a neighbor. Years later, Jeff bought it back and restored it. He used it for tractor pulls for many years, and now that it is an antique, he proudly displays it at the Kansas State Fair.

Over the years, new and more modern tractors were purchased to keep up with their growing wheat farm. Their family was growing, too. They incorporated the farm with their son Lynn, and recently their grandson, Dustin, joined as the newest partner. We asked Jeff what he likes about the newest tractors. "They are more powerful and they move fast," he told us. Zelma added, "The GPS systems now installed on tractors make the work go more smoothly and easily. And the boys can read a

newspaper while the tractor guides itself!"

The old Caterpillar and the Case are proudly displayed on the farm as reminders of the past and their service to the land. Zelma still helps to "keep the books" for the family business. And, while Jeff still drives the tractor that pulls the grain cart during the harvest and keeps the Bad Boy mower busy, he leaves most of the work to Lynn and Dustin.

Banana Muffins with Brown Sugar-Walnut Topping

What to do with those overripe bananas? Make jumbo banana muffins! Warm muffins are a satisfying treat for brunch, breakfast, or even a bedtime snack. The addition of white whole wheat flour gives the muffins a hearty texture. Chopped walnuts are folded into the batter and more are mixed with butter, flour, brown sugar, and cinnamon for an irresistible topping.—Jayni

MAKES 12 MUFFINS

2 cups unbleached all-purpose flour
1 cup white whole wheat flour
1 tablespoon baking powder
½ teaspoon baking soda
½ teaspoon salt
½ teaspoon fresh-grated nutmeg
½ teaspoon cinnamon

½ cup butter, softened
1 cup packed light brown sugar
2 eggs
3 overripe bananas (about 1 generous cup), mashed
1 teaspoon vanilla extract
1¼ cups buttermilk
½ cup walnuts, coarsely chopped or broken

Brown Sugar-Walnut Topping:
¼ cup packed light brown sugar
¼ cup all-purpose flour
½ teaspoon cinnamon
3 tablespoons butter, chilled
¼ cup walnuts, finely chopped

Spray two, 6-cup jumbo muffin pans with cooking spray. In a large bowl, combine the flours, baking powder, baking soda, salt, nutmeg, and cinnamon. Set aside.

In a large mixing bowl, cream the butter and brown sugar with a mixer on medium-high speed until light and fluffy. Beat in the eggs, one at a time. Beat in the mashed bananas and vanilla extract. Add the buttermilk and mix well. Using a large spoon or rubber spatula, gently fold the dry ingredients and ½ cup chopped or broken walnuts into the banana mixture until all dry ingredients have been incorporated. Avoid overmixing or the muffins will be tough. Spoon the batter into the muffin cups, filling them about two-thirds full.

Brown Sugar-Walnut Topping: In a small bowl, combine the brown sugar, flour, and cinnamon. Cut in the butter using a pastry blender. Fold in the finely chopped walnuts.

Sprinkle 2 or 3 teaspoons of the topping mixture over the un-baked muffins. Bake the muffins in a 375-degree oven for 23 to 25 minutes, or until an inserted toothpick comes out with moist crumbs. Take the muffins out of the oven and let them stand for 5 minutes before removing them from the pans, taking care not to disturb the topping. Cool the muffins on a wire rack.

Chocolate Waffles

Sharon Davis says her chocolate waffle recipe is a favorite with the after-school groups to whom she teaches cooking and baking. Sharon suggests serving the waffles sprinkled with confectioner's sugar, along with a fresh fruit blend, or topped with vanilla yogurt and warmed cherries.

"This recipe is a personal favorite—very tried and true—with our family plus many Kansas kids!"
—Sharon Davis, family and consumer sciences educator, Home Baking Association, Manhattan

MAKES 12 WAFFLES

2 cups white whole wheat flour*
½ cup sugar
3 tablespoons baking cocoa
2 teaspoons baking powder
¼ teaspoon salt
½ cup chopped nuts (optional)

1½ cups low-fat milk
¼ cup unsalted butter, melted
¼ cup vegetable oil
1 teaspoon vanilla extract
2 large eggs, separated

CONTINUED ➡

To measure the white whole wheat flour, fluff the flour, spoon into a 1-cup dry measuring cup, and level off. In a medium bowl, whisk together the flour, sugar, cocoa, baking powder, and salt. Add the chopped nuts, if using. Set aside.

In a 4-cup liquid measuring cup or bowl, add the milk, melted butter, vegetable oil, and vanilla extract, and whisk to combine. Separate the eggs, reserve the whites, and add the yolks to the milk mixture. Whisk until well blended.

Put the 2 egg whites in a medium glass or metal mixing bowl. Beat them with a clean whisk or electric mixer to form stiff peaks.

Before combining all ingredients, brush the waffle irons with vegetable oil and preheat. Warm the plates in a 175-degree oven, or lowest temperature possible, to keep the waffles warm as you make them.

Stir the milk mixture into the dry ingredients just until well blended. With a large spoon, gently fold the egg whites into the batter until they disappear.

Scoop ¼ cup of batter onto each waffle iron grid, close the lid, and bake as the waffle iron instructions direct.

Serve the waffles hot with a topping of your choice.

* White whole wheat flour is preferred, but 1 cup traditional whole wheat flour plus 1 cup all-purpose flour may be substituted.

Black Walnut Coffee Cake

Barbara Watkins makes her coffee cake with a black walnut filling and topping. Black walnut trees are native to Kansas, and the nuts are appreciated for their rich, earthy flavor.

"My backyard patio is surrounded by three large black walnut trees. The squirrels and I battle for the custody of the fall harvest. This is my favorite coffee cake, and I modestly call it 'the world's best.' I serve it often for brunch with friends and family."—Barbara Watkins, Lawrence

12 SERVINGS

Black Walnut Filling and Topping:
½ cup sugar
1 teaspoon cinnamon, Vietnamese
    cinnamon preferred
½ cup black walnuts, chopped

½ cup butter, softened
1 cup sugar
2 eggs
1 cup sour cream
2 teaspoons vanilla extract

2 cups all-purpose flour
1 teaspoon baking powder
1 teaspoon baking soda
¼ teaspoon salt

Black Walnut Filling and Topping: Combine the sugar, cinnamon, and chopped black walnuts. Set aside.

Place the softened butter in a large mixing bowl. Add 1 cup of sugar and, using a mixer, cream until light and fluffy. Beat in the eggs, one at a time. Blend in the sour cream and vanilla extract.

Sift together the flour, baking powder, baking soda, and salt. Stir the dry ingredients into the batter until smooth.

Spoon half of the batter into a greased and floured 9-inch baking pan. Sprinkle about two-thirds of the walnut filling and topping mixture over the batter. Spoon the remaining batter into the pan. Top with the remaining walnut mixture.

Bake the coffee cake in a 325-degree oven for 40 to 45 minutes, or until a cake tester or toothpick inserted in the center comes out with moist crumbs.

Variation: English walnuts may be used in place of black walnuts in this recipe.

Purple Pride Quick Bread

Cynthia Falk created this recipe for K-State fans, and it makes a tasty treat for tailgate parties. This one-bowl quick bread recipe is easy enough for beginner bakers. One bite of this purple-colored sweet treat will have K-State fans cheering!—Cindy Falk, nutrition educator, Kansas Wheat, Onaga

16 SERVINGS

1 large egg
½ cup sugar
1 cup 2 percent low-fat milk
3 tablespoons unsalted butter, softened
½ teaspoon salt
3 teaspoons baking powder
2¼ cups all-purpose flour
1 teaspoon orange or lemon zest
½ cup fresh blueberries

2 tablespoons granulated or sparkling white sugar (optional)

Spray the bottom of an 8½ × 4½-inch loaf pan with nonstick cooking spray and set aside.

In a large mixing bowl, whisk the egg. Stir in the sugar, milk, softened butter, salt, baking powder, flour, and orange or lemon zest. Mix just until the dry ingredients are moistened. Blend in the blueberries. Spread the batter in the prepared loaf pan.

If desired, sprinkle 2 tablespoons granulated or sparkling white sugar on top of the batter. Bake the quick bread in a 375-degree oven for 50 to 55 minutes, or until a toothpick inserted in the center of the bread comes out clean. Cool for 10 minutes. Carefully remove the bread from the pan. Slice and serve warm, fresh from the oven.

Tip: Another way to test for doneness is by checking the internal temperature with a food thermometer. Quick bread should reach 210 degrees when done.

Reece's Sweet Cornbread

Ron and Sharyna Reece were ecstatic at the idea of opening a restaurant and expanding on their passion for cooking, serving, and sharing their favorite dishes with others. In 2012, these longtime caterers opened Reece's Cafe in Alden.

"This recipe is not a traditional cornbread recipe—it's sweet and more like cake. It took a lot of testing over the years to get it just right, but it's oh-so-good and a perfect pairing with just about any entrée! We serve it every Sunday at the cafe due to popular demand."—Sharyna Reece, Reece's Cafe, Alden

24 SERVINGS

6 eggs
1½ cups milk
1½ cups half and half
¾ cup canola or vegetable oil

3¾ cups all-purpose flour
2¼ cups cornmeal
2 tablespoons baking powder
2½ cups sugar
1 teaspoon ground cinnamon
1½ teaspoons salt

1 tablespoon butter

Preheat the oven to 350 degrees. Spray an 11 × 15-inch baking pan with nonstick cooking spray and set aside.

In a large mixing bowl, add the eggs, milk, half and half, and oil and whisk until well combined.

In a separate large bowl, combine the flour, cornmeal, baking powder, sugar, cinnamon, and salt. Add the dry ingredients all at once to the wet ingredients and mix with a large spoon until smooth.

Pour the mixture into the prepared baking pan and bake for 30 to 35 minutes, until the center springs back when touched, or an inserted toothpick comes out clean. Butter the top of the corn-bread and serve warm.

Option: This recipe can also be prepared as muffins.

Variation: The following ingredients can be added to the corn-bread or corn muffins: corn kernels, grated cheese, diced jalapeño peppers, or salsa of choice.

Chapter 11
Refrigerator Pickling, Condiments, and Marinades

Refrigerator pickling a jar or two of a favorite vegetable, making a flavorful condiment, or marinating vegetables in the refrigerator doesn't have to be difficult and time consuming. The key is to make small batches.

Most cooks today don't have the time to put up bushels of vegetables and process dozens of jars the way past generations did. The recipes in this chapter allow you to capture summer's glory, as did Kansans in the past, but do it a jar or two at a time and with simple methods, as with "Spicy Bread and Butter Refrigerator Pickles," or "Pickled Green Tomatoes." If you have sweet corn in your garden, consider a condiment like "Summer Corn Relish," and if the tomatoes are overflowing, try making "Tomato-Ginger Chutney" or "Jane's Chili Sauce."

No messy water bath processing is necessary for these recipes. Simply sterilize the jars, heat the pickling solution, and pour it over the prepared vegetables—or spoon the condiment into jars and allow them to self-seal. Storing the jars in the refrigerator is a must, and using them sooner, rather than later, is best.

Another easy way to get the most out of vegetables is to immerse them in a marinade. Concoctions like "Marinated Cucumbers with Mint" or "Lemon Zucchini" will keep in the fridge for a few days, and you can use them as a garnish for a main course, put them in salads or on sandwiches, add them to a relish tray, or serve them as a refreshing snack.

Spicy Bread and Butter Refrigerator Pickles

These days, most people don't have the time to can dozens of jars of pickles the way earlier generations did. Still, the opportunity beckons to make crunchy pickles from the bounty of cucumbers in your garden. Just a few sliced cucumbers will fill a quart jar and be ready to eat in just twenty-four hours by using the refrigerator pickling method. Let the kids help out—it's a great summer garden project! Refrigerator pickles will keep two to three weeks, but the tasty slices seem to disappear long before then. Serve the pickles with burgers, sandwiches, or straight from the jar at a summer picnic.—Jayni

MAKES 1 QUART

12 ounces small pickling cucumbers, or other small variety

½ medium red bell pepper, seeded and diced

½ small onion, thinly sliced

2 or 3 garlic cloves, peeled

Pickling Liquid:

2 cups apple cider vinegar

1 cup sugar

2 teaspoons kosher salt

½ teaspoon cayenne pepper

½ teaspoon mustard seeds

½ teaspoon celery seeds

½ teaspoon pickling spice

½ teaspoon turmeric

Rinse the cucumbers thoroughly and remove any blemishes. Cut off and discard stem and blossom ends. Slice the cucumbers into ⅜-inch slices and place them in a large bowl. Add the diced pepper, sliced onion, and garlic cloves to the bowl. Toss to combine and pack the mixture into a sterilized 1-quart canning jar.

Pickling Liquid: Pour the vinegar into a large saucepan. Stir in the sugar, kosher salt, cayenne pepper, mustard seeds, celery seeds, pickling spice, and turmeric. Heat over medium-high heat, stirring occasionally, until the sugar dissolves and the pickling liquid comes to a boil. Reduce the heat to low and simmer for 3 to 4 minutes. Pour the hot liquid over the cucumber mixture, leaving ½-inch headspace. Wipe the jar rim to remove any sticky liquid and cover with a canning lid. Tighten the screw band until snug but not overly tight. Allow the jar to self-seal and cool to room temperature before storing in the refrigerator.

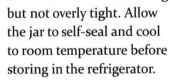

The pickles will be ready to consume in 24 hours. Store in the refrigerator up to 3 weeks.

Pickled Green Tomatoes

In late summer as the garden begins to fade, I look at the little green tomatoes that refused to ripen. Rather than give them over to the squirrels, I pickle them. It's easy to do. The hard part is waiting a week until they are fully flavored. —Frank

MAKES 1 QUART

1 pound small green tomatoes
½ teaspoon celery seeds
¼ teaspoon mustard seeds
½ teaspoon crushed red pepper
1 fresh dill sprig
1 tablespoon onion, diced
2 bay leaves

Pickling Liquid:
4 garlic cloves, peeled
1 cup apple cider vinegar
1 cup water
⅓ cup sugar
1 tablespoon kosher salt

Wash the tomatoes thoroughly and remove any stems or blemishes. Halve or quarter them to make bite-size pieces. Put the tomatoes into a sterilized 1-quart canning jar. Add to the jar the celery seeds, mustard seeds, crushed red pepper, dill sprig, diced onion, and bay leaves. The jar should be full, but nothing should extend above the jar's threads.

Pickling Liquid: Combine the garlic, vinegar, water, sugar, and salt in a saucepan. Bring to a boil over high heat and let boil for 3 minutes, until the sugar is dissolved and the garlic begins to soften. Pour the hot liquid over the tomatoes, leaving ½-inch headspace. Wipe the jar rim to remove any sticky liquid and cover with a canning lid. Tighten the screw band until snug but not overly tight. Allow the jar to self-seal and cool to room temperature before storing in the refrigerator.

The pickled tomatoes will be ready to consume in 1 week. Store in the refrigerator up to 1 month.

Refrigerator Pickled Beets

Backyard gardeners may harvest their beets while they are still very small—just the right size for pickling. You can also find small beets at farmers' markets in the spring and early summer. This easy refrigerator version makes one jar and eliminates the need for processing in a water bath. Refrigerate the pickled beets and use them within a month for the best flavor. They are delicious served on salads or as a colorful garnish on dinner plates.—Frank and Jayni

MAKES 1 PINT

1 pound fresh small beets, 1¼ to
    1½ inches in diameter preferred
2 to 3 tablespoons olive oil
Salt and black pepper, to taste
2 to 3 fresh rosemary sprigs
2 to 3 fresh thyme sprigs

½ small onion, thinly sliced

Pickling Liquid:
1 cup white wine vinegar
½ cup water
½ cup sugar
1 teaspoon kosher salt
¼ teaspoon mustard seeds
½ teaspoon pickling spice
12 black peppercorns
1 small bay leaf

Trim off all but ½ inch of the beet tops and leave the roots intact to prevent bleeding while roasting. Rinse well and pat dry with paper towels. Place the beets on a piece of heavy-duty aluminum foil large enough to hold them in a single layer. Drizzle them with 2 to 3 tablespoons of olive oil and sprinkle with salt and pepper. Lay the rosemary and thyme sprigs on top. Seal the foil tightly to form a packet and place it on a baking sheet. Roast the beets in a 400-degree oven for 40 to 50 minutes, until tender, but still firm. While the beets are still warm, remove the remaining tops and roots and peel them. If the beets are small, leave them whole. If using medium to large beets, cut them in halves or quarters.

Pack the beets and sliced onion in a sterilized 1-pint canning jar.

Pickling Liquid: Pour the vinegar and water into a large saucepan. Stir in the sugar, kosher salt,

CONTINUED ➡

mustard seeds, pickling spice, peppercorns, and bay leaf. Heat over medium-high heat, stirring occasionally, until the sugar dissolves and the pickling liquid comes to a boil. Reduce the heat to low and simmer for 3 to 4 minutes. Pour the hot liquid over the beets and onion, leaving ½-inch headspace. Wipe the jar rim to remove any sticky liquid and cover with a canning lid. Tighten the screw band until snug but not overly tight. Allow the jar to self-seal and cool to room temperature before storing in the refrigerator.

The beets will be ready to consume in 3 days. Store in the refrigerator up to 1 month.

Summer Corn Relish

A spoonful of this brightly colored relish adds a taste of summer to many foods. Serve it on hot dogs or tacos, as a topper to grilled chicken, add it to salads, or simply serve it as a garnish to any warm weather meal.—Frank

MAKES 1 PINT

3 ears sweet corn (1½ cups kernels)

Pickling Liquid:
⅓ cup apple cider vinegar
⅓ cup sugar
½ teaspoon mustard seeds
¼ teaspoon celery seeds
1 teaspoon kosher salt

¼ cup red onion, cut into small dice
½ cup red bell pepper, seeded and diced
1 jalapeño pepper, seeded and finely diced

Trim the dried tassels off the ears of corn, but do not shuck them. Place 2 ears of corn in a microwave oven and cook on full power for 2 minutes. Turn the ears over and cook for 1 to 2 minutes more, to desired doneness. Repeat with the remaining ear of corn, reducing the cooking time to 1 minute on each side, or to desired doneness. Let the ears rest for 3 to 5 minutes on the countertop. To shuck, hold the warm ears with a tea towel or paper towels and grasp the leaves and silks together with your fingers as you shuck them. Cut the kernels off the cobs using a sharp knife and place them in a bowl. Measure 1½ cups of kernels.

Pickling Liquid: In a 2-quart saucepan, combine the vinegar, sugar, mustard seeds, celery seeds, and salt.

Bring the pickling liquid to a boil over medium heat. Add the red onion and boil for 1 minute. Add the red bell pepper and jalapeño and boil for 2 minutes. Finally, add the corn kernels and boil for 3 minutes more. As it cooks, the corn should release enough liquid to cover the mixture as it gently boils.

Remove the corn relish from the heat and pour it immediately into a sterilized 1-pint canning jar, leaving ½-inch headspace. Wipe the jar rim to remove any sticky liquid and cover with a canning lid. Tighten the screw band until snug but not overly tight. Allow the jar to self-seal and cool to room temperature before storing in the refrigerator.

The relish should come to full flavor in 3 days. It will keep for 1 week in the refrigerator.

Tomato-Ginger Chutney

This potent mixture of tomatoes cooked with aromatic spices, fresh ginger, vinegar, and sugar is slow-simmered to make a flavorful condiment. Serve it as an accompaniment to a cheese and meat tray; as a garnish for chicken or turkey; or to liven up a cheese, ham, or chicken sandwich. We like to make this chutney at the height of the tomato season when we have extras—or some not-so-pretty ones—to use up.—Frank and Jayni

MAKES 1 PINT

6 medium fresh tomatoes

2 tablespoons canola or olive oil
1½ cups onion, chopped
1¼ teaspoons salt
½ teaspoon crushed red pepper
½ teaspoon ground cinnamon

¼ teaspoon ground clove
¼ teaspoon cardamom seeds, crushed

¾ cup white wine vinegar
¾ cup sugar
1 ounce (2 packed tablespoons) fresh ginger, peeled and finely chopped
2 garlic cloves, finely chopped

CONTINUED ➡

Bring a large pot of water to a boil over high heat. Wash the tomatoes, remove the stems, and cut an "X" in the blossom end. Lower the tomatoes into the boiling water for 15 to 30 seconds, until the skins begin to loosen. With a slotted spoon, transfer the tomatoes to a bowl of ice water and cool briefly. Drain and remove the skins and cores. Chop the tomatoes on a cutting board, reserving the juice. Measure 3 cups of tomatoes, including their juice, and set aside.

Heat the oil in a large saucepan over medium heat. Add the onion and cook for 3 minutes, stirring frequently. Add the salt, crushed red pepper, cinnamon, clove, and cardamom seeds. Stir and cook the mixture for about 2 minutes more.

Add the chopped tomatoes, vinegar, sugar, ginger, and garlic. When the mixture comes to a boil, reduce the heat to low. Adjust the heat as needed to maintain a slow, steady simmer, stirring occasionally. Cook until the mixture thickens, about 1 hour. Stir the mixture more frequently during the last 20 minutes of cooking to prevent burning.

Pour the chutney into in a sterilized 1-pint canning jar, leaving ½-inch headspace. Wipe the jar rim to remove any sticky liquid and cover with a canning lid. Tighten the screw band until snug but not overly tight. Allow the jar to self-seal and cool the chutney to room temperature before storing in the refrigerator.

The chutney will be ready to consume in 24 hours. Store in the refrigerator up to 1 month.

Jane's Chili Sauce

Jane Wohletz says she has always loved gardening and tends to grow more produce than her family can eat. "Fourteen years ago, my family and I decided to start selling our wonderful produce at the Lawrence Farmers' Market under the name 'Tomato Allie.' We have enjoyed every aspect of this and now sell produce at three different farmers' markets as well as at the you-pick strawberry patch on our farm, Wohletz Farm Fresh," says Jane. "I think we have the best-tasting tomatoes in Kansas! I recommend going to your local farmers' market during July and getting fresh tomatoes to make this chili sauce. Ask the local farmers if they have tomato seconds or canning tomatoes, which are very ripe tomatoes and make the best sauce—plus they are usually less expensive."—Jane Wohletz, Lawrence

MAKES APPROXIMATELY 3 TO 4 PINTS

2 quarts fresh tomatoes

2 medium onions, cut into small dice

2 medium green bell peppers, seeded and cut into small dice

¾ tablespoon salt

¼ teaspoon cayenne pepper

¼ teaspoon allspice

¼ teaspoon cinnamon

¼ teaspoon mustard powder

½ teaspoon ground ginger

½ cup distilled white vinegar

Rinse and stem the tomatoes. Place them in a clean sink and close off the drain with the stopper. Bring a large pot of water to a boil over high heat. Pour the boiling water over the tomatoes. This will cause the tomato skins to blister for easier peeling. Drain the water and peel the tomatoes when they are cool enough to handle. Coarsely chop them and measure 2 quarts.

Transfer the tomatoes to a large pot and smash them with a potato masher or the back of a large spoon. Add the diced onion and green pepper. Stir in the remaining ingredients. Boil the mixture rapidly over medium heat for 1 to 1¼ hours, or until slightly thickened. Stir occasionally.

Remove the chili sauce from heat and skim off any foam. Immediately pour the chili sauce into three or four 1-pint sterilized canning jars, leaving ½-inch headspace. Wipe the jar rims to remove any sticky liquid and cover with a canning lid. Tighten the screw bands until snug but not overly tight. Allow the jars to self-seal and cool to room temperature before storing in the refrigerator.

CONTINUED ➡

Store in the refrigerator up to 1 month.

Option: This chili sauce can be frozen for later use in freezer-safe containers or storage bags.

Marla's Joy's Hot and Spicy BBQ Sauce

"At Marla's Joy, we use this barbecue sauce on our smoked brisket hoagie and our pulled pork, but it can also be used on ribs, burgers, and most anything one likes barbecue sauce on."—Chef G, Marla's Joy, Concordia

MAKES 3 CUPS BBQ SAUCE

3 tablespoons packed brown sugar
2 cups ketchup
2 teaspoons molasses
6 tablespoons butter
2 teaspoons cayenne pepper
1 teaspoon celery salt
2 tablespoons liquid hickory smoke
4 tablespoons Worcestershire sauce
3 teaspoons dry mustard
¼ teaspoon salt
¼ teaspoon black pepper
½ cup water
1 (7-ounce) can chipotle peppers in
  adobo sauce

Place the brown sugar, ketchup, molasses, and butter in a medium-size saucepan. Stir in the cayenne pepper, celery salt, liquid hickory smoke, Worcestershire sauce, dry mustard, salt, pepper, and water. Remove 4 chipotle peppers from the can of chipotle peppers in adobo sauce and add them to the mixture. Bring the mixture to slow boil over medium heat. Using a whisk, break up the chipotle peppers while stirring. When the mixture begins to boil, reduce the heat to low and simmer for 10 minutes, stirring occasionally. Remove the pan from the heat.

Using a whisk, push the sauce through a wire-mesh strainer into bowl to remove the pepper skins and seeds from the sauce. Pour the barbecue sauce into a covered container and store in the refrigerator.

The sauce may be stored in the refrigerator for up to 1 month.

Creamy Lemon Dill Sauce

Those who like the combination of lemon and dill will find this sauce easy to make, and its versatility lends it to a number of dishes.

"We make this creamy lemon dill sauce at Marla's Joy to serve with our house-made crab cakes and our almond trout."—Chef G, Marla's Joy, Concordia

MAKES 3 CUPS SAUCE

2 cups mayonnaise
4 tablespoons chopped fresh dill, or
    4 teaspoons dried dill
2 teaspoons dried parsley
¾ teaspoon garlic, minced
2 tablespoons lemon zest
4 teaspoons fresh lemon juice
1 cup buttermilk

Place the mayonnaise, dill, parsley, garlic, lemon zest, and lemon juice in a large bowl. Whisk in the buttermilk. Cover and refrigerate for at least 4 hours, but overnight is best.

Store the sauce in the refrigerator for up to 1 month.

Marinated Cucumbers with Mint

Gardeners like to grow cucumbers because they are easy to manage and are terrific producers. If purchasing cucumbers, buy fresh-picked ones from your local farmers' market in the summer. Choose cucumbers that are firm and blemish-free. Small to medium ones will be more crisp and have fewer seeds.

Marinated cucumbers are an old family favorite, but adding some fresh chopped mint gives them a modern twist. Serve them as a garnish to a summer meal, add them to salad greens, or serve on burgers, hot dogs, or sandwiches.—Jayni

6 TO 8 SERVINGS

½ cup apple cider vinegar
¼ cup water
¼ cup sugar
Pinch of sea salt
Pinch of freshly ground black pepper

2 or 3 small to medium (about 12 ounces) cucumbers
½ medium yellow onion (sweet variety), thinly sliced

1 tablespoon fresh mint leaves, finely chopped

CONTINUED ➡

Combine the vinegar, water, sugar, salt, and pepper in a medium glass bowl. Whisk or stir until the sugar is dissolved.

Peel the cucumbers and trim the ends. Using a mandolin slicer or sharp knife, slice the cucumbers into very thin rounds, about ⅛ inch thick. Place the sliced cucumbers and onion in the vinegar mixture. Stir in the chopped mint. Cover and refrigerate for at least 2 hours before serving.

To serve, remove the sliced cucumbers and onion from the marinade with a slotted spoon. Use within 2 to 3 days for the best flavor.

Lemon Zucchini

Thinly sliced, marinated zucchini is a refreshing way to enjoy this popular summer vegetable. Choose super-fresh, small, firm zucchini to ensure a crisp texture and vivid color. The marinated zucchini adds bold color to salads. It also replaces pickles in sandwiches or works well as part of a relish tray.—Frank and Jayni

6 TO 8 SERVINGS

1 (6-ounce) green zucchini
1 (6-ounce) yellow zucchini

Marinade:
2 tablespoons lemon juice
⅛ teaspoon sea salt
2 tablespoons extra-virgin olive oil

Slice the zucchini into rounds, about ⅛ inch thick, using a mandolin slicer or sharp knife. Place the zucchini in a bowl.

Marinade: Pour the lemon juice into a small bowl. Add the salt and whisk in the olive oil.

Pour the marinade over the zucchini and toss to combine. Cover and refrigerate for 3 hours, or overnight. Toss once or twice while marinating.

To serve, remove the zucchini slices from the marinade using a slotted spoon. For the best flavor and crunchiness, use within 3 days.

Zucchini: Too Much of a Green Thing

In Kansas, there is not much a gardener can rely on. When spring comes around, we poke seeds into the earth and imagine the harvest of our dreams. Each year, we say to ourselves, "The spring days will be warm and the gentle rains will be perfectly timed. There will be no hail, no high winds, no late frost, and no pests. Yes, this year will be the best!"

In reality, all Kansans know the only reliable thing about the weather is that it will change, and you'd be better off to plan for all the above. Yes, spring will be warm, including a chance of frost, hail, and high winds. Yes, it will be too dry before it rains too much. And, of course, there will always be pests. The tender lettuce leaves may freeze, the corn may blow down, and the squirrels may steal your tomatoes, but, at the very least, you will always have—zucchini. Hurrah! Well, hurrah up to a point.

At first, the zucchini vines spread across the garden and burst into a beautiful display of yellow blossoms. From the blossoms, the small, tender squash will begin to form. The experienced gardener takes this opportunity to harvest the blooms instead of the fruit. Zucchini blossoms make a great appetizer when stuffed, battered, and deep-fried. And that would be a tasty end to the year's zucchini crop, if you were wise—but that's not me! I'll be harvesting those tender, young bright green squash. It's a versatile vegetable that can be eaten fresh, sautéed, stuffed, and marinated. There is an endless variety of ways to use zucchini because this vegetable never seems to come to an end. Ignore these plants for just a few days and zucchini the size of baseball bats suddenly appear. Large zucchini are less desirable because they can be bitter, watery, and full of pith and large seeds. They don't make good baseball bats either.

Kansans don't believe in wasting food, so what's a gardener to do? Giving them away to friends and coworkers often results in a polite wave, signaling no thanks. Once, I walked my dog very early in the morning—well, in the dark—and while I was out, I thought, "Why not *share* a few zucchini by leaving them on my neighbor's porch?" I returned home, proud of my generosity (and shrewdness) only to find a few zucchini on my porch. There will always be pests.—Frank

Moroccan Carrots

A traditional combination of spices used in Moroccan cooking—cumin, paprika, and cayenne pepper—jazzes up the sweet flavor of carrots. These marinated carrots can be served as a side dish, added to a salad, or eaten as a healthy snack—Frank and Jayni

6 TO 8 SERVINGS

1 pound carrots, peeled and sliced
    into ⅛-inch-thick rounds

¼ cup olive oil
1 garlic clove, minced
2 tablespoons lemon juice
1 teaspoon toasted cumin seed*,
    crushed
½ teaspoon paprika
½ teaspoon salt, or to taste
¼ teaspoon cayenne pepper
2 tablespoons fresh cilantro leaves,
    chopped

Steam the sliced carrots, or boil them in a pot of water for 3 to 4 minutes, until tender-crisp.

Drain the carrots and place them in a bowl. While they are still warm, add the olive oil and toss to coat. Add the garlic, lemon juice, cumin, paprika, salt, and cayenne pepper and toss to combine. Taste and adjust seasonings, if needed. Add the chopped cilantro and toss again.

Serve the carrot salad warm, room temperature, or chilled. If not consuming right away, cover and refrigerate. Best if used within 3 days.

*Toasted cumin seed: Place the cumin seed in a small skillet over medium-low heat. Toast the cumin, shaking the skillet frequently, until lightly browned and fragrant. Cool and coarsely crush in a mortar with pestle or in a spice grinder.

Chapter 12
Desserts

"Life is short; eat dessert first," as the adage goes, flips the natural order of things. Scientists claim that we eat dessert at the end of a meal because it aids in digestion. Our parents used dessert as the reward for eating our vegetables. We see the logic of both views—bring on the vegetables: carrot cake, zucchini bread, pumpkin pie—*then* we'll have dessert! While you're digesting that, this chapter will fulfill all your sweet dreams.

Though Kansas is known as the wheat state, fruits such as apples, peaches, and berries are readily grown in the eastern half of the state. There are many opportunities to visit "you-pick" farms or purchase local fruits at farmers' markets. To take advantage of freshly picked fruit, try these fruit-laden beauties with a twist: "Peach Tart with Lavender Crust," "Concord Grape Pie," and "Gluten-Free Apple Galette." If cobbler is your thing, make "Apple Butterscotch-Walnut Crumble," "Blackberry and Pear Skillet Cobbler," or "Cinnamon-Cherry Cobbler with Almond Crunch Topping."

When it comes to cake, zucchini gets into the act, as in "Dark Chocolate Zucchini Cake," or, for those who don't have time to bake, try "Microwave Zucchini Cake." For a special dinner, wow your guests with "Muscat Cake," made with a local Kansas Muscat wine, or bake a "Cranberry-Orange Holiday Cake" for a festive occasion.

If your craving leans toward rich and creamy, head for the kitchen and whip up "Caramel Pumpkin Crème Brûlée," "Burnt Sugar Custard with Crispy Caramel-Sea Salt Topping," or "Eggnog Bread Pudding with Rum Drizzle."

Only homemade ice cream can satisfy the yearn to churn, so consider "Homemade Vanilla Ice Cream with Roasted Strawberries," "Fresh Peach Ice Cream," and for a holiday treat, "Peppermint Ice Cream."

Strawberry Patch Pie

"I have great memories of picking strawberries with my mom and brothers when I was a little girl. These memories have spurred me to grow two acres of strawberries and open my own you-pick strawberry patch on our farm. I love everything about gardening and fresh strawberries. I want to share this wonderful experience with others in hopes of creating fun family memories for many!"
—Jane Wohletz, Wohletz Farm Fresh, Lawrence

6 TO 8 SERVINGS

Pie Shell:
1½ cups all-purpose flour
¼ teaspoon salt
¼ cup chilled butter, cut into small cubes
¼ cup chilled vegetable shortening
4 to 5 tablespoons ice water

Strawberry Sauce:
2 pounds (about 4 cups) fresh strawberries, hulled, rinsed, and drained
1 cup water
¾ cup sugar
3 tablespoons cornstarch

Sweetened whipped cream

Pie Shell: Combine the flour and salt in a medium bowl. Using a pastry cutter, cut the butter cubes and shortening into the flour until the mixture resembles coarse crumbs. Using a fork, stir in ice water, a tablespoon at a time, until the dough can be formed into a ball. Shape the dough into a disk. Wrap in plastic wrap and chill in the refrigerator for at least 30 minutes before using.

Roll out the chilled dough on a lightly floured surface to about ⅛-inch thickness. Gently fold the dough in half and place it in a 9-inch pie plate, unfold, and gently press it into the plate. Decorate the edges by crimping the dough between your thumb and index finger. Prick the top and sides with a knife or fork. Bake the pie shell in a 450-degree oven for 10 to 12 minutes, until lightly browned. Remove the shell from the oven and cool on a baking rack. Do not fill until cool.

Strawberry Sauce: Measure out about 8 ounces (approximately 1 heaping cup) of the

CONTINUED ➡

fresh strawberries. Quarter the berries and place them in a small bowl. Mash with a potato masher. You should have about 1 cup of mashed berries. Transfer the mashed berries to a saucepan. Add 1 cup of water and cook over high heat for about 2 minutes, stirring occasionally. Reduce the heat, if needed, to prevent the mixture from boiling over. Combine the sugar and cornstarch in a small bowl. Slowly stir it into the mashed strawberry mixture. Cook and stir over medium to medium-low heat until the mixture is thick and bubbly. Remove the pan from the heat and cool the strawberry sauce to room temperature. (For a deeper red pie, add a few drops of red food coloring.)

Place half of the remaining whole strawberries into the baked and cooled pie shell. If the strawberries are very large, cut them in half. Pour half of the strawberry sauce over the berries. Layer with the remaining strawberries and sauce. Chill the pie for at least 1 hour before serving.

Serve slices of the strawberry pie topped with a dollop of whipped cream.

Concord Grape Pie

My Aunt Lorraine always grew Concord grapes on her farm to make jam. When I was a youngster, she let me pick a few grapes to taste. In spite of the Concord's bitter skin and seeds, they yield a true grape flavor. Concord grapes are easy to grow if you have a fence, trellis, or arbor to train them on, and sometimes you can find them at farmers' markets and grocery stores in mid- to late summer. If you spot Concord grapes or a similar variety, I'd suggest making this delicious pie. Though the seeds must be removed, it's easy to flick them out with the point of a sharp knife, and the effort will reward you with a unique treat.—Jayni

8 SERVINGS

Pie Shell:
2 cups all-purpose flour
½ teaspoon salt
⅓ cup chilled unsalted butter, cut into small cubes
⅓ cup chilled vegetable shortening
5 to 7 tablespoons ice water

Grape Filling:
4 cups Concord grapes, or similar variety
1 tablespoon lemon juice
⅔ cup sugar
¼ cup all-purpose flour

2 tablespoons butter, diced

Pie Shell: Place the flour and salt in a large bowl and stir to combine. Using a pastry cutter, cut the butter cubes and shortening into the flour until the mixture resembles coarse crumbs. Using a fork, stir in ice water, a tablespoon at a time, until the pastry can be formed into a ball. Divide the dough into two equal portions and shape each portion into a disk. Wrap in plastic wrap and chill in the refrigerator for at least 30 minutes before using.

Grape Filling: Seed the grapes by cutting them in half, and using the sharp point of a knife, flick them out. Place the grapes in a large bowl. If the skins slip off while seeding, add them to the bowl. Before adding the lemon juice, check the grapes, and if they have released a large amount of liquid (enough so that it might run over while baking the pie), pour off some of it. Add the lemon juice to the grapes. Combine the sugar and flour in a small bowl. Stir the mixture gently into the grapes, just until combined.

Roll out one chilled pastry disk on a lightly floured surface to about ⅛-inch thickness. Pick up the dough by folding it loosely in half. Place it in a 9-inch pie plate, unfold, and gently press it into the plate. Pour the grape filling into the pie shell. Scatter the cubed butter over the grapes. For the top crust, roll out the remaining pastry disk to ⅛-inch thickness. As before, fold the dough in half and place it over the filling. Unfold and trim off the excess dough. Crimp the edges together. Prick the top with a knife or fork to allow the steam to escape.

Bake the pie in a 400-degree oven for about 40 minutes, until lightly browned and bubbly.

Peach Tart with Lavender Crust

Preparing this simple rustic tart is an easy way to enjoy fresh peaches during the height of their short, but very treasured, season. The peaches are peeled and sliced, then seasoned with only a sprinkling of sugar, so that they retain their true, fresh flavor. This recipe has a lavender pastry under the peaches, which gives the tart a slightly mysterious, but delicious, taste without overpowering the peaches.—Frank and Jayni

8 TO 10 SERVINGS

Pastry Dough:
1 cup plus 2 tablespoons all-
    purpose flour
1 tablespoon sugar
⅛ teaspoon salt
2 teaspoons dried lavender, minced
½ cup chilled unsalted butter, cut
    into small cubes
3 to 4 tablespoons ice water

2 pounds fresh peaches

2 tablespoons sugar

2 tablespoons peach jam
1 teaspoon water

Pastry Dough: Place the flour, sugar, salt, and minced lavender in a food processor bowl and blend briefly to combine. Add the cubed butter and process just until the mixture is crumbly, about 10 seconds. Add the ice water and pulse a few times, just until the pastry dough is moist and begins to hold together. Transfer the dough to a piece of plastic wrap and gently pat it into a thick disk. If the dough is too sticky, add 1 or 2 tablespoons of flour. Wrap and refrigerate for 1 hour or more.

Bring a pot of water to a boil over high heat. Prepare a bowl of ice water. Wash the peaches. Cut an "X" in the blossom end of each peach. Gently lower the peaches into the boiling water for about 15 seconds to loosen the skins. Remove them from the water with a slotted spoon and immediately place them in the bowl of ice water to cool briefly. Carefully peel off the skins. Slice the peaches in half, remove the pits and cut them into ½-inch-thick slices.

To make the crust, place the chilled pastry dough between two pieces of waxed paper sprinkled with flour for easier rolling. Roll the dough into a circle about 12 to 13 inches in diameter. Carefully transfer the dough to a 12-inch pizza pan.

Arrange the peach slices on the dough in concentric circles, starting 1½ inches from the edges and working towards the center. Crimp the outer edges of the dough. Sprinkle 2 tablespoons of sugar evenly over the peaches. Bake the peach tart in a 375-degree oven for about 40 minutes, until the crust is golden brown and the peaches are tender-firm. Place on a wire rack to cool.

Place the peach jam in a small microwave-safe container, add 1 teaspoon of water to thin the jam, and warm it in a microwave oven for a few seconds. Brush the jam lightly over the tart. Serve the tart slightly warm or room temperature.

Gluten-Free Apple Galette

"Several years ago I discovered I most likely have celiac disease, so now I avoid all wheat and other grains with gluten. Since then, I have begun to cook with other types of flours. One of the most challenging aspects of using gluten-free flours in making pastry crusts is that they do not bind together as strongly as regular flours. Adding a small amount of xanthan gum helps with this. This recipe uses culinary parchment paper to roll the dough and to transfer it to the baking sheet without breaking it."—Sandra Schumm, Lawrence

8 SERVINGS

Crust:
½ cup brown rice flour
½ cup almond meal flour
⅓ cup quinoa flour
1½ teaspoons xanthan gum
½ teaspoon salt
2 tablespoons sugar
6 tablespoons cold unsalted butter, diced
1 egg
1½ to 2 tablespoons ice water

Filling:
½ cup apricot preserves
2 tablespoons water
3 or 4 Pink Lady apples, or apples of choice
2 tablespoons sliced almonds

Vanilla ice cream or crème fraîche (optional)

Crust: Put all dry ingredients in the bowl of a food processor and pulse once to mix. Add the diced butter and pulse 5 or 6 times, until the mixture is crumbly. Add the egg and turn on

CONTINUED

the processor. Add 1½ tablespoons of water through the feed tube while the processor is running, until the mixture begins to form a ball. If the dough is too dry and does not come together in a ball, add a bit more water. Remove the dough from the processor bowl. If it is too sticky, knead in more brown rice flour. Pat the dough into a flat disk about 2 inches thick. Wrap in waxed or parchment paper and chill in the refrigerator for at least 1 hour.

Preheat the oven to 450 degrees. Dust a large piece of parchment paper and the rolling pin with rice flour. Roll out the dough on the parchment paper to ⅛-inch thickness and about 14 inches in diameter. Keep turning the dough and dusting the paper and rolling pin with rice flour as you roll out the dough. Trim the outside edge to make a more uniform circle if needed, and use trimmings to fill any holes or cracks. Slide the parchment paper with the dough onto a flat baking sheet.

Filling: Warm the apricot preserves with 2 tablespoons of water in a small pan over low heat. Using a pastry brush, brush about half of the mixture onto the rolled out dough, stopping 2 inches from the edges. Peel and core the apples and cut them into ⅛-inch slices. Fan the apples slices down the center of the dough, slightly overlapping the rows, and stopping 2 inches from the edges. Continue with as many apple slices as needed to completely cover the dough. Fold the 2-inch border of dough over the apple slices. Brush the remaining apricot preserve mixture over the apples and the folded over dough. Sprinkle the sliced almonds over the exposed apples. Dust any extra flour off the parchment paper and trim the paper to about the size of the baking sheet so that the over-hanging edges don't burn.

Place the baking sheet with the apple galette in the center of the oven and immediately reduce the oven temperature to 400 degrees. Bake for 30 minutes, or until the crust is golden and the apples are tender and bubbly. Cool for about 20 minutes.

Transfer the galette on the parchment paper to a serving plate. Carefully loosen the edges of the galette from the paper and pull the paper out from under it. Cut the apple galette into wedges and serve with vanilla ice cream or a spoonful of crème fraîche, if desired.

Vertacnik's Apple Strudel

Dave and Wendy Vertacnik planted twenty-five apple trees in 1983. Their orchard has now grown to one hundred trees. Take a stroll through this beautiful you-pick orchard in late August through October, and you'll find a variety of apples to choose from like Golden Delicious, Honeycrisp, Jonathan, Jonagold, Granny Smith, Cameo, Fuji, Gold Blush, and Gala.

Wendy uses apples from their orchard to make this apple strudel recipe. "My mother-in-law taught me how to make the strudel when we visited her during the holidays many years ago. Our favorite apple to use for this recipe is the Golden Delicious."—Wendy Vertacnik, Vertacnik Orchard, Lawrence

16 TO 20 SERVINGS

1½ cups all-purpose flour
¼ teaspoon salt
1 egg
½ cup tepid water
1 tablespoon melted butter

Filling:
1 cup plain dried breadcrumbs
1 cup plus 2 tablespoons melted
    butter, divided
1 teaspoon lemon zest

8 apples, peeled, cored and finely
    chopped
1 cup sugar
1 teaspoon cinnamon

Sift the flour and salt into a large bowl. Combine the egg and water and add gradually to the flour as you work the dough with your fingers. Slowly knead the dough on a floured work surface until it no longer sticks to the surface, about 15 minutes. Form the dough into a ball and place it in a large bowl. Brush the top of the dough with 1 tablespoon of melted butter, turn, and brush again. Cover the bowl and let the dough rest in a warm place for 1 hour. The dough can also be refrigerated overnight, but let it come to room temperature before rolling it out.

Filling: In a small bowl, combine the breadcrumbs, ½ cup of the melted butter, and lemon zest.

The apples should be prepared just before, or while the dough is being rolled out, to prevent the apples from releasing their juices, which can make the strudel soggy. (An extra pair of hands would be helpful.) Place the chopped apples in a bowl and stir in the sugar and cinnamon.

Lay a clean sheet over a table measuring at least 36 × 48 inches. Lightly dust the sheet with flour and begin to roll the dough to

CONTINUED ➡

flatten it. Then pull the dough (using your hands, palms up first), stretching it until it is paper-thin. (You should be able to read a newspaper through it.) Allow the dough to hang over the table a few inches, if necessary. Brush or splatter the dough with ¼ cup of the melted butter. Gently spread the breadcrumb mixture over the dough, up to the last 10 inches of one long edge. Spread the apple mixture evenly over the breadcrumbs. Cut off any thick edges of the dough, if needed. Starting at the long edge of the dough containing the apple mixture, turn the edge of the dough in ½ inch and roll up the dough over the filling by pulling gently on the sheet with both hands. It will roll automatically as the sheet is raised. When done, press and seal the edges of the dough.

Line a large baking sheet with parchment paper (for easier cleanup) and brush with 2 tablespoons of melted butter. Slide the rolled strudel into the pan in an "S" shape. Brush the top of the strudel with the remaining ¼ cup of melted butter.

Bake the strudel in a 450-degree oven for 20 minutes, then lower heat to 350 degrees and bake for 40 minutes more, until golden. Cool, and cut the strudel into 2-inch slices to serve.

Option: If you don't have a table or workspace large enough to roll out the dough, divide the dough in half. Roll out each half to about 18 × 24 inches and fill each as directed, with half of the breadcrumbs and apple mixture.

A Recipe for Disaster

Give me a recipe for coq au vin, beef bourguignon, or eggs Benedict and I'll whip it up in no time! But a recipe for dessert in my hands is a recipe for disaster.

Early on in my forty-two-year marriage, I tried my hand at pies, pastries, and cakes made from scratch. My creations were met with pleasant smiles, polite waves of "no thanks," or faint apologies alluding to diets and calorie counts. But the day we caught the dog licking the filling out of the pie but leaving the crust, I decided I was done! Not even the dog would eat my piecrust.

So for years, my only venture into dessert was to make the simplest of cookies and box cupcakes for our daughters. Every few years, I would try again to bake something airy and irresistible, only to have it collapse and be eaten by the garbage can rather than my family. When it came to desserts, Mrs. Smith and Marie Callender became my new best friends.

A few years ago, my husband was returning from a consulting trip, so I decided to surprise him by making his favorite dessert, a red velvet cake. So the process began: I hauled out my dusty stand mixer, lined up all of the ingredients, preheated the oven, and I was off! Just mixing the batter was an experience. Red food coloring erupted out of the mixing bowl to splatter what looked like blood, all over the cabinets and me. My kitchen looked like a murder scene, and guess who was the victim. But I did not let that stop me. The sinister red batter was poured into three round cake pans and placed into the oven. When the timer went off, I took them out. The three cakes looked more like pancakes, except they were hard—more like Frisbees, perhaps—but I was determined to finish my surprise.

The runny icing I had made earlier was poured on each layer, the layers were stacked, and the remaining icing was mopped over the top to drizzle down the sides of what appeared to be a sticky, deformed stack of three Frisbees. There was no time to pause for idle admiration. I couldn't wait; I had to have a bite! So I cut a wedge, took a bite, and began to chew, and chew, until my taste buds scolded me. This is *not* like any cake I have ever eaten. It was beyond bad, more like sickening, repulsive, the *worst*—I spit it out. Yet again, all of my hard work was a total disaster. I stared at that pitiful-looking mess and made the decision to go ahead and surprise, or rather shock, my husband with his favorite dessert.

The second my husband walked in the door, I told him I had a surprise for him. "Something red," I whispered. Of course his mind went straight to something red—but also skimpy and romantic. As he began to get frisky, I quickly told him I had made his favorite dessert, red velvet cake. His response, "Oh honey! That's great! How did it turn out?" I answered with, "Amazing! It's the best dessert I've ever eaten, absolutely delicious!" I handed him a slice. He cut into it, took a bite, and started to chew. He paused, smiled, and chewed some more. I could tell he didn't want to hurt my feelings, so I managed to keep the joke going a little longer until I doubled over with a big belly laugh. The bite was still wallowing around in his mouth but he finally choked it down and asked, "Are you sure this is red velvet cake?"

I dumped the entire cake in the trash. I've never attempted to make another red velvet cake. I've decided to stick with what I do best: the main course. And, instead of preparing something sweet, I'll go straight to a dessert of red, skimpy, and romantic. It's a sure hit every time!—Karen Waite, Lawrence

Apple Butterscotch-Walnut Crumble

If you're lucky enough to live near an apple orchard, take advantage of the opportunity to pick your own at the peak of ripeness. This apple crumble tastes best made with full-flavored, sweet-tart apples such as Jonagolds or Jonathans.—Frank and Jayni

8 SERVINGS

2 pounds (5 to 6 medium) apples
½ cup sugar
1 tablespoon all-purpose flour

Topping:
¾ cup all-purpose flour
¾ cup rolled oats
¼ teaspoon cinnamon
½ cup packed brown sugar
⅓ cup chilled butter, diced
⅓ cup butterscotch chips
⅓ cup walnuts, coarsely chopped

Vanilla ice cream

Peel and core the apples. Slice them into ¼-inch-thick slices (about 6 cups sliced apples) into a large bowl. In a small bowl, combine ½ cup sugar and the 1 tablespoon of flour. Pour the mixture over the apples and toss to combine. Set aside.

Topping: In a large bowl, combine the ¾ cup flour, rolled oats, cinnamon, and brown sugar. Using a pastry blender, cut in the butter until the mixture resembles coarse crumbs. Stir in the butterscotch chips and walnuts.

Pour the apple and sugar mixture evenly into a 13 × 9-inch baking dish. Cover the apples evenly with the topping mixture. Bake the crumble in a 350-degree oven for 45 to 50 minutes, until browned and bubbly.

Serve the crumble warm or room temperature in stemless cocktail glasses or dessert bowls with vanilla ice cream.

Blackberry and Pear Skillet Cobbler

Dessert doesn't have to be a production. This skillet dessert, featuring blackberries and pears, can be put together quickly just before dinner and baked while the family eats. The beauty is that it can be served from the hot skillet at the table.

Blackberries are easy to grow in Kansas and, with proper care, these shrubs can produce fruit for ten years or more. In late June to August, you-pick farms offer blackberries, ripe for the picking.—Jayni

6 SERVINGS

6 ounces blackberries
2 teaspoons sugar, divided
2 small to medium pears
1 tablespoon lemon juice

5 tablespoons butter, divided
1 cup all-purpose flour
½ cup sugar
1 teaspoon baking powder
½ teaspoon salt
1 egg
½ cup buttermilk

Sweetened, lightly whipped cream, for topping

Place the blackberries in a small bowl. Add 1 teaspoon of sugar and toss to combine. Peel the pears, core, and cut into 1-inch cubes. Place them in a separate bowl, add the lemon juice, and toss to combine. Add the remaining teaspoon of sugar and toss again.

Melt 1 tablespoon of the butter over low heat in a 10-inch stainless steel or iron skillet. Remove the skillet from the heat. Combine the flour, sugar, baking powder, and salt in a mixing bowl. In a separate bowl, beat the egg with a wire whisk. Whisk in the buttermilk. Melt the remaining 4 tablespoons of butter in a small container in a microwave oven and whisk it into the egg and buttermilk mixture. Pour the buttermilk mixture into the flour mixture and stir until all dry ingredients have been incorporated. Avoid overmixing.

Pour the batter into the skillet, gently smoothing with a rubber spatula to cover the bottom of the skillet. Scatter the pear cubes evenly over the batter, followed by the blackberries.

Bake the cobbler in a 350-degree oven for 40 to 45 minutes, until lightly browned and an inserted toothpick comes out with moist crumbs. Serve the cobbler warm and top each serving with a dollop of whipped cream.

Cinnamon-Cherry Cobbler with Almond Crunch Topping

There is only one way to improve this cobbler made with tart, bright red pie cherries and a crunchy almond topping. Serve it warm, with a scoop of vanilla ice cream.—Frank and Jayni

8 TO 12 SERVINGS

5 cups tart pie cherries, pitted
  (fresh, or frozen and thawed)
1 teaspoon almond extract
1 cup sugar
3 tablespoons all-purpose flour
1 teaspoon cinnamon

Almond Crunch Topping:
1½ cups all-purpose flour
3 tablespoons sugar
2 teaspoons baking powder
¼ teaspoon salt
⅓ cup chilled butter
1 egg, slightly beaten
½ cup milk
½ cup whole almonds, coarsely
  chopped

Place the cherries in a large bowl. Sprinkle them with the almond extract and stir gently. In a small bowl, combine the sugar, flour, and cinnamon. Pour the mixture over the cherries and stir gently to combine. Pour the cherry mixture into an 11 × 9-inch baking dish.

Almond Crunch Topping: In a large bowl, combine the flour, sugar, baking powder, and salt. Cut in the butter with a pastry blender until the mixture is crumbly. Combine the beaten egg and milk in a small bowl. Stir it into the flour and butter mixture just until the mixture is moistened. Using a large spoon, drop 12 equal mounds of the batter on top of the cherries. Make four rows, with three mounds in each row. When baked, this will make natural divisions for serving. Sprinkle the coarsely chopped almonds evenly over the topping.

Bake the cobbler in a 400-degree oven for 25 to 30 minutes, until the topping is golden brown and the cherry filling is thick and bubbly. Serve warm or room temperature.

Muscat Cake

Grape vineyards and wineries have popped up all over the state of Kansas and many have tasting rooms where you can sample their wines. When looking for a sweet wine to use in this cake recipe, we had to look no farther than two nearby wineries. Holy-Field Vineyard & Winery in Basehor grows Valvin Muscat grapes and produces a lovely sweet wine of the same name, and BlueJacket Crossing Vineyard & Winery in Eudora produces a wine called Kansas Transplant, made with the juice of Moscato grapes. Both are pleasantly sweet white wines with hints of stone fruit and citrus, which adds a unique flavor to this moist cake and its glaze. A small glass of the chilled wine pairs nicely with the cake.—Jayni

12 TO 16 SERVINGS

1 cup butter (2 sticks), softened
2 cups sugar
4 eggs
2 teaspoons vanilla extract

2 cups all-purpose flour
½ teaspoon baking powder
½ teaspoon salt
½ cup Muscat, Moscato, or other
    sweet white wine

Muscat Glaze:
1 cup powdered sugar
¼ cup Muscat, Moscato, or other
    sweet white wine

1 bunch red or green grapes, sep-
    arated into small clusters, for
    garnish

Prepare a 9-inch springform pan by greasing the sides and bottom. Cut parchment or waxed paper to fit the bottom of the pan, place it in the pan and grease the top side of the paper. Dust the interior of the pan and paper with a small amount of flour and tap out the excess.

In a large bowl using a mixer, beat the butter until light and fluffy. Add the sugar and beat well. Blend in the eggs, one at a time. Mix in the vanilla extract.

In a separate bowl, combine the flour, baking powder, and salt. Add the dry ingredients to the butter and sugar mixture alternately with the wine, ending with the dry ingredients.

Pour the batter into the prepared springform pan. Bake in a 350-degree oven for 55 minutes, or until a thin wooden skewer or toothpick inserted into the center of the cake comes out with very moist crumbs.

Cool the cake in the pan on a cake rack for about 10 minutes. Remove the pan sides from the base and continue cooling. When the cake is cool enough to handle, carefully remove the

CONTINUED ➡

base and peel off the parchment or waxed paper. Return the cake to the cake rack to glaze.

Muscat Glaze: In a small bowl, combine the powdered sugar and ¼ cup of wine, stirring or whisking until smooth. Using a toothpick, poke holes in the top of the cake and pour the glaze over it. If some of the glaze pools in the center of the cake, brush it to the outer edges using a pastry brush. Let the glaze soak into the cake for at least 30 minutes before serving. Transfer the cake to a cake plate. Cover, if serving later.

Garnish the cake plate or individual servings with small clusters of red or green grapes.

A Taste of the Vine

Kansas is home to approximately thirty-five wineries, with more on the way. Though winemakers in Kansas have endured some snickers in the past, a sip in the tasting room usually turns skepticism into sales. Tasters new to Midwestern wines may not be familiar with some of the hybrid varietals. Kansas winemakers grow grapes with names like "Norton," "Chambourcin," "Seyval Blanc," "Chardonel," and "Vignoles." More familiar grapes such as Cabernet Sauvignon, Merlot, and Chardonnay do not perform as well due to the shorter growing season and the lower winter temperatures. Kansas wines range from sweet to dry, light to robust, and possess the typical characteristics of wines made everywhere.

Holy-Field Vineyard & Winery, near Basehor, has been producing wines for sale to the public since 1994. Currently, the vineyard has seventeen acres of grapevines in production. A few other wineries have come and gone before them, so currently Holy-Field holds the title of the oldest winery in Kansas. It has received many regional and international awards over the years, including six prestigious Jefferson Cup Invitational Wine Competition Awards.

It all started back in 1986 when Les Meyer and his daughter, Michelle Meyer, planted their first few rows of vine stock. "We started growing grapes to make wine for ourselves," Michelle tells us and adds with a chuckle, "but I like to say it was because my dad liked to dig holes." After college, Michelle pursued a career in the business world, but her love of wine and working outdoors called her back to the rural life. Her enthusiasm for the grape bursts forth when she talks about the vineyard, her dedication to making serious wines, and her affection for their customers.

Les, Michelle, and Mandy Hampton, their dedicated employee whom they consider family, do it all. Though she can jump in to help with anything, typically Mandy pours wine in the tasting room, manages the gift shop, and cooks dinners for events. Michelle and Les tend to the vineyard and hand-harvest the grapes with the help of volunteers on their popular "Picking Sundays." Afterward, they press, age, and bottle their wines on the property.

Since the Meyers first opened for business, visitors, far removed from farm life, have expressed curiosity about how the grapes are grown and picked.

The Meyers, as do many wineries across the state, invite volunteers to join in the grape harvest in late summer. Afterward, the Meyers treat the picking crews to a buffet lunch and a glass or two of sangria made with Holy-Field wine. Many of the volunteers will return to taste the vintage they helped to pick.

Wine enthusiasts will find that most Kansas wineries are a short drive from nearby urban centers such as Wichita and Kansas City and along I-70 to Manhattan. However, grapes are grown and tasty wines are made in eastern Kansas from Lancaster to Galena and as far west as WaKeeney. Making wine in any locale requires dedicated study, experimentation, and hard work, and the Kansas climate presents it own unique challenges for Midwestern wine producers. There may not be an ancient chateau or a coastal mountain range as a backdrop to these vineyards, but a visit to the tasting room often includes something that is quite exclusive—a personal conversation with the winemaker.

Cranberry-Orange Holiday Cake

"The flavor combination of cranberry, toasted pecans, orange brandy, and freshly ground nutmeg makes this Bundt cake the perfect dessert to serve during the holiday season!"—Julene DeRouchey, assistant nutrition educator, Kansas Wheat Commission, St. Marys

16 SERVINGS

½ cup butter, softened
1¼ cups sugar
2 large eggs

2 cups all-purpose flour
1 teaspoon baking powder
1 teaspoon baking soda
½ teaspoon salt
1 teaspoon nutmeg, freshly grated

1 cup sour cream
1 tablespoon orange brandy
1 tablespoon orange zest
¼ cup toasted pecans*, chopped

1 (8-ounce) can whole berry cranberry sauce, divided

Glaze and Garnish:
1 cup confectioners' sugar
1 tablespoon orange brandy
¼ teaspoon vanilla extract
Extra toasted pecan pieces, for garnish

Preheat the oven to 350 degrees. Lightly grease and flour a 10-inch (12-cup) Bundt pan.

In a large mixing bowl, beat together the butter and sugar with an electric mixer. Beat in the eggs one at a time.

In a medium-size bowl, combine the flour, baking powder, baking soda, salt, and nutmeg. Add to the creamed mixture and mix well.

Add the sour cream, orange brandy, orange zest, and ¼ cup toasted pecan pieces.

Pour half of the batter into the prepared pan. To swirl the cranberry sauce, drop half of the sauce by tablespoons onto the batter and use a butter knife to swirl it throughout the batter. (Do not swirl the cranberry sauce too deep or too close to the edge of the pan.) Top with the remaining batter. Swirl the remaining cranberry sauce on top. Smooth the batter with a spatula.

Bake the cake for 40 minutes, and then tent with aluminum foil to prevent overbrowning. Bake an additional 10 to 15 minutes, until an inserted cake tester or toothpick comes out clean. The cake will be a light golden brown all over. Cool the cake in the pan on a wire rack for 1 hour, then loosen carefully and invert onto a cake serving plate. Cool completely before glazing.

Glaze and Garnish: Place the confectioners' sugar, orange brandy, and vanilla extract in a small bowl. Whisk the ingredients together until smooth. Thin the glaze with more orange brandy, if needed. Scoop the glaze into a small plastic storage bag and seal. Snip a tiny hole in one corner of the sealed bag. Drizzle the glaze over the top of the cake. Garnish with extra pecan pieces.

*Toasted Pecans: Place the pecan halves on a microwave-safe plate and microwave on high for 2 to 4 minutes, or until lightly browned.

Variation: As an alternative to the glaze, sprinkle the cake with confectioners' sugar.

Dark Chocolate Zucchini Cake

"My grandparents from Pittsburg always had a huge garden and an abundance of zucchini every year. Grandma would try to find creative ways to use it because she hated to see anything go to waste. She gave me her recipe for a chocolate zucchini cake when I got married thirty-seven years ago. Over the years, I have modernized the recipe by using dark chocolate instead of milk chocolate. This cake is so rich you can only eat a small piece!"—Linda Wilson, Weir

12 TO 16 SERVINGS

½ cup butter, softened
½ cup vegetable oil
1¾ cups sugar
2 eggs
1 teaspoon vanilla extract
½ cup buttermilk

2½ cups unsifted, all-purpose flour
¼ cup dark cocoa powder
½ teaspoon pumpkin pie spice
½ teaspoon baking powder
¼ teaspoon salt

2 cups zucchini, finely shredded
1 (10-ounce) bag dark chocolate
    chips, divided

CONTINUED ➡

Place the butter, oil, and sugar in a large mixing bowl and beat with an electric mixer until well blended. Beat in the eggs, vanilla extract, and buttermilk.

In a separate bowl, combine the flour, dark cocoa, pumpkin pie spice, baking powder, and salt. Add the dry ingredients to the batter and blend until well combined.

Stir the shredded zucchini and half of the dark chocolate chips (5 ounces) into the batter.

Spoon the batter into a greased and floured 13 × 9-inch baking dish. Bake in a 325-degree oven for 40 to 45 minutes, or until an inserted toothpick comes out clean. Transfer the cake from the oven to a wire baking rack and, while still hot, sprinkle the remaining chocolate chips over the top. Let them melt and spread evenly over the cake.

Variation: Dark chocolate frosting can be substituted for the chocolate chip topping.

Microwave Zucchini Cake

"Our garden produces lots of zucchini, and my mom and I worked together to create this recipe. I had never baked in the microwave before, but I've now made this recipe many times. It is one of my favorites. I love that it is quick to make, and I don't have to use the oven!"—James DeRouchey, Pottawatomie County 4-H Club, St. Marys

8 TO 10 SERVINGS

3 eggs
1½ cups sugar
¾ cup canola oil
2 teaspoons vanilla extract
2 cups zucchini, grated

1½ cups all-purpose flour
½ cup whole wheat flour
½ cup quick cooking oats
1 teaspoon salt
¼ teaspoon baking powder
1½ teaspoons baking soda
2 teaspoons ground cinnamon
½ teaspoon ground nutmeg

Glaze:
½ cup powdered sugar
1 teaspoon vanilla extract
1 tablespoon sweet cream coffee creamer, or heavy whipping cream

In a large mixing bowl, blend the eggs and sugar together with a whisk or large spoon. Stir in the oil, vanilla extract, and grated zucchini.

In a separate bowl, combine the flours, oats, salt, baking powder, baking soda, cinnamon, and nutmeg. Stir the dry ingredients into the zucchini mixture.

Pour the batter into a lightly greased and floured 12-cup microwave-safe Bundt-style pan. Microwave the cake on high power for 10 to 13 minutes. The cake is done when a cake tester or toothpick, inserted near the middle of the cake, comes out clean, and the cake begins to pull away from the sides of the pan. Cool the cake for 10 minutes in the pan. Loosen the edges and invert the cake onto a serving plate to finish cooling.

Glaze: In a small bowl, combine the powdered sugar, vanilla extract, and sweet cream coffee creamer or heavy whipping cream. Add more coffee creamer or heavy whipping cream if needed to achieve a pourable consistency.

Drizzle the glaze over the cake when it is completely cooled.

Chef G's Snickers Cheesecake

Gary Bottarini, also known as Chef G, is the executive chef at Marla's Joy in Concordia. His cheese-cake is one of the most popular desserts on the menu.

"I arrived in Concordia in 2011 from the San Francisco Bay area and was blessed to meet restaurant owner Marla Jorgensen. With her vision for the overall dining experience and my passion for cooking, we have created a one-of-a-kind dining delight right here in small-town Kansas. We welcome you to come and enjoy our bistro and a fine dining experience in north-central Kansas, where we do everything with heart. It's worth the trip."—Chef G, Marla's Joy, Concordia

12 SERVINGS

Crust:
2 cups finely crushed Nilla Wafers
6 tablespoons butter, melted

30 "fun size" Snickers bars, frozen

3 (8-ounce) packages cream cheese, room temperature
2 large eggs
½ cup sugar (Baker's sugar recommended)
1½ teaspoons vanilla extract

Crust: Preheat the oven to 350 degrees. Place the wafers in a sealed storage bag. Using a rolling pin, finely crush the wafers and pour them into a medium-size bowl. Add the melted butter and mix well. Firmly press the mixture into the bottom of a 9-inch springform pan. Place the pan on a baking sheet and bake for 10 minutes. Let cool for 10 minutes.

After cooling the crust for 10 minutes, remove the wrappers from fifteen of the frozen Snickers bars, place them in the food processor, and blend until finely crushed. If the Snickers bars begin to clump, put the processor bowl in the freezer for 10 minutes, then blend them again. Spread the crushed Snickers over the wafer crust. Set the processor bowl aside to process the remaining Snickers bars later.

Place the cream cheese in a mixing bowl and blend with a mixer until smooth. Add the eggs, sugar, and vanilla extract, and mix well. Pour the mixture evenly over the crushed Snickers. Bake the cheesecake for 40 minutes. When it is removed from the oven, it will not be firm.

As soon as you take the cheesecake out of the oven, remove the wrappers from the remaining fifteen frozen

Snickers bars. Place them in the food processor and blend until finely crushed. Spread the crushed Snickers evenly on top of the warm cheesecake. Let cool for 45 minutes, and then refrigerate in the springform pan for at least 4 hours before serving.

To serve, run a small knife between the cheesecake and the springform pan ring. Remove the ring and cut the cheesecake into twelve slices.

Caramel Pumpkin Crème Brûlée

"Fall is my favorite time to develop the dessert menu at Harry's in Manhattan. We had this crème brûlée on our dessert menu a few years ago, and it quickly became a favorite with our customers as well as our staff."—Pastry Chef Kirsten Spear, Harry's, Manhattan

8 SERVINGS

10 tablespoons granulated sugar, divided
3 cups heavy cream

2 tablespoons light brown sugar
½ teaspoon sea salt
¼ teaspoon ground ginger
⅛ teaspoon ground clove
½ teaspoon ground cinnamon
¼ teaspoon nutmeg, freshly grated
5 ounces pumpkin puree

6 egg yolks
¼ cup Frangelico, or similar hazelnut liqueur
1 teaspoon vanilla extract

8 teaspoons sugar, for topping

Preheat the oven to 300 degrees. Place eight shallow, 5-inch round, oven-safe ramekins in a roasting pan. Heat a pot of water to boiling.

To caramelize the sugar, place a pot on the stove over medium-high heat. Have oven mitts handy. Add 5 tablespoons of the granulated sugar to the hot pot. Shake the pan gently as the sugar begins to melt. Move the sugar around with a heat-safe spatula as necessary. When all of the sugar has melted, let the sugar cook, undisturbed, until dark in color. It will begin to smoke. Using oven mitts, immediately remove the pan from the heat and whisk in the heavy cream. Caution: The caramel will splutter and the cream will produce very hot steam. Whisk until the caramel is incorporated into the cream. If you have any hardened lumps of caramel, they will melt down in the next step.

Place the pot of cream back on the stove and add the remaining

CONTINUED ➡

5 tablespoons of granulated sugar, brown sugar, sea salt, spices, and the pumpkin puree. Bring the mixture to a simmer over medium heat.

Meanwhile, place the egg yolks in a heat-safe bowl. When the cream comes to a simmer, turn off the heat. Whisk about 1 cup of the cream into the egg yolks, pouring it in a slow, steady stream while constantly whisking. Whisk the tempered egg yolks back into the remaining cream mixture. Add the Frangelico and vanilla extract.

Fill the ramekins ¾ of the way full and place the roasting pan in the oven. Fill the roasting pan halfway up with the boiling water. Bake until the custard has set, but is still slightly jiggly in the very center, about 45 minutes, but check the custard after 30 minutes.

Carefully remove the roasting pan from the oven and cool until the ramekins can be picked up. Cover and refrigerate the custards for at least 4 hours, or up to 2 days.

To serve, sprinkle about 1 teaspoon of sugar over the top of each custard and brûlée (caramelize) with a culinary torch by moving the flame constantly, 1 to 2 inches from the surface, until the sugar browns and bubbles. Or, as an alternative, place the ramekins on a sheet pan and place under the oven broiler to brown.

Burnt Sugar Custard with Crispy Caramel-Sea Salt Topping

Burnt sugar pie is an old-time favorite in Kansas. We've taken the idea and modernized it by doubling down on the caramel flavor and serving it in the style of crème brûlée. We sprinkle a pinch of sea salt on top with the sugar and torch it for a crispy topping.—Frank and Jayni

6 SERVINGS

Burnt Sugar Custard:
2½ cups half and half
⅔ cup sugar, divided

6 egg yolks
½ teaspoon vanilla extract

Topping:
¼ cup sugar, divided
Sea salt

Place six round, 5-inch crème brûlée ramekins in a large roasting pan or baking dish, or use two smaller baking dishes. Set aside. Preheat the oven to 325 degrees and heat a pot of water to just below boiling while making the custard.

Burnt Sugar Custard: Pour the half and half in a saucepan and set aside. Melt ⅓ cup of the sugar in a small skillet over medium heat. Gently shake the pan as the sugar begins to melt. When it is mostly melted and begins to color, stir gently as the sugar begins to caramelize. Do not let the sugar scorch. When it reaches a medium mahogany color, slowly pour the mixture into the half and half, stirring. The mixture will bubble up a bit and the caramelized sugar will clump. Add the remaining ⅓ cup of sugar and heat the mixture over medium heat, stirring until the caramelized sugar, and the added sugar, dissolves and the mixture is hot and steamy, just below boiling. Remove the pan from the heat.

Place the egg yolks in a medium bowl and whisk until blended. Stirring constantly, ladle some of the hot half and half mixture into the egg yolks a few drops at a time. If added too quickly, the eggs will curdle. Slowly add all of the half and half mixture, stirring constantly. Pour the mixture through a fine wire-mesh strainer into a large glass measuring cup, 4-cup or larger, to remove any curdled egg. Stir in the vanilla extract.

CONTINUED ➡

Pour the custard mixture into the ramekins. Carefully pour enough hot water (not boiling water) into the pan to come halfway up the sides of the ramekins. Place in a 325-degree oven and bake the custards for about 25 minutes. The custard is done when the center jiggles slightly when gently shaken.

Transfer the pan of ramekins from the oven to a countertop. Using a large metal spatula, carefully lift the ramekins from the hot water and place them on a cooling rack. Cool to room temperature. Cover the ramekins with aluminum foil and chill in the refrigerator for several hours before serving.

Topping: When ready to serve, caramelize the tops of the custards by using a culinary torch, or the oven broiler. Sprinkle 2 teaspoons of sugar evenly over each custard. Using a salt grinder, grind a few sprinklings of slightly coarse sea salt over the custards. If using a torch, brown the sugar on each custard, keeping the flame moving about 1 to 2 inches from the surface, until the sugar bubbles and browns. If using the oven broiler, put the ramekins on a sheet pan and place them under the broiler until bubbly and browned.

Let the custards cool for 5 minutes before serving.

Bittersweet Chocolate Custard

A classic chocolate custard is a favorite of both children and adults. It's an easy make-ahead dessert for company or a family meal. We prefer the taste of bittersweet chocolate for the custard and like to garnish each serving with a fresh strawberry. When chilled, this custard makes a tasty afternoon treat with a cup of coffee or tea.—Frank and Jayni

6 SERVINGS

2 cups half and half
½ cup sugar
4 ounces bittersweet chocolate chips

6 egg yolks
½ teaspoon vanilla extract

Sweetened whipped cream
6 small fresh strawberries

Preheat the oven to 350 degrees and heat a pot of water to just below boiling while making the custard.

Heat the half and half and sugar in a saucepan over medium heat, stirring occasionally until hot and steamy, just below boiling. Reduce the heat to low and immediately whisk in the bittersweet chocolate until completely melted. Remove the pan from the heat.

Place the egg yolks in a medium bowl and whisk until well blended. Stirring constantly, ladle some of the hot chocolate mixture into the egg yolks a few drops at a time. If added too quickly, the eggs will curdle. Slowly add all of the chocolate mixture, stirring constantly. Pour the mixture through a fine wire-mesh strainer into a 4-cup glass measuring cup to remove any curdled egg. Stir in the vanilla extract.

Pour the chocolate custard into six (4-ounce) custard cups or ramekins. Cover the tops with aluminum foil and place them in a large baking dish. Pour in the hot (not boiling) water to a depth of 1 inch. Place in the oven and bake for 30 minutes. The custard is done when the center jiggles slightly when gently shaken.

Remove from the oven and, using tongs or an oven mitt, lift the custard cups from the hot water and place them on a wire rack. Remove the foil tops and cool to room temperature.

CONTINUED ➡

Serve the custard warm or cover with foil and chill for several hours before serving. When ready to serve, top each custard cup with a dollop of sweetened whipped cream and garnish each with a whole strawberry.

Eggnog Bread Pudding with Rum Drizzle

Eggnog is a popular drink during the holiday season and, when we've sipped enough, we like to use the remaining nog to make this bread pudding. The rum sauce, drizzled over the bread pudding just before baking, glazes the top and makes a light crunchy coating when served warm from the oven.—Jayni

8 SERVINGS

1 loaf hearty white bread, European-style preferred

1 whole egg
3 egg yolks
½ cup sugar
2½ cups eggnog*
1 teaspoon vanilla extract
⅛ teaspoon salt

Rum Drizzle:
3 tablespoons brown sugar
3 tablespoons light corn syrup
3 tablespoons dark rum

Butter, for the baking dish

Slice the bread into 1-inch slices. Remove most of the crusts and cut into 1-inch cubes. Measure 6 cups of the bread cubes, lightly packed, and place them in a large bowl. Set aside.

In a separate bowl, whisk the whole egg, egg yolks, and sugar together using a wire whisk, until the mixture turns a light yellow color. Whisk in the eggnog, vanilla extract, and salt. Pour the mixture over the bread cubes and turn gently to combine. Let the mixture stand for 20 minutes, turning two or three times to make sure all cubes of bread are well soaked in the eggnog mixture. While the bread is soaking, make the rum drizzle.

Rum Drizzle: Combine the brown sugar, light corn syrup, and dark rum in a small saucepan. Heat over medium heat, stirring constantly, until the mixture simmers and the brown sugar is dissolved. Reduce the heat to low and simmer slowly for 4 to 5 minutes, just until the mixture lightly coats the back of a spoon. Pour the rum mixture into a 1-cup glass measuring cup and set aside.

Generously butter an 8- or 9-inch baking dish. Pour the soaked bread into the baking dish. Drizzle the rum drizzle evenly over the top.

Place the bread pudding in a 325-degree oven and bake for 45 to 50 minutes, or until it is lightly browned on top and somewhat firm, but jiggles slightly in the center when the pan is gently shaken. If the top needs more browning, place the bread pudding about 6 inches under the oven broiler and broil for about 30 seconds. Serve warm or room temperature.

* For rich and creamy bread pudding, choose a rich, thick eggnog.

Variation: In place of eggnog, 2½ cups of half and half may be substituted. Add ¼ teaspoon fresh-grated nutmeg and increase the sugar to ¾ cup.

Ginger-Nib Cookies

Chef Megan Garrelts and her husband, Chef Colby Garrelts, have combined their culinary talents to create two successful restaurants, Bluestem in Kansas City, Missouri, and Rye in Leawood, Kansas. Early on, while working in pastry kitchens, Megan decided to focus her career on the sweeter part of the meal.

Megan's richly flavored cookies, made with the alluring combination of molasses, dark beer, fresh ginger, chocolate, and fragrant spices, are rolled in a mixture of sugar and cocoa nibs for a delightfully textured finish. Serve the cookies with a cup of coffee or tea.—Chef Megan Garrelts, Bluestem and Rye, Leawood

3 DOZEN COOKIES

½ cup unsalted butter, softened
½ cup light brown sugar
⅓ cup blackstrap molasses
2 tablespoons dark beer
1 large egg
2 tablespoons fresh ginger, peeled and grated

1¾ cups all-purpose flour
1 tablespoon, plus 1 teaspoon cocoa powder
1 teaspoon baking powder
1 teaspoon ground ginger
1 teaspoon ground cinnamon
1 teaspoon ground allspice
7 ounces dark chocolate, melted

½ cup granulated sugar
½ cup cocoa nibs (also known as cacao nibs)

CONTINUED ➡

In a mixing bowl of a stand mixer fitted with a paddle, cream together the butter, brown sugar, and molasses. Add the beer, egg, and fresh ginger and mix until thoroughly combined.

In a small mixing bowl, whisk together the flour, cocoa powder, baking powder, ground ginger, cinnamon, and allspice. Slowly mix the dry ingredients into the creamed butter mixture. Fold in the melted chocolate.

Cover the cookie dough, transfer it to the refrigerator, and chill until the dough becomes firm enough to scoop, about 1 hour.

Preheat the oven to 350 degrees. Place the sugar and cocoa nibs in a food processor and pulse until the cocoa nibs are slightly ground. Pour the mixture into a medium bowl and set aside.

To make the cookies, scoop the cookie dough and roll into 1- to 1¼-inch balls. Roll the dough in the sugar and cocoa nib mixture. Place them on a baking sheet and bake for 8 to 10 minutes.

Transfer the cookies to a wire rack and allow them to cool slightly. The cookies are best eaten slightly warm, fresh from the oven, or they can be stored in an airtight container for 2 to 3 days.

Farmhouse Oatmeal Cookies

"My grandparents' farm near Geneseo, with its cattle, wheat, and big vegetable garden, is the place of my best food memories. My grandma always cooked big meals for the family and for anyone who was working on the farm. She somehow found time to make amazing cinnamon rolls and pies for the local restaurant as well as treat us to fancy cakes, baked Alaska, and pancakes in the shape of animals—always with raisin eyes! Now in her mid-90s, my strong, fun-loving grandmother still likes to bake these cookies, which makes everyone happy."—Staci Garman, Lawrence

4 DOZEN COOKIES

3 cups rolled oats
3 cups all-purpose flour
2 teaspoons baking soda
1 teaspoon ground cinnamon
½ teaspoon ground cloves
½ teaspoon salt

2 cups dark raisins
⅔ cup milk
2 eggs
1 teaspoon vanilla extract (optional)
1 cup (two sticks) butter, softened
2 cups sugar

Place the oats in a food processor and blend them until they have a look of part flour, part oats. Pour the oats into a large mixing bowl. Add flour, baking soda, cinnamon, cloves, and salt. Mix to combine.

Add the raisins to the food processor and process them until they are finely chopped and begin to stick together. Add the milk, eggs, and vanilla extract, if using, and pulse several times. Add the softened butter and sugar and pulse again, just until mixed. Spoon this mixture into the dry ingredients and stir just until well combined. If the dough is too sticky to form into balls, cover and refrigerate for 30 minutes or more.

Scoop up the dough with a tablespoon and form into balls. Place them on a lightly greased cookie sheet and press down with your fingers, or the back of a spoon, to flatten the tops. Bake the cookies in a 350-degree oven for about 12 minutes, or until light golden brown. Let the cookies rest on the baking sheet for a minute or two, then transfer them to a baking rack to cool. The cookies will be soft.

Grilled Peaches with Mint Mascarpone and Raspberry Coulis

In the summer months, when the peaches and raspberries are fresh and local, try this summertime treat. Prepare the mint mascarpone and raspberry coulis ahead, and grill the peaches just before serving.—Frank and Jayni

6 TO 8 SERVINGS

Mint Mascarpone:
½ cup mascarpone
2 teaspoons fresh mint leaves,
    minced
2 tablespoons sugar

Raspberry Coulis:
6 ounces fresh raspberries
2 tablespoons sugar, or more to
    taste

3 or 4 large peaches, ripe but firm
2 tablespoons melted butter
Sugar

Fresh mint sprigs, for garnish

Mint Mascarpone: Place the mascarpone, mint, and sugar in a small bowl and whisk to combine. Cover and chill for at least 30 minutes to allow time for the flavors to blend.

Raspberry Coulis: Purée the raspberries in a blender or food processor with 2 tablespoons of sugar. Taste and add another tablespoon of sugar, if needed. Set a wire-mesh strainer over a bowl. Pour the puréed raspberries through the strainer to remove the seeds, pressing the purée through with a rubber spatula. Set aside.

Cut each peach in half, from top to bottom, and twist gently to open. Using a melon ball cutter or small spoon, scoop out the pit and the tough flesh from the center of each peach half to create a shallow dip for the filling. Brush the cut sides with the melted butter and sprinkle with sugar.

Prepare a gas or charcoal grill for cooking over high heat. Place the peach halves cut side down on the cooking grate and cover the grill. Cook for 2 to 3 minutes, until lightly browned. Using a metal spatula, turn the peaches over and grill for 2 to 3 minutes more, until the skins are browned and begin to loosen. Transfer the peaches to a plate, cut side down, and use tongs to pull off the skins.

To serve, pour a small puddle of raspberry coulis on each dessert plate. Place a peach half cut side up in the raspberry puddle.

Place about 1 tablespoon of the mint mascarpone in the center of each peach half. Drizzle extra coulis over each. Garnish with mint sprigs.

Option: As an alternative, peel and slice the grilled peaches and layer them in footed dessert dishes or stemless cocktail glasses with the mint mascarpone and raspberry coulis. Garnish with mint sprigs.

Fresh Peach Ice Cream

Long gone are the days when the older men in the family would sit beneath a shade tree and churn the ice cream in a wooden bucket with crushed ice and salt. Sleek, modern ice cream makers have replaced the hand-cranked models of the past, and ice cream can now be churned in minutes. Still, under the canopy of a large shade tree remains a pleasant spot for the family to enjoy a bowl of homemade peach ice cream on a warm summer afternoon. When making this ice cream, remember: The better the peaches, the better the ice cream.—Jayni

MAKES 1½ QUARTS ICE CREAM

2 cups fresh ripe peaches (about 1½ pounds), peeled, pitted and very finely chopped
1 tablespoon lemon juice
½ cup sugar

Custard:
2 cups half and half
1 cup heavy cream
¾ cup sugar

4 egg yolks

½ teaspoon vanilla extract

Combine the chopped peaches, lemon juice, and ½ cup of sugar in a large bowl. Cover and refrigerate for 8 hours, or overnight, to allow the juices to accumulate.

Custard: Pour the half and half, cream, and sugar into a large saucepan. Heat over medium-high heat, stirring until the sugar is dissolved. Continue heating, stirring occasionally, until the mixture is very hot and steamy, just below simmering. Remove the pan from the heat.

In a medium bowl, beat the egg yolks lightly. In a slow stream, pour about 2 cups of the hot half and half and cream mixture into the egg yolks, stirring constantly. (Adding the hot liquid gradually will prevent the eggs from curdling.) Pour the egg

CONTINUED ➡

yolk mixture slowly into the saucepan of the remaining cream mixture, stirring constantly. Cook the custard over low heat, stirring continually, until it thickens slightly and coats the back of a spoon (170 to 175 degrees), 10 to 15 minutes.

Strain the custard into a large bowl to remove any curdled bits. Cool for about 30 minutes. Stir in the vanilla extract. Cover and refrigerate overnight, or until well chilled.

When ready to make ice cream, pour the chilled peaches into a wire-mesh strainer placed over a bowl to strain the juice from the peaches. Stir the peach juice into the custard. Return the peaches to the refrigerator to keep them cold until ready to use.

Freeze the custard in an ice cream maker according to the manufacturer's directions. When the ice cream is fairly firm and nearly done, add the chilled peaches and continue freezing until firm. Transfer the ice cream to a sealed, freezer-safe container and place in the freezer for at least 2 hours before serving. This allows time for the ice cream to firm up.

A Meal Worth Boasting About

In 1941, following the Dust Bowl of the 1930s, and with commercial irrigation established, State Representative Will Christian bragged that he could prepare an entire dinner using only foods grown and produced in Grant County. To prove his point, he invited some fellow legislators and the lieutenant governor to a dinner at his ranch. The dinner was a success, and Will and his wife, Nora, continued to host this annual event until his retirement from the Kansas Legislature.

In 1962, the Grant County Chamber of Commerce and several local citizens revived the dinner, naming it the Grant County Home Products Dinner, to which the public and elected politicians were invited. Along with the fresh produce, the number of diners also began to grow. The following year, the first "modern" dinner menu was served, and today approximately fifteen hundred people sit down to what has to be the largest annual farm-to-table meal in Kansas.

For more than fifty years, the menu has remained much the same, though some new items have been added over the years. Barbecue beef is the main course, served with scalloped potatoes, baked pinto beans, candied squash, cherry tomatoes, sweet corn, whole wheat rolls, strawberry jam, cheese, watermelon, ice cream, and milo doughnuts. And so, every year for the dinner, it takes approximately eight hundred pounds of beef, four hundred pounds of potatoes, one hundred pounds of pinto beans, fifty squash, four thousand cherry tomatoes, a pickup load or two of sweet corn, eighteen hundred whole wheat rolls, forty pounds of strawberries, ninety pounds of cheese, fifty watermelons, thirty-eight gallons of ice cream, and two thousand milo doughnuts.

This is no small task. Planning for the dinner, held the third Tuesday in September, begins in November. Marieta Hauser, director of the Grant County Chamber of Commerce in Ulysses, oversees the annual event. "We serve nearly fifteen hundred people food that is produced and prepared in Ulysses. It takes about seven hundred volunteers, fifty clubs, and a rotating committee of eight people about eleven months to coordinate the event," Marieta explains. "The committee picks the entertainment, chooses a theme and artwork, coordinates with local farmers to grow the produce, and solicits donations from local businesses. The donations are used to buy supplies and the beef from the local grocery store who cuts and wraps it for us."

The first work day for the committee and the volunteers is "corn day," around late July or early August when the sweet corn is picked, shucked, cut off the cob, cooked, and put in the freezer for storage. Over the following weeks, the committee coordinates the gathering of potatoes and pinto beans, and the collection of wheat flour for the rolls and milo flour for the doughnuts from local farmers. During the week before the dinner, the committee swings into full action, picking tomatoes, squash, and watermelons and distributing the products to local clubs, churches, and schools to be prepared for the dinner. Additionally, the committee is responsible for cooking the barbecue beef the night before the event.

In addition to the food, tables and chairs for fifteen hundred must be set up in the Grant County Civic Center along with decorations. A commemorative button featuring the current year's artwork is the admittance ticket. The money raised supports scholarships for local Grant County youth who have graduated from high school and are attending college. Following the event, the committee coordinates the cleanup of the civic center and the kitchen, and the return of decorative items.

After more than fifty years, the people of Ulysses still take pride in putting on the Grant County Home Products Dinner, which brings the community together. Marieta Hauser tells us that nearly everyone in the community is involved in some way. Now, and just as before, it's an event worth boasting about!

Homemade Vanilla Ice Cream with Roasted Strawberries

The secret to making velvety smooth gourmet-quality ice cream is to first prepare a rich custard. Chill the custard overnight before freezing it in an ice cream maker the following day.

Roasting the strawberries deepens their flavor and makes a luscious topping for homemade ice cream. The most flavorful strawberries can be grown in a backyard garden and picked at their peak of ripeness. Or purchase them at a you-pick strawberry patch or your local farmers' market.
—Frank and Jayni

MAKES 2 QUARTS ICE CREAM

Custard:
4 cups half and half
1½ cups sugar

6 egg yolks

2 cups heavy cream
1½ teaspoons vanilla extract

Roasted Strawberries:
1 pound fresh strawberries, rinsed, hulled, and halved or quartered
2 tablespoons sugar
1 tablespoon Triple Sec, or other orange liqueur
2 teaspoons white balsamic vinegar
Dash of salt and black pepper

Custard: Pour the half and half and sugar into a large saucepan. Heat over medium-high heat, stirring until the sugar is dissolved. Continue heating, stirring occasionally, until the half and half is very hot and steamy, just below simmering. Remove the pan from the heat.

In a large bowl, beat the egg yolks lightly. In a slow stream, pour about 2 cups of the hot half and half into the egg yolks, stirring constantly. (Adding the hot liquid gradually will prevent the eggs from curdling.) Pour the egg mixture slowly into the saucepan of the remaining half and half, stirring constantly. Cook the custard over low heat, stirring continually, until it thickens slightly and coats the back of a spoon (170 to 175 degrees), 10 to 15 minutes.

Strain the custard into a large bowl to remove any curdled bits. Stir in the 2 cups of heavy cream and vanilla extract. Cool for about 30 minutes. Cover and refrigerate overnight, or until well chilled.

Freeze the custard in an ice cream maker according to the manufacturer's directions. Transfer the ice cream to a sealed, freezer-safe container and place in the freezer for at least 2 hours before serving. This allows time for the ice cream to firm up.

Roasted Strawberries: About an hour or two before serving the ice cream, roast the strawberries. Place the halved or quartered strawberries in a bowl. Add the sugar and gently toss to combine. Add the Triple Sec, white balsamic vinegar, salt, and pepper. Toss again and pour the mixture into a shallow baking dish. Roast the strawberries in a 375-degree oven for 15 minutes, stir, and continue cooking for about 10 minutes more, until the strawberries are very tender and fragrant.

Serve the roasted strawberries warm or room temperature over the homemade vanilla ice cream.

Peppermint Ice Cream

When the holidays roll around, and peppermint candies are easy to find, it's the season to make our favorite ice cream. To make it more fun, we like to serve it in cones instead of bowls.—Frank and Jayni

MAKES 1 QUART ICE CREAM

Custard:
4 cups half and half
4 egg yolks
1 cup sugar

2 teaspoons peppermint extract
4 to 5 drops red food color (optional)

½ cup crushed peppermint candy
(about 22 candies)

Custard: Pour the half and half into a large saucepan and heat over medium-high heat until very hot and steamy, just below simmering. Remove the pan from the heat. Place the egg yolks and sugar in a large mixing bowl. Using a wire whisk, whisk until the mixture is pale yellow and falls into ribbons when the whisk is lifted from the bowl. In a slow stream, pour about 2 cups of the hot half and half into the egg yolks, stirring constantly. (Adding the hot liquid gradually will prevent the eggs from curdling.) Pour the egg mixture slowly into the saucepan of the remaining half and half, stirring constantly. Cook the custard over low heat, stirring continually, until it thickens slightly and coats the back of a spoon (170 to 175 degrees), 10 to 15 minutes.

Strain the custard into a large bowl to remove any curdled bits. Cool for about 30 minutes. Add the peppermint extract and, if desired, a few drops of red food color to obtain a soft pink color. Cover and refrigerate overnight, or until the custard is well chilled.

Crush the peppermint candy. Place it in a covered container and chill in the refrigerator until ready to use.

When the custard is well chilled, stir in the chilled crushed peppermint candy. Freeze the custard in an ice cream freezer according to manufacturer's directions. Transfer the ice cream to a sealed, freezer-safe container and place in the freezer for at least 2 hours before serving. This allows time for the ice cream to firm up.

Easy Lemon Ice Cream

Shari Paynter likes to prepare this quick and easy-to-make lemon ice cream on a hot summer day. A small scoop or two of this rich and refreshing ice cream is just the right amount to serve after dinner. Simply whisk the ingredients together and freeze in a container—no churning required!—Shari Paynter, Tonganoxie

4 TO 6 SERVINGS

2 cups whipping cream
1 cup sugar
2 tablespoons lemon zest
¼ cup fresh-squeezed lemon juice

Pour the whipping cream into a mixing bowl. Whisk in the sugar. Add the lemon zest and juice and continue to whisk until the sugar is dissolved.

Pour the ice cream mixture into a freezer-safe container. Cover tightly and place in the freezer for at least 8 to 10 hours for soft, easy-to-scoop ice cream. If frozen overnight, the ice cream will be very firm, so set it out for 5 minutes to soften slightly before scooping.

About the Authors

Frank and Jayni Carey have been a team in the kitchen since they first met. Together, the couple has authored two cookbooks. *The Kansas Cookbook: Recipes from the Heartland* was published in 1989 by the University Press of Kansas, and *The Easier You Make It, The Better It Tastes!* was published in 1994 by Better Homes and Gardens Books. Jayni is the author of *The Best of Jayni's Kitchen*, published in 2008 by Sunflower Publishing, a division of The World Company.

Jayni Carey was the host for thirteen seasons of a weekly cooking show, *Jayni's Kitchen,* produced by Free State Studios for Channel 6, a division of WOW, Lawrence, Kansas. *Jayni's Kitchen* has won seven Mid-American Cable Television Association Awards and a Silver Telly Award. She has also taught cooking classes on a variety of cuisines.

Frank Carey was the director of technology for the School of Education at the University of Kansas for twelve years. Currently, he is an information technology analyst specializing in video conferencing, database development, and managing audio-video responsibilities. Frank also worked behind the scenes of *Jayni's Kitchen*, assisting Jayni with recipe development, photography, and B-roll video.

Together, Frank and Jayni continue to pursue their interest in the foodways of Kansas, testing new recipes, gardening, and travelling in search of delicious things to eat.

Recipe Credits

The following recipes by Jayni Carey were originally featured in the program *Jayni's Kitchen*, produced by Free State Studios in Lawrence, Kansas.

"Chipotle Meatballs"
"Toasted Baguette Slices"
"Sun-Dried Tomato Spread"
"Winter Tomato Soup"
"Mussels Steamed in White Wine"
"Lamb Chops with Cheese Grits"
"Potato Salad with Green Beans"
"Eggplant Stacks"
"Potato Gratin with Apples and Walnuts"
"Deluxe Sweet Potatoes"
"Grilled Flank Steak with Chimichurri Sauce and Farro Pilaf"
"Grilled Beef Tenderloin Filets with Red Wine Sauce"
"Fennel-Roasted Pork Loin with Blackberry-Red Wine Sauce"
"Roast Chicken with Quinoa-Vegetable Pilaf"
"Grilled Duck Breasts with Port Wine Sauce"
"Planked Ruby Trout with Orange Butter, Citrus, and Rosemary"
"Spicy Lime Shrimp with Coconut Rice"
"Moroccan Carrots"
"Apple Butterscotch-Walnut Crumble"
"Cinnamon-Cherry Cobbler with Almond Crunch Topping"
"Bittersweet Chocolate Custard"
"Grilled Peaches with Mint Mascarpone and Raspberry Coulis"
"Peppermint Ice Cream"

Index of Contributors

Index

Wheat State Wine Co., Winfield, KS, 214
White Whole Wheat Bread, 253–254
Whole Grain Wheat 'n' Oats Bread, 251–252
Williams, Janet (Keller), 186
wineries, 214, 318–319

Winter Tomato Soup, 15
Winter Veggie Roast, 103
Wohletz Farm Fresh, Lawrence, KS, 297, 305

yellow squash, ground beef-stuffed, with tomato-oregano topping, 174–175. *See also* squash

zucchini
blossoms, 301
cake, dark chocolate, 321–322
cake, microwave, 323
corn casserole, 110
gratin, 111
growing, 301

hippie lasagne, 106–107
lemon, 300
salad, 62
sautéed, with tomato, 88
summer veggies baked in phyllo pastry, 107–108
See also squash